Arnulfo L. Oliveira Memorial Library

UTB
TSC

GOD'S
MECHANICS

GOD'S
MECHANICS

How Scientists and Engineers
MAKE SENSE OF RELIGION

Brother Guy Consolmagno, S.J.

JB **JOSSEY-BASS**
A Wiley Imprint
www.josseybass.com

Published by Jossey-Bass
A Wiley Imprint
989 Market Street, San Francisco, CA 94103-1741—www.josseybass.com

Wiley Bicentennial logo: Richard J. Pacifico

Jossey-Bass books and products are available through most bookstores. To contact Jossey-Bass directly
call our Customer Care Department within the U.S. at 800-956-7739, outside the U.S. at 317-572-3986,
or fax 317-572-4002.

Anecdote about the Saint Joseph statue in Chapter Six contributed by Bruce F. Emmer

Jossey-Bass also publishes its books in a variety of electronic formats. Some content that appears in
print may not be available in electronic books.

Library of Congress Cataloging-in-Publication Data
Consolmagno, Guy, date.
  God's mechanics : how scientists and engineers make sense of religion /
Guy Consolmagno.—1st ed.
    p. cm.
  Includes index.
  ISBN 978-0-7879-9466-2 (cloth)
1.   Religion and science. 2.   Consolmagno, Guy, 1952-   I. Title.
  BL240.3.C68 2007
  201'.65—dc22   2007019067

Printed in the United States of America
FIRST EDITION
HB Printing 10 9 8 7 6 5 4 3 2 1

Contents

PART FOUR
WHY WOULD A TECHIE BE A CHRISTIAN? 131

PART FIVE
THE CONFESSION OF A VATICAN TECHIE 201

GOD'S
MECHANICS

Introduction:
The Lord of the Techies

IT WAS AFTER a long, exhausting day at a science-fiction convention that an old friend of mine from my MIT student days and her husband caught me up with a surprising question. "Could you explain," they asked me, "how this religion stuff in your life actually works?"

Now, I had already written about my life and work in a book called *Brother Astronomer.* After hearing endlessly about the "eternal war" between science and religion, I figured that merely demonstrating the existence of a lot of people like me, who flourish as scientists while practicing a religion, should be proof enough that science and religion can be perfectly compatible. Indeed, this empirical evidence ought to have been far more convincing than any drawn-out philosophical argument.

But that didn't go far enough for my friends. They already understood that a person like me *could* exist. They knew I *did* exist. But what they wanted to know was *how.* What were the nuts and bolts of how I actually made it all work together?

They're interested in religion, now, in a way they never were when they were young punk MIT engineers who knew it all. They're getting older; they're raising a family. And they're asking me, because along with my being a Jesuit brother (and a friend), I am also, like them, a *techie.*

That's what makes my answer—this book—different from a typical book of apologetics. This book explains a techie's religion.

What's a techie? Someone who makes his or her living as an engineer or a scientist, yes; but it's broader than that.

To a lot of nontechies, the word techie might imply nothing more than a computer geek, but that's missing the whole point.

For one thing, techies' interests are broader than computers; there's a whole world of technology-related activities, from aeronautics to zoology, that techies might be engaged with. But more important than that, techies do more than just make a living off of technology. They actively enjoy the stuff. It's their source of play. (And while some of us still cringe at the word *geek,* nearly every techie I know is proud to wear the techie tag.)

Who is a techie? Anyone whose Christmas list includes tools. Anyone who spends more time fiddling with things attached to their TV than actually watching TV. Anyone who still has a bit of the kid inside and still wants to take Dad's watch apart.

A techie is someone whose orientation toward the world is extremely pragmatic, logical, and—most of all—functional. Where an artist might ask, "Is it beautiful?" or a philosopher would ask, "Is it true?" the question behind a techie's worldview is "How does it work?" Techies see the world in terms of processes to be understood and jobs to be done—problems to be solved. We want to know where to find the gears and levers and why they are arranged that way. We also ask, "Does this arrangement of gears and levers do the job it was designed to do?"

Think of that famous photograph of Buzz Aldrin standing on the moon. You could be inspired by the symbolism of humankind's quest for adventure or impressed with the courage (and cleverness) of both the astronauts and the whole raft of people who got them up to the moon. But if, in addition to all those other emotions, you find yourself wondering why that dry lunar soil is sticking to his knees, you're a techie.

I'm a techie; I know my tribe. I spent seven years at MIT (earning two degrees and spending three years as a postdoc), and I loved every minute of it. I have worked with scientists and engineers all my adult life. My friends are the kinds of people who break codes for fun, go camping with telescopes, build home-brew rockets and homemade robots. For Christmas they give their kids rocks—really cool rocks.

My friends didn't want me to try to convert them to my religion. Nothing turns us techies off faster than proselytizing; we'd just as soon figure things out for ourselves, thank you very much. But like me, they're fascinated with the ways people live their lives and how they make things work. Technical people recognize the value of seeing sample problems worked out, and they value having concrete data on which to work. So an unabashedly honest description of how religious techies have figured things out, when it comes to our religions, can be accepted as grist for their data mill. Not "this is how you must live" but rather "this is how we live—here's how the parts fit together."

But there's more to this book than simply a description of how religion works for a scientist or an engineer. Seeing how a techie understands religion can provide some very revealing insights to the rest of the world about how the techie mind works.

The techie worldview is incredibly important to the larger, nontechie society. We depend on technology to provide our light and heat, the food we eat, the ways we move about and stay in touch with each other. But even more, over the past two centuries, technical and scientific advances in understanding the universe have shaped the assumptions, the language, and the dreams of society as a whole. These include our understanding of the great religious questions.

In recent years, a laudable effort has been made to discuss issues of science in a theological context—for instance, the series of conferences cosponsored by the Vatican Observatory in Castel Gandolfo and the Center for Theology and the Natural Sciences at Berkeley. This is, in effect, bringing science to the philosophers. One result of these conferences (besides a series of thick and at times impenetrable proceedings) is a realization that the techie worldview can seem utterly alien, and even off-putting, to many nontechies. Yet it is a worldview so deeply ingrained in us techies, so "intuitively obvious to the casual observer," that most of us techies are equally mystified at people who don't understand it.

Indeed, to people who don't understand the scientific or engineering mind-set, the questions a techie would ask and the techie manner of asking them can often sound threatening or dismissive, even though such questions are nothing of the sort. But without understanding the attitudes and assumptions behind the questions, it's hard to come up with good answers. To the extent that there is still a rift between science and religion among my fellow scientists and engineers, it's because most religion teachers and writers are woefully inept at explaining religion in terms that make sense to a techie. Certainly, this is true of most of our Sunday school teachers!

The cliché supposes that all techies are hard-nosed materialists. But anyone who's read a techie Usenet list—or the heated commentaries in *Nature*—knows better. Religion enters into our conversations all the time. It is an important part of our lives, even for people who never set foot inside a church. It's part of the society we live in, it's part of the way we were brought up, and it's a response to a human hunger as basic as food and sex.

Techies are human; we have the same hungers as anyone else. But especially, we have the hunger to know. We want things to make sense. And this book will show the kinds of answers that some of us have developed that make our religions make sense. And maybe it will reveal to the rest of the world what "making sense" means to us.

PART ONE

Why Would a Techie Believe in God?

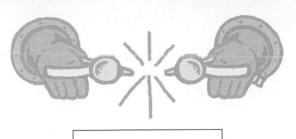

CHAPTER 1

How Techies Believe

≷ Proof or Belief? ≶

A Baptist preacher, visiting Vermont, approached a Yankee farmer leaning on a fence post by the side of the road.

"Brother," he asked the farmer, "do you believe in Baptism by immersion?"

The Yankee farmer chewed on a blade of grass and then spit it out.

"Believe in it?" he replied. "Dang, I've seen it!"

I'm like that Vermont farmer. I'm an empiricist. I believe what I see.

Yet I also believe in things I can't see: electrons and black holes, for instance. They are theoretical constructs that allow me to explain the things I do see.

So does God fit into that category?

Even an atheist has to believe that the concept, at least, of "God" does exist, whether or not that concept is true or useful or the best way to approach things. Like the Yankee farmer, he merely needs to observe what we all have witnessed: some people do believe in God.

And some of those believers are hard-nosed, rational, dyed-in-the-wool techies—scientists, engineers, people whose deepest desire is to know how things work.

When I became a Jesuit brother, a member of a Roman Catholic religious order, I had been a scientist for fifteen years, yet—as is typical in our culture—most of my friends and colleagues had no idea I practiced a religion. But once they found out I was a Jesuit, a surprising number came up and started telling me about the churches they attended. Religious belief appears to be just as prevalent among people working in technical fields as it is in the general community from which those people come. On the one hand, few British scientists are churchgoers, but then few Brits of any stripe go to church nowadays. On the other hand, scientists in, say, Chicago, seem to follow the national trend, with about half of them being regular church attendees. I recall a memorable dinner with half a dozen MIT professors where, over coffee, every one of them chimed in with complaints about the organists at each of their churches—some things are universal in all religions!

For what it's worth, in my experience astronomers are more likely than biologists to be believers. But several surveys, more scientific than my anecdotal experiences, have confirmed that in academic settings, the real atheists are to be found in English Literature departments.

Given that observation, an atheist (or anyone else) might want to ask, "How do these people, who are so dependent on empirical reasoning, find belief ... believable?"

The answers I come up with here may not be the real answer to the question of why techie believers do believe. Heck, I don't even know if the motives I talk about here are exactly why I believe either; I only assert that they are some of the reasons I use to justify my religion to myself. But the real roots of one's personal faith are hard to untangle.

Choosing to believe or not to believe is wrapped up in so many things: family background; what the "religious people" we grew up around were like; our preconceptions and prejudices about one religion or another; the sort of self-image we want to project to the world. Some of our claim to religion, or lack of it, is simple posturing: "Look at me, I'm a rebel" or "I'm a good girl" or "I'm too smart for that stuff" or "I'm too humble to deny any possibilities." Some of the choice is a response to the religious desires of the people we live with, the people we love: our parents, our spouse, or even our children. And some of it is sincere angst, an honest attempt to deal with—or avoid—the scary questions of life.

The point is, within every individual, the good motives and bad motives are so intimately mixed together that it's impossible to separate them out. That's what it means to be human.

But I would expect that even the most skeptical of atheists would concede that good motives for believing in God could exist. Any person of reason should be able to appreciate that belief in at least some sort of God is one viable choice. Just as I can at least understand intellectually why someone might enjoy a movie or a hobby or a kind of food that doesn't necessarily appeal to me, I should hope that even the most severe skeptic will grant me the observation that some reasonable people can and do believe in God and that for them, positing the existence of some sort of God is not wholly illogical.

This is the only really "proselytizing" part of this book: I'm asking you to acknowledge that there could be legitimate reasons for belief in some sort of greater being (or beings). If I can't convince you that theism is not an unreasonable assumption for someone to adopt, you should put this book down right now; the rest of the chapters will make no sense to you, or worse, you'll read things into them that aren't there. Nevertheless, I do not insist that you personally adopt any sort of theism yourself, much less mine.

I understand, you may be suspicious. Whenever people hear that I am a Jesuit scientist who writes popular books, I get the impression they assume that I'm planning to write the great "science and religion" book that will Explain It All. It's not clear what they're actually expecting me to explain. Or to whom. A lot of people, I am afraid, are looking for a book that will use science to "prove" religion—*their* religion, of course.

But such a book would be a misapprehension of what science is all about. And any faith that is "proved" by science would be a poor imitation of a real religion.

Back when I was a student at MIT, I had the chance to sit in a radio studio at Boston University while two hippie radio announcers—this was a long time ago—with a show called Cosmic Vibrations or some such thing, were interviewing a young up-and-coming astronomer from Cornell named Carl Sagan. He had just published his first book, *Cosmic Connections,* and

I guess they thought with a title like that, he must be a fellow cosmic voyager. But a series of answers from him made it quite clear that whatever their vibrational modes, he was on a distinctly more mundane wavelength. Finally, in frustration, one of the hippies shot at him, "you're just a Western scientist!"

"Western New York," admitted Carl from Cornell.

Now, I may disagree with Carl Sagan's personal theology; he stopped shy of calling himself an atheist only on the grounds that, as he put it, "an atheist is someone who knows more than I do." But in this case, I'd say he had a valid point. I, too, am a Western scientist, and not just because my doctorate is from Arizona. And I, too, get fed up with people who try to dress up their theology with scientific-sounding jargon. It rings false.

Science is not in the business of dealing with specific religious questions. That would be science making the same mistake that religion made with Galileo. (Don't get me started on Galileo. . . .) Science can't prove or disprove religious tenets any more than religion can prove or disprove a scientific discovery.

Furthermore, any "religion" based on science would be subservient to science and prone to collapse when its underlying science is replaced by next year's model. We've already seen that happen throughout history, with the passage of time and new discoveries inevitably revealing the absurdity of such science-based philosophies.

It's a mistake that has been made too often already. In the thirteenth century, when the Moors were expelled from Spain, they left behind libraries with the writings of Aristotle and other ancients, books that hadn't been seen in the non-Muslim world for centuries. Aristotle's view of how the universe worked was decidedly different from what is found in the Bible. But then Saint Thomas Aquinas did such a good job of reconciling the two that within a hundred years, it seemed like Christianity was actually based on Aristotelian physics. A few centuries later, when Galileo and Newton came along and made Aristotle's physics obsolete, that was regarded, ironically, as a threat to Christianity. And that led to a new kind of religion, Deism, based on Newton's ideas of a clockwork universe, which was popular for another few hundred years until quantum theory showed up the shortcomings of Newton's physics. Now there's a rush of people who want to equate quantum uncertainty with free will. Some people never learn.

⇝ Proof and the Scientist ⇜

Conflating this year's latest physics with theology is just a thinly disguised attempt to use science to "prove" the existence of God. And most assuredly, that is something I am *not* at all interested in trying to do. Such proofs are useless; a "God hypothesis" cannot be subjected to "scientific" or rational proof.

The famous medieval proofs of God, such as those of Aquinas or Anselm, are not proofs in this sense. Rather, they are demonstrations that belief in God is reasonable to anyone steeped in Aristotelian philosophy, or they are expressions of delight that God does exist. They may use the format of a mathematical proof to communicate philosophical information, but they never actually claim to be rigorous mathematical proofs.

For one thing, a supernatural God would be bigger than any natural, logical system—that's what *supernatural* means. The supernatural is, by definition, above, outside of, or bigger than the natural. So trying to pin down or limit, to prove or disprove, the supernatural in terms of what's natural is a pointless exercise.

For another, we know that every logical proof must start with some assumed axioms or self-evident truths. Change your axioms, and you can prove whatever you want. In practice, it's the "whatever you want" that comes first, and that determines the axioms you decide to adopt. In essence, it is not God that you find at the end of your logic; rather, your God is the unshakable axiom that you used when you started your chain of logic. Belief comes before the explanations.

Consider how you decide about something mundane, like buying a car. You may choose the Firebolt over the Nimbus because it offers better gas mileage. But on what basis did you decide that gas mileage was more important than, say, resale value? And is mileage important to you because it saves you money or because it saves the ecology? And why do you want to save money—out of greed or to feed your family better? Each reason is based on a previous reason. But this chain of reasons can't go on forever; there has to be some ultimate value, some initial axiom that you believe in before you start your chain. A different but still perfectly logical chain of reasoning could lead to a completely different conclusion if you change your starting value. Otherwise, everyone would buy the same car.

And sometimes you don't even realize what those initial axioms are. Sometimes you lie to yourself. You may say your ultimate value is feeding your family when in fact what is more important to you is feeding your ego. The Firebolt comes in a snazzy red that gets your pulse going, but its only socially correct benefit is its marginally better gas mileage, so you then "decide" that mileage is the most important factor in your decision.

The one thing that you can't do is use your logic to justify itself. "Of course gas mileage counts more than anything else. You want proof? Just look at the Firebolt in my driveway." The fact that you bought the Firebolt may demonstrate that you think (or pretend to think) that mileage is the most important value; it doesn't prove that your sense of values was correct.

The same logic is true for buying a philosophical system. For instance, look at the way that Newton's laws of physics describe the universe. Everything, from the motions of the planets to the reactions of the chemicals in our brains, is governed (they say) by rigid, inflexible laws; give me the precise location and velocity of each particle in the universe and a complete description of all the forces acting on it, and I can calculate the outcome of every future action, completely and irrevocably determined by the laws of cause and effect. Newton's worldview does lead to a mechanistic, deterministic view of life; all things, down to the atoms that mirror the thoughts in our brains, are slaves to the cold equations. So does this prove that there is no freedom, that everything in life is predetermined? No; that kind of determinism is just the assumption we started with when we adopted the Newtonian view of the universe.

Likewise, start with the assumption that everything is chance, the way that some formulations of quantum theory describe things (once we found the places where Newtonian physics failed in describing how the universe actually behaves), and you have no problem "proving" that life is random and meaningless. Again, all you're doing is recovering the assumption you started with.

The eighteenth-century argument from design, recently repackaged as "intelligent design," falls into the same trap. Only when you assume a designer God in the first place does the evidence of design "proving" His existence leap out at you. Yes, the order in the universe can be seen as consistent with the assumption of an "intelligent designer"; it's a fine consistency argument. But it proves nothing—atheists can also come up with their own self-consistent explanations with no place for a designer. (And relying on design as your demonstration of God's existence carries with it the danger that you'll stop looking any further for explanations of why things are the way they are. The argument from design, if held too rigidly, can become very limiting of both your view of nature and your view of God.)

Most fundamentally, striving for a "scientific" proof of the existence (or nonexistence) of God is a meaningless ambition, because in fact science just doesn't do "proofs" the way that mathematics or philosophy does. No assumption, assertion, or conclusion of science is ever held to be unassailable.

Science in itself never deals with certainties. Rather, we scientists are satisfied if we can come up with a theory that's merely consistent with what we think we've observed up to now. Even long-held axioms like conservation of mass ("no matter is ever created or destroyed") have been found to be incomplete in the light of new experimental evidence. As an example from my own field of astronomy, for a generation everybody studying solar systems knew that rocky planets like Earth and Mars are found close to the sun, while gas giants like Jupiter and Saturn were farther out; this was a fundamental starting point in every theory of how planets were formed. Then we learned how to detect planets around other stars and found hundreds of cases where gas giants orbit very close to their stars. Time to rethink our theories.

Everything in science is always subject to further review. Even our experimental data can be found to be biased by unsuspected error, and their interpretation can be distorted by our theoretical preconceptions. (It turns out that star systems with gas giant planets close to their stars are the easiest kinds of systems to discover. Have we found so many of them only because they are easy to find, or is the overwhelming number of such systems evidence that this is a fundamental characteristic true for most stars with planets? We still don't know.)

Indeed, sometimes the fact that the evidence is merely "not inconsistent with" our theory is good enough to let us keep believing in that theory. We can measure the law of gravity over small distances in the lab or very large distances on the scale of planets and stars; we assume the same law holds for intermediate distances simply in the absence of any data to the contrary. But we could be wrong.

Science is successful only as a way of approaching the truth asymptotically, as it were, getting closer and closer without ever quite fully arriving there; it's constantly self-correcting because it continually recognizes its need to correct itself. That works only if you admit from the beginning that you don't already have the truth, whole and completely understood, and that you'll never have the truth in that way. This humility in the face of the universe is an essential element of a properly functioning techie mind-set.

If you limit yourself to science, you always have to accept the possibility of a God—and the possibility of no God. Even Carl Sagan knew that. Neither belief in God nor the denial of God is necessary to do science. And in any event, choosing to believe or not believe in the God axiom comes first, before you even start to do the science.

≳ Faith in Reason ≲

On the other hand, Stephen Jay Gould in his book *Rocks of Ages* makes an argument, often heard, that an impermeable barrier stands between the worlds of science and religion and that neither can make useful contributions to the other's realm. But certainly that can't be entirely true. For one thing, our contemporary understanding of the universe means that we must recognize today that any God responsible for creating it must be much bigger than they could possibly have imagined in 1000 B.C. That shouldn't be surprising or disturbing. After all, the picture of God I had when I was five years old was pretty limited, too. (So was my understanding of science.)

More profoundly, without a certain philosophical predisposition, I would have no reason to think that science was worth doing, much less possible to do. It has been argued that belief in a creator God who is reported to have looked at his creation and called it "good" is what gave early Jews, Christians, and Muslims the motivation—or at least the political cover—to get the resources they needed to do pure science, to study the universe just for its own sake.

Believing in a capricious God, a God of chaos who constantly changes the rules of the universe, would play havoc with some of the other assumptions we believe in as scientists because science relies on being able to count on the stability of certain rules. But even that doesn't disprove the existence of such a chaotic God. Perhaps instead it's the axioms of science that we techies choose to believe in that are not correct. I can't prove that every scientific law isn't just a long string of coincidences. But instead I tend to believe the opposite, that a sufficiently long string of coincidences is evidence of a scientific law.

It's important to remember that the scientist is no stranger to belief in and of itself. We believe our yardsticks are actually a yard long. We believe in the authority of the CRC Handbook when we look up physical constants or standard formulas. We believe that the laws of physics that worked yesterday will still work the same way tomorrow. Sometimes we even believe our data.

More subtly, scientists and engineers start every new project with a belief that a solution does exist. We believe that there is an objective reality and that in at least some limited way we can make progress in understanding the truth about that objective reality. That's a huge assumption to swallow. Some nontechnical people are just as happy thinking that "everything is illusion" or "reality is what you make of it yourself." Solipsism—the philosophical theory that suggests that the universe is just a projection of an individual's own imagination—starts with the mind-set that "I am the only mind that exists." The story goes that one such-minded amateur philosopher once said to George Bernard Shaw, "I am a Solipsist, and most of my friends are, too." Shaw was understandably amused.

Most fundamentally, underlying every logical system, every scientific data point, are the nonrational human beings whose desires, intuitions, and hunches led them to do that bit of science in the first place.

When you take a hard look, you realize that most of our work is shot through with nonrational behavior. When I say "nonrational," I don't mean "irrational." Our nonrationality is in fact quite reasonable. It's necessary, because our very rationality itself relies on insight: we techies usually start our problem solving with a hunch—an insight about where we should look to find the solution, what the answer is going to look like, how this problem will parallel or differ from similar problems of our experience. Without those hunches, we have no idea where to start. And without knowing ahead of time what the solution is going to look like, we would have no way of recognizing it once we found it; we'd have no idea when to stop looking.

If you don't think this is the case, try teaching physics to first-year college students. You can have a classroom full of incredibly bright kids, but until they have developed their own set of intuitions, they find physics utterly mysterious. That's why freshman physics and engineering classes concentrate on examining previously solved problems: the point is to force-feed some "canned" experience into the students, cramming into them many examples of solutions that work, in the hope that these students will become more able to recognize a given sort of problem (and how to solve it) when they see one. What we are teaching isn't a collection of facts or formulas; I'd let my students bring equation sheets to the exams and they'd still manage to flunk the test. No, what is being presented in physics class is the habit of intuition.

Reason itself is based on intuition. "All men are mortal; Socrates is a man; therefore, Socrates is mortal." But how do you know that all men are mortal? Or that Socrates is a man? And what spark inside you allows you to deduce that this demands that Socrates must be mortal? Each of these steps involves a nonrational intuition.

"Cats are small and black and furry; this animal is small and black and furry; therefore, this animal is a cat." It takes a bit of education to be able to name all the flaws in that syllogism. But if you don't learn to do so, you're likely to find yourself cuddling up to a skunk.

We know that in practice our logic alone is untrustworthy; our habits of intuition are imperfect, our premises are incomplete, and sometimes we misstep. That's why we also demand experimental evidence.

Notice how we techies handle the things we believe. First of all, we always recognize that we could be wrong. Logic can be flawed. Tables have been known to contain misprints. Hunches sometimes turn out to be mistaken. Next, we allow our beliefs to be tested by results. If we get an answer that works, it confirms our trust in the data, and it strengthens our preconceptions the next time we're looking for a hunch. We allow our beliefs to be confirmed by our experience. And finally, we're a whole lot more comfortable with our results if there is more than one line of evidence leading to the same conclusion.

At a fundamental level, these attitudes and practices are fraught with philosophical peril (as you'll see). There is actually no logical support for that kind of reasoning, and trying to construct a mathematical proof with arguments like that would get you laughed out of a mathematics department. (It's like the joke of the physicist's proof that all odd numbers are primes: "Three is prime, five is prime, seven is prime, nine must be experimental error, eleven is prime, . . .") Indeed, every obsolete theory in the history of science— which is littered with obsolete theories—is an example of a well-established idea supported by multiple lines of evidence and good observational data that seemed to work for a while but still turned out to be wrong. Yet for most everyday techie activities, most of the time, this way of thinking seems to work.

A big reason that the techie way of proceeding works is that we pay attention to everyone else in the community of science and engineering. We love this techie stuff, and we love showing it off and watching other techies strut their stuff even when it isn't in our corner of the playground. Our work isn't finished until it's been presented to the larger community. And almost always, what we do is done as a part of a team. We check our results against what others have done. Implicit in this is the unspoken but fundamental techie assumption that one answer is the right answer, objectively and demonstrably right, and anything that disagrees with that answer is wrong. And we're more interested (usually) in finding the right answer than in stroking our own egos.

Sure, sometimes the lone outcast is the only one to get it right; but let's face it, that doesn't happen very often. If everyone else's calculations come up with 7 and you get 700, then everyone—including you—will agree on whose result you're going to check first to look for the mistake. It is illogical to assume that you're always smarter than everyone else (even if, alas, it's an all-too-common techie failing).

And so, simply by force of habit or out of comfort and trust in familiarity, the same techniques can be applied by a scientist or an engineer to understanding what God is or at least what God might be. The techie credo is to keep an open mind but trust your common sense. Compare what you hear with what you've actually experienced of how the universe works. And listen to not only your own common sense but also the experiences and common sense of the rest of the world.

If most of the people in most of the world over most of human history have believed in some sort of God, that doesn't prove that there must be a God. But it's a reasonable presumption that all those people must be getting some good out of believing in one. So let's see what good that might be, from a techie perspective.

CHAPTER 2

Where God Is Useful

≥ If God Is the Answer, What Was the Question? ≤

We techies are pragmatic people, and we must have pragmatic reasons to believe in anything. When we judge a theory, we ask, "What data does this theory try to explain? And how well does it do the job?" So how would someone with this approach evaluate the proposition that what we call God really exists?

As the famous German theologian Karl Rahner once pointed out, the mere fact that there is a word for "God" in almost every language on Earth ought to raise some questions. Why was that word invented? What is it supposed to do? What things do I see that the concept "God" helps to explain? Belief in God must resolve some issues, fit some data, solve some problems, answer some questions.

Granted, in some cultures "gods" were invoked to explain phenomena of nature that we can now explain in scientific terms: our ancestors had a god of thunder, a god of growing crops, and so forth. But science only barely does away with that sort of theism; to most people, invoking a physical law like the conservation of energy is every bit as abstract, arbitrary, and alien as any nature god. And even those rare few of us whose life and work allow us to actually understand the implications of the conservation of energy also recognize the limits of that explanation. After all, science only explains how the universe works; it can't explain why it works that way.

But more important, even in the most primitive of religions, "God" is invoked for reasons that have nothing to do with earthquakes and lightning. "God" suggests itself as an answer to the sorts of deep, personal questions that every human being confronts at some time in life.

What are some of those questions? What does believing in God answer? What problems does it solve?

I can think of many questions to which some sort of God is a reasonable answer. I'll give three of them here. (None of these questions are original to me, of course; similar issues were explicitly raised by Immanuel Kant back in the 1700s. If I say anything original in this book, I apologize.) I don't say that God is the only possible answer to these questions. I merely claim that it is a reasonable answer, one that works for some people, sometimes. Your mileage may vary.

Question One: Why Is There Something Instead of Nothing?

The first question is a "cosmic" question. Why does existence exist?

Why is there time? Why is there space? And how is it that we exist, to be aware of the existence of time and space, and to be able to wonder why they exist?

"Why is there something instead of nothing?" This question was asked by Leibniz in *The Principles of Nature and Grace, Based on Reason* (1714); as coinventor of The Calculus, he certainly qualifies as an eighteenth-century techie. But in fact his question is essentially the same concept raised by Aquinas (God as the Prime Mover) and Descartes ("I think, therefore I am"). This question does not insist that there is a point to existence, which is an assumption of a later question, and in any event something that I cannot prove. Rather, it merely notes the fact of existence and asks, how did this happen?

Any natural cause that I can find or imagine for the existence of the universe (and my own personal existence) that fits within the universe begs the question.

If you say we're the creations of some superbeing from Alpha Centauri, perhaps figments of its bored imagination, you still have to ask where that superbeing came from.

If we're accidents of the universe, you still have the universe to explain. If ours is but one in an infinite set of possible universes, we still need to explain why any of those universes should be. Even if you say the universe just is and always was, you still have to deal with the fact that it is.

If you say we resulted from a quantum fluctuation in a primordial vacuum, you still have to ask why the primordial vacuum existed. Why did the dimensionalities of space arise so that there could be a place for the vacuum to be, and where did the time come from, within which it could fluctuate and change? And how were the laws of quantum physics defined such that these fluctuations eventually resulted in *me*, in all my glory?

Nothing within the universe itself can exist to explain the fact that it exists.

So how does this lead to a suggestion of a God? By definition. We'll simply define God as the answer (which we otherwise can't fathom) for why there's something instead of nothing. God is the Prime Cause, the First Mover.

The interesting thing about such a definition of God is that of necessity, this God is somehow outside of, greater than, and independent of the universe. This God is nothing contained in this universe. So one might still happily be an atheist, if by that you mean that you don't believe in any God within this universe, because there's nothing about our answer that by itself demands that such a God has any presence in this universe except to cause it to be.

Indeed, the ancient Romans, who persecuted Christians for being "atheists," had a point. A supernatural God makes all the pagan nature gods look ridiculous—mere jealous creations of poets, figments of too much wine. Worse, it renders them unnecessary. And of course, by ridding the world of the gods of weather and crops, the culture suddenly had room to ask questions about natural, repeatable causes and effects. That's what made science possible.

It's odd, but until Christianity came along, atheism was never considered a reasonable option. Even the ancient Hebrews worried about leaving Yahweh for other gods, not about abandoning all belief in God altogether. According to the Psalms, "The fool says there is no God"; atheists in that time were madmen.

Of course, pure atheism in itself doesn't make much sense today either. While there is no intellectual contradiction in recognizing the possible existence of an otherwise unknown or even unknowable God, if you are certain that there is no God, you must have a pretty clear picture of the God you don't believe in. You can never rule out the possible existence of unimagined gods.

(There's a story about an Italian atheist philosopher, on his deathbed and as cranky and ornery as ever. A preacher from a New Age sect came to his bedside to try to convince the free-thinker of the wisdom to be found, at last, in his new religion. Finally, disgusted by the New Age preacher, the atheist leaned up, pointed to the door, and sent him packing, crying, "I don't believe in the Catholic God, and that's the real God! Why should I believe in yours?")

Atheism is not to be confused with agnosticism, which is merely stating that you don't know what to believe. But agnosticism is no answer to the "Why is there something instead of nothing?" question. Of course you don't know the answer; ultimately, no one knows. The question may not have an answer; not every question does. That's one of the joys of language: it allows for the creation of nonsense. "What's the difference between a duck?" "Why is a mouse when it spins?" But if you accept that the question "Why is there something instead of nothing?" is not completely nonsense, like a jabberwock or a purple cow; if you accept that an answer exists even if you suspect we'll never know what it is; then you essentially already believe in some sort of God.

Question Two: What Do I Want, and Why Do I Want It?

The second question for which "God" is a possible answer is another classic. What do I care about? What am I looking for in life? What am I ultimately longing for? What drives me? What gives me the impetus to get up in the morning and face another day?

This question starts with the assumption that everyone has at some level an indescribable longing that never seems to be satisfied; and it asks, what is this longing all about, really?

Is that a valid assumption? Are we all beset by unsatisfiable longings for some inexplicable something? Well, the hunt to satisfy such longings makes up the plot of three-quarters of all literature. It's the hunger that drives Odysseus for twenty years; it's the intangible goal symbolized by the ever-sought Holy Grail. You can find it in modern popular literature from romances to science fiction, from coming-of-age novels to 1960s pop songs. The dream always seems to be to escape from whatever is trapping you in the mundane, to chase after that mysterious something "out there"— preferably with the gorgeous partner of our dreams at our side. Philosophers call this the "search for the transcendent."

There's another side to the question, by the way. I could equally wonder not only what I am longing for but also where this longing is coming from in the first place—not just what I care about but also why I care.

My question pair thus identifies God with either the transcendent that we're searching for or, more subtly, the reason behind the fact that we're searching for a transcendent. This two-pronged "attack" of the transcendent into our mundane lives was described by the German theologian Karl Rahner (again), who used two hard-to-translate German words to describe it: the thing-we-all-are-aiming-for (*das Wovorher*) and the thing-inside-us-that's-the-source-of-why-we're-searching (*das Woraufhin*).

But rather than spouting German theology at you, I can put it in a much simpler form. God is what turns you on—or at least what is behind whatever turns you on. It's what gets you up in the morning and what you dream about in bed at night.

Every one of us has a religion, whether we think we do or not. For some of us, it's Islam; for others, it's Elvis (as noted in G. Dennis O'Brien's very funny book, *God and the New Haven Railroad—and Why Neither Is Doing Very Well*). But note exactly what I am saying now: if Elvis is your religion, that's different from saying that Elvis is your god. Rather, Elvis is what you've chosen to use to reach out to that indefinable something that you do feel closer to when you're all alone with the video player watching *Blue Hawaii* late at night. Ultimately, you worship that "indefinable something"; Elvis is just the way you've found to get closer to it.

This sort of longing is uniquely human. It's different from your cat's longing for tuna, your dog's longing to be petted. For one thing, tuna satisfies the cat; but at the end of the night, when you turn off the TV, even those two hours with Elvis leave you feeling a little unsatisfied. Despite his best effort, you still go to bed feeling lonesome tonight.

Of course, most of us are not worshipers at the Church of Elvis. The places where we look for the transcendent can be much more mundane and much more immediate.

There are the obvious religion substitutes: wealth and power, political causes, football teams, rock stars. Sometimes we madly throw ourselves into sex and drugs and rock-and-roll as a way to try to drown out this insistent attack of the transcendent, as if satiating the hungers of the body would still the hunger of the soul. Sometimes, instead of alcohol or cocaine, we overindulge in more socially acceptable "drugs," like our work or our families. (And then being forced into retirement or having your kids rebel against your overbearing presence becomes all the more unbearable.)

The philosopher who searches for truth is caught by this desire. The artist who searches for beauty, the romantic searching for love, the mathematician searching for elegance—all are responding to a need for something bigger than the ordinary.

One of the clearest expressions of this unsatisfied thirst for the transcendent is our desire for justice. "If God is good, why is there evil in the world?" asks the skeptic; but the very question presupposes not only a God but also an absolute of right and wrong. In his famous book of popular apologetics, *Mere Christianity*, C. S. Lewis uses this universal sense of "fairness" as the pointer to God. The equation can be turned a slightly different way: the presence of evil in the world—which any day's newspaper will demonstrate—proves that transcendent justice is sometimes most sharply apparent when it is absent.

Teenagers are often unimpressed by the use of justice as a proof of a good God, precisely because their sense of right and wrong is still at an in-between stage. They can see that their (or their younger siblings') childhood cries of "it's not fair" were often just juvenile expressions of selfishness, and so they may well be tempted to extrapolate that any such thing as "fairness" or "justice" is based on selfishness and is purely relative. (And of course writers from Ayn Rand to Hugh Hefner have capitalized on this idea, identifying selfishness with justice; it's not surprising that adolescents find their work so appealing.) Perhaps it's not fair to expect much more from someone who's still going through the early stages of moral development. Justice, like logic or physics, does not come naturally to the human animal. It is learned through experience. And that takes time.

Taste in anything takes time to develop. If we cringe at the music of the younger generation, it's not because it is any louder or more vulgar than what we listened to at that age but precisely because we're embarrassed to admit that we did listen to equally bad stuff, though we have since learned to tell the difference. It can be great fun to go back as an adult and experience our favorite childhood films or books; it's sometimes surprising to see what stands the test of time and what does not.

But because it takes learning to appreciate these transcendentals, we can never be certain that what we are experiencing isn't merely a set of social conventions. The fact that virtually every human society has held a number of these conventions in common is, if not highly suggestive, at least consistent with the claim that they are more than just conventions. But that still is no proof. Indeed, a sense of beauty or elegance or justice may simply provide some sort of biological evolutionary advantage, resulting in its being programmed into our genes. (Certainly guys with no sense of beauty or truth have a harder time getting dates—or at least they would, if there were any justice in this world!)

The problem of evil is a more mature and more profound attack on this notion of transcendent justice, however. How can a good God exist if he allows horrors like the Holocaust to occur? Tougher yet, how do we reconcile a good Creator with the existence of natural disasters like tornadoes and earthquakes? These questions cannot be dismissed by glib replies that "it has something to do with free will" or "someday we'll understand, but these things are beyond us now"—even though, maddeningly enough, both of those trite statements are probably true. The problem of evil is a question we have to come back to later, in another context, to explore more fully. For now, we merely acknowledge it. And we can point out that it doesn't deny the existence of a transcendent; it merely questions how that transcendent works.

The fact that such questions do bother us is itself an example of the kinds of urges I am talking about. It's one of the things that make us human. (Cats don't care about the Holocaust.) And all I claim now is that God could be defined as the source, and the object, of that urge for transcendence. These urges do not prove the existence of God, but they are demonstrations of— not inconsistent with—the possible existence of a transcendent, which we can choose to identify as God. At the very least, they raise questions about the origin and goal of those urges, for which some sort of God is one possible and not unreasonable hypothesis.

Question Three: How Do I Make Sense of My Life?

Our third question is the final classic: Who am I, and what am I supposed to be doing?

The second question, "What do I care about, and why do I care?" was very personal, as opposed to the more universal first question about how it happened that there is a me and a life and a universe in which to live it. But this third question unites the first two. Given this cosmos and the transcendent urges I feel in it, what am I supposed to be doing about it all? Who am I, and who am I supposed to be? Is there something I was supposed to be doing, and a Someone who knows what it is, even if maybe that Someone neglected to tell me about it?

The classic experience of the "identity crisis" is a standby of college sophomore angst and Woody Allen films. We see the chubby middle-aged executive trying to squeeze himself into a fire-engine-red sports car and knowingly smile to ourselves. We can laugh because we've all been there in some way or another.

That desire to know who we are and what is expected of us is a powerful human urge. It's the basis of our fascination with astrology and self-help books, as if our birth date or our favorite color is the key that can give us the instant answer to self-knowledge. "Know your place," sneers the villain who wants to crush the plucky young hero of the melodrama; but the hero is resisting the evil overlord precisely because he does know his place and he's confident that it doesn't happen to be where the villain would put him.

A confident knowledge of our place and our purpose in this world is one of the strengths of tradition (as Fiddler on the Roof reminds us). And we get understandably upset when, like Bob Dylan's Mr. Jones, we find ourselves someplace where we don't belong and we don't know why that is.

So where does God fit into this question?

Believing in God allows us to make sense of this yearning for place. We can identify God as the external standard against which we can measure not only where we are, in a metaphysical sense, but also where we're going (and at what speed). God becomes our metaphysical frame of reference. We can use God as the source of the order in a universe that has a place for us. Perhaps someone has assigned us our identity and purpose, and that is who we'll call God. Or at the very least, we can postulate a God who observes the choices we make and applauds (or cringes) at the way we make our own places for ourselves.

Or we can recognize the sense of alienation that every human being feels at times and conclude that wherever it is we really belong, it isn't here. And then we can define God as the unknown "whatever" whose presence defines the place where we will finally fit in.

Now notice, even more than the other questions, this argument has absolutely nothing to do with a "proof" of God's existence. Using God as an answer to the question "How do I orient myself in this universe?" makes sense only if you already hypothesize the existence of God. But as I cannot emphasize often enough, I am not the least bit interested in trying to prove the existence of God. I am trying, instead, to explain the utility of such a belief to a believer. And one of the greatest utilities of believing in God is that it provides precisely this sense of logic, order, and purpose.

That sense of purpose is especially useful because the universe can otherwise seem terribly purposeless. And that's a feeling that most people just don't like to live with.

"Deal with it," the agnostic can say, with justification. "It's a meaningless universe, and if there is any meaning at all, it's what we make for ourselves." That is a possible response to the question. But belief in God is another possibly valid answer. We don't have the external data to prove absolutely one of these answers or the other. We have to make our choice. Given what we know, either choice could be true.

But each choice has its consequences.

Notice what is missing in all the arguments to this point. In none of these three questions do we hypothesize a pie-in-the-sky God. In no case do I suggest that you should believe in God as a way of ensuring some sort of personal salvation or an eternal life of happiness after death. (That kind of belief comes later, as a result of one's theology, not as a motivation for it.) Nor do I suggest that believing in God is a way to satisfy your longing for revenge on your enemies or to provide hope that we will be reunited with departed loved ones.

You don't have to believe in life after death to believe in God. The Sadducees, a large party of devoutly believing Jewish religious leaders at the time of Christ, did not believe in life after death. (Jesus, of course, disagreed with this view, but that's a different issue.) Even without an afterlife or a Judgment Day, the fact of our existence and the nature of our human longings are enough to suggest the possible existence of some sort of external deity. And a God who was the source of our existence and our longings and our meaning is one whom we would by definition rank as the most important thing in our lives.

And finally, before we start to tease out their weak points, note one final strength in the three questions in this chapter: they represent multiple lines of argument supporting the same theory. We've focused on three different questions that the "God" hypothesis seems to be able to handle.

To a scientist, this is a telling point. We're used to perfectly good-looking theories turning out to be wrong because of some minor effect that we've forgotten, so we like to have more than one independent line of argument in support of the same theory. It's not enough to judge that certain meteorites come from Mars simply because they contain trapped Martian gas; it helps that they also have the same minerals as seen on Mars's surface and radionuclide ages that imply an origin from a Mars-sized planet. In the same way, the idea that postulating the existence of God is one possible answer to the "Why is there something instead of nothing?" question is nice enough, but seeing that the same God postulate also helps us understand the source of our deepest desires and even gives us a direction to look for meaning in our lives emphasizes that it's a very useful postulate indeed.

That's techie thinking. It's not philosophical or mathematical thinking. The fact is, none of those arguments is conclusive; and logically speaking, even an infinite number of inconclusive arguments still don't constitute a conclusive proof. But techies are not looking for proof. They're looking for confidence. And the more problems that a particular proposed hypothesis can handle, the more confidence we have that there's truth to be found in it.

CHAPTER 3

Good Science, Bad Philosophy

⋚ Complications and Confusions ⋛

None of the classic questions asked in Chapter Two has a conclusive or unique answer. None of the answers that I gave in that chapter, which claimed that belief in God can provide a possible solution to those questions, is even close to completely satisfactory. Remember, I never said I could answer those questions. I merely pointed out that these are the sorts of questions that can suggest to someone that the hypothesis of God might be a possible, useful way to proceed.

But it's a way to proceed that has its own potholes for the unwary. If there's one thing I hate about religion books, it's that arrogant attitude of smug satisfaction that we get when we think we've produced the ultimate answers to all the deep questions that have bothered the greatest thinkers of the ages. If the answers were so simple, those questions wouldn't still be with us. And the same is true here.

If you do assume that God exists in order to help you answer the three questions posed in Chapter Two, you run smack into some classic philosophical conundrums. The difficulties are well documented and well worth taking a look at. I'm going to go over just some of them—as with the questions themselves, I could hardly be exhaustive—and I'm going to take them in reverse order. (The most interesting trap for techies is found in our answer to the first question—why there is something instead of nothing. We'll spend the last two parts of this chapter digging into it further.)

We asked, "How do I make sense of my life?" and postulated that there is something called God that gives my life its orientation. Fine. *But whose life is this, anyway?*

What about predestination versus free will? Does the existence of a God who determines my "place in the universe" mean that my life choices have already been mapped out? Is everything predestined? Or do I get judged on how close I come to guessing God's secret plan for me? If God does have a plan for me, why does he make it so hard for me to figure it out? And what if I don't like it—don't I have a say in this?

For one thing, we are limited in our choices. We are limited by the laws of physics and by the constraints of the time and place in which we live. I will never be a basketball all-star. I will never be a courtier to King Louis XV of France. I will never flap my arms and fly to the moon. Free will is not the ability to choose anything imaginable but merely the ability to choose among a set of limited possibilities.

But clearly, the problem is deeper than that. Just as Newton's deterministic mechanics, when extrapolated to the physics and chemistry of the human brain, has a hard time explaining free will, likewise the very postulate of an all-knowing, all-powerful God who defines the purpose in our life, makes free will hard to understand. Yet if we don't have free will, any further argument is pointless (since we would not be free to accept or reject those arguments). Our experience in life gives us every reason to believe (and no particular reason to doubt) that we are free agents. Indeed, our desire for freedom, our repugnance at the idea of being a slave—no matter how happy—is a fundamental data point, telling us that our understanding of this omnipotent life-defining God, like our understanding of Newtonian physics, is missing something essential if it doesn't account for free will.

It's a sticky point, with no easy way out. If we assume the existence of God as the answer to who defines our life, we must recognize that this God must be consistent with the observational fact of our freedom to make that definition for ourselves. That's a tricky kind of God to imagine. But then, no one ever said it would be easy.

Another question that used God as an answer asked, "What do we want, and why do we want it?" OK, suppose there is a God who is the source of some of our deepest urges. *Is every urge an urge from God?* Obviously not.

The medievals understood this point. They described the different urges that seem to come from outside one's own person as "spirits," angels and devils. To them, angels and devils were not cartoon concepts or characters in some fantasy TV show but descriptions of actual, ordinary, mundane experiences.

A model student takes a gun to school and kills two of his friends. A lover in anger says the one cruel remark she knows is most likely to hurt the one she loves. A dieter deliberately walks into an ice-cream shop.

One of the characteristics of actions like these is that we know darn well that we shouldn't do them, that they're stupid, that the momentary pleasure of the act—if there is any pleasure to it at all—is nothing compared to the miserable consequences. We know that the hot fudge sundae is never as good as it looks, that the pornographic film will not satisfy our lusts, that the alcohol won't make our hurt go away. Cigarettes taste ghastly, ruin your health, and cost a fortune, but millions of people smoke them anyway. We play the lottery despite the odds. Yet at times we feel an overwhelming urge to do these things. What gets into us? Watching it happen to someone else, we ask, "Whatever possessed him to do that?" Does our modern psychobabble tell us anything more than what the ancients meant when they said that such a person was "possessed by a devil"?

At other times, these outside impulses are strokes of genius. Some of the greatest acts in history occurred when ordinary people gave themselves over completely to extraordinary ideas: Mother Teresa going to India, Einstein imagining a ride on the crest of a light wave, Rosa Parks refusing to give up her seat on the bus.

But worst of all, there are ideas that on the surface look like good plans, noble projects, or bold and original thoughts but underneath serve to do nothing but stoke our egoism and paranoia. When does sadism masquerade as "tough love"? At what point does "protecting the weak" cross the line and become an enervating paternalism?

Where do these impulses come from? And how do we tell the good ones from the bad?

These questions have plagued people since the dawn of humanity. One of the advantages of being part of an organized religion, as we'll discuss in Part Two, is that most religions have developed techniques to differentiate between good and evil and more subtly between urges that merely seem good and those that really are good.

But the point here is that once you have adopted some goal other than self-interest to guide your actions, you can be left with some tricky situations. You're liable to make mistakes; indeed, mistakes are inevitable. And that opens up the whole realm of sin, of guilt, of the need for forgiveness and redemption, and the need to forgive and redeem others. It's a can of worms, and there's no getting away from it.

Finally, we asked, "Why is there something instead of nothing?" If the existence of the physical universe is our demonstration of God's existence, the answer to our first question, can't we use the evidence of science to determine what God must be like? *Are the laws of science the same as the laws of God?* Is science just experimental theology?

This is perhaps the most insidious temptation of them all for the technically literate person.

One obvious fallacy is to extrapolate from the latest and still tentative discoveries of contemporary science to justify some already held prejudice. In the nineteenth century, social Darwinists used the brand-new theory of evolution to justify their greedy, rapacious version of capitalism. The Nazis used the same theory to justify eugenics and other horrors, convinced as they were of their own racial superiority. (If today many good religious people who, alas, are scientifically naïve, are suspicious of evolution, can you blame them? The abuse of the theory of evolution by pseudo-scientists has given the nonscientists a very understandable reason to distrust what started out as a perfectly innocent and quite valid observation of nature.)

But even well-intended extrapolations from science can lead to wildly wrong philosophical results. As I mentioned earlier, we scientists are used to confirming our theories with results; if the right answer comes out, we think that this confirms our starting hypotheses. But in fact, although this method works in a rough-and-ready way in science, generally speaking, that's not a logically valid deduction. Simply having a workable system that handles most day-to-day problems does not at all imply that our system is ultimately correct. After all, most engineers never have to look beyond Newtonian physics, and yet we all know there comes a point where Newton's laws no longer work.

The trouble is that the failure of our assumptions (like the failure of Newton's laws) are most likely to occur precisely where we are extrapolating from the everyday world to extreme cases. And the philosophical issues of origins and meaning and the ultimate longing of the soul are precisely those sorts of extreme questions. It's just at the point of the "religious" questions that we should be most cautious in extrapolating from our scientific experience, recognizing that it is precisely there where our assumptions are most likely to fail us.

This is a rather unsettling result, especially to us techies who are understandably proud of our reasoning ability.

≥ Defining the Universe, with Two Examples ≤

The history of science and philosophy is full of examples of the failures of that sort of extrapolation

Around the year A.D. 500 in India, a great mathematician and astronomer named Aryabhata published a book on geometry and astronomy. It was based on both his own work and the accumulated wisdom he'd inherited from the Greeks; through them, he had access to data on planetary positions going back to the Babylonians. A thousand years before Copernicus, Aryabhata proposed that Earth spins; he said that what we perceive as the daily motion of the stars rising and setting is the evidence of this spin. Unlike Copernicus, he still had the Ptolemaic system of planets moving around Earth, but the spinning-Earth-and-fixed-stars universe was a major departure from Aristotelian physics, one that led to enormous controversy in India for the next several hundred years.

Whether it was this idea of a fixed set of background stars or some other unspoken motivation (his surviving writings are sketchy, to say the least), the observational data available to him and his advanced understanding of geometry led him to calculate the length of time it takes for the moon, Mercury, Venus, Mars, Jupiter, and Saturn to make one complete circuit of the heavens, relative to those fixed stars. And he gives these numbers in his book to a remarkable degree of accuracy, even compared to present-day known values (his figures are off by less than 1/100,000th in some cases). This is important science, of a quality that would not be equaled for more than a thousand years.

Yet there is a problem with his data. It's the way he presents these numbers. The trouble is, he wants to express the period of, say, Mars, in terms of an Earth year; but the period of Mars is not some exact number of Earth years long. It's approximately 1.8807 years, according to our best data to date. We express the fraction of a year by all those numbers past the decimal point, and it's understood that whatever uncertainty remains in that data lies in the last significant figure. (The uncertainty is not in our precision of measurement but in the motion of Mars itself. Because of perturbations by other planets, its period will vary ever so slightly from year to year.)

But Aryabhata didn't have the decimal point to use because mathematicians hadn't invented it yet. So how could he express the period of Mars? He was very clever. He could do it as a ratio. For instance, he could say that in 205 Earth years you'll find Mars making 109 circuits of the heavens. Do the arithmetic, and you find that this ratio matches the modern figure to within the tiny variation noted earlier.

Of course, it's not correct in the sixth decimal place. It couldn't be—no planet's orbit would be—because no planet orbits the sun with a period that is a perfect ratio of a round number of Earth years (nor is any period constant to that precision, for that matter). The period of each planet, expressed in terms of an Earth year, is always a slightly varying number whose values beyond the decimal point never occur in a repeating pattern. It is a number that cannot be precisely expressed as a ratio—it's what is known as an *irrational* number.

That's not surprising to us. Irrational numbers, like pi and the square root of 2, occur all the time in nature. When it turns out that two planets' orbits actually do make a simple ratio, we immediately look for the gravitational perturbations that could force planets into such a state because a simple ratio of planetary periods is not generally what we would expect. (The ratio of the periods of Neptune and the "dwarf planet" Pluto, for example, really is 2/3, on average, given the fluctuations in their orbits. Understanding how orbiting bodies get "captured" into resonances like these is one of the goals of modern planetary orbital theory. And the fact that Pluto is so small that it could be trapped in such a state is one of the arguments for why it is only a dwarf planet.)

Aryabhata didn't know all that. He just knew that these ratios—hardly simple numbers in themselves, measured to a sixtieth of a circle—did match a thousand years' worth of data. And given ratios such as these for each planet, like astronomers before him going back to the Babylonians, he took the next obvious step of comparing all the ratios against a common period. In essence, he multiplied all these ratios together to find the common denominator of the ratios for all the planets together. With the Babylonian data, this works out to be 4.32 billion Earth years.

What does this common denominator mean? If the planets all really did orbit with periods in perfect ratios to Earth's period, 4.32 billion years would represent the amount of time it would take for the whole system of planetary positions to repeat itself.

Now, put yourself into the ancient Hindu cosmology, one that accepted the astrological idea of human and earthly events being controlled by the positions of the planets. If the planets repeat their positions every 4.32 billion years, as the best astronomy of those days implied, then this calculation provided "solid scientific proof" that life on Earth was indeed trapped in an endless cycle, relentlessly and inevitably repeating itself. And science even gave us the length of time between cycles of the universe: 4.32 billion years!

Later Hindu astrologer-astronomers speculated about when exactly the time was when all the planets started out perfectly lined up, how long it would be (given current planetary positions) before this perfect lineup would occur again, and what this would mean for the future of humanity.

Knowing what we know today, that planetary periods are not perfect ratios, we immediately see the fallacy of this argument. Planetary positions never repeat. There was no moment when all the planets were perfectly aligned, nor will there be in the future. There is no scientific basis for the concept of a repeating solar system or a repeating cycle of human existence.

Yet this version of Hindu philosophy seemed to be backed up by a science that was not only good for its day but darn impressive by modern standards. The numbers it was based on were good to four or five significant figures! What more could you ask for?

Now move ahead eleven hundred years and consider Johannes Kepler, the man whose laws of planetary motions made the heliocentric system actually work. Copernicus had proposed a system where the sun was the center of the solar system and Earth moved around it, but the Copernican system was still a system of circular orbits. And so just like Ptolemy before him, in order to match the actual observed positions of the planets, he had to assume "epicycles"—the planets moved in little circles around their "average" circular orbits. And he had to assume "eccentric" circles, circular orbits that were centered not exactly on the center of the solar system but on some point offset from that center. Even the sun itself did not sit at the exact center but rather did a small circular dance about its average position.

None of this was satisfactory to Kepler. The problem for him wasn't one of inelegance; rather, it was a theological problem. Kepler, you see, had a very peculiar notion of God's place in the universe. Unlike the standard theologies of his day, Catholic or Protestant, Kepler's personal mysticism told him that everything in the physical world exactly mirrored, or paralleled, the spiritual realm. Thus to him the light of the sun represented in some real way, more than just symbolically, the Holy Spirit pouring itself upon Earth. And the source of this light, the sun, was to his thinking the physical manifestation of God the Father himself!

As he explained in a letter to his friend Herwart von Hohenburg (quoted in Job Kozhamthadam's wonderful book *The Discovery of Kepler's Laws*), among the reasons for adopting his theory for the orbits of the planets was the mystical significance of the structure of the celestial sphere: "The center is the origin and beginning of the sphere. Indeed, the origin has precedence everywhere and is by nature always the first. When we apply this consideration to the most Holy Trinity, the center refers to the image of God the Father. Hence the center of this material world-sphere should be adorned by the most ornate body, that is the Sun, on account of light and life."

It would hardly be fitting, reasoned Kepler, for God the Father to make this eccentric little dance around the center of the universe. God the Father had to be the center, in a literal sense. So Kepler went searching for an astronomical system that allowed the sun, and therefore God the Father, to remain fixed. Eventually, he hit upon replacing the circles and epicycles of Copernicus with elliptical orbits, and the rest is history.

Kepler the philosopher also proposed an interesting axiom of philosophy. He maintained that no true deduction can be made from false premises. We merely note in passing that his deductions of planetary motions in elliptical orbits have stood the test of time far better than his odd theological premises.

Kepler's theology was considered ludicrous by most people even in his own day; indeed, it probably prevented a lot of scientists from paying attention to his orbital theories at that time. Certainly no one takes it seriously today. But it served to inspire him to a breakthrough in understanding the motions of planets, which in turn inspired and confirmed Newton's mechanics—one of the single biggest breakthroughs in the history of science. (Newton's personal theology, by the way, was also pretty strange.)

In Aryabhata's case, good science was used to support a philosophical picture of the cosmos that almost certainly is not accurate. In Kepler's case, a highly improbable theology directly led to excellent science. Comparing these two cases, we can deduce that at the very least, there is no clear-cut relationship between the quality of one's science and the quality of one's theology.

≫ The Inverse Problem ≪

The stories I have just recounted are examples of what's known as the "inverse problem." Science regularly comes up against this situation. In geophysics, for instance, you can measure the gravity field at Earth's surface and then try to deduce what ore masses or rock structures below the ground produced that gravity field, but there is no one unique array of ore masses that gives rise to the measured gravity anomalies. The problem is said to be "under-determined": though many possibilities can be ruled out, there remain any number of different possible starting conditions that could give rise to the same gravity field. Only one of those start-ing conditions is true.

The point is, of course, that Kepler was exactly wrong: it's quite possible to start with false premises and still arrive at a true conclusion.

Back in 1865, James Clerk Maxwell derived his famous equa-tions uniting electricity and magnetism (predicting the electro-magnetic wave nature of light, which led to the possibility of radio, the transmission of AC power, and just about everything else we use in electronics today) by assuming that the "ether" behaved like a regular fluid, with a finite density, compressibility, and so forth. His theory led to Einstein's theory of relativity, which in turn showed that there was no such thing as an "ether." Yet our electri-cal appliances still work, regardless.

In 1800, astronomers used Bode's law of planetary positions to look for a planet between Mars and Jupiter, and the first aster-oid Ceres was discovered; a hundred years later, Clyde Tombaugh was guided by Percival Lowell's calculations to discover Pluto. We now know that in both cases, the theories were completely unjus-tified; it turns out that neither Pluto nor the asteroids have the properties that the theories used to predict them actually pre-dicted. But the coincidences in position did occur; the asteroids and Pluto are still out there even though the theories that led to their discovery have been discarded.

Of course, even in science, not every false assumption will inevitably lead to a true conclusion. As with the inverse prob-lem, we can rule out lots of possibilities that will never work. But still, it is striking to see how differently philosophy and physics behave. Physics seems to be pretty robust; if your starting assump-tions are not too far away from reality, you have a good chance of stumbling somewhere close to the truth. Physics converges on the truth. Philosophical implications based on that physics, by contrast, exhibit what could be called extreme sensitivity to starting conditions. Reminiscent of mathematical chaos, a slight change in your philosophical assumptions can result in a radically diverging outcome.

Science is an approximation of the truth. The art of the scientist, and even more of the engineer, is knowing how close is close enough—when does the job we're trying to do demand higher precision, and when is such precision a waste of time? But inevitably, scientific results carry with them a small degree of uncertainty. That is precisely why they are so dangerous to use as the basis of one's philosophy, given this extreme sensitivity to starting conditions in philosophy.

Every scientific "fact," every data point, has—spoken or unspoken—error bars, those little lines on the graph that show the range of uncertainty in the data. No scientific number is perfect. No measurement is perfect. And every scientific theory, no matter how good or useful, is at best only an approximation of the truth. It can be a phenomenally good approximation, but phenomenally good is not the same as perfect. If you try to extrapolate too far from your data, you're very likely to go wrong. A religion based on the best science of its day is almost certainly a false religion.

Indeed, Michael Buckley in his book *At the Origins of Modern Atheism* suggests that the atheism of the eighteenth and nineteenth centuries arose precisely because the religious thinkers of those times tried to base their religion on the new certainties of Newton and Leibniz. In some cases, they tried to fit the traditional idea of an omnipotent, active God into the gaps where the new physics was not yet successful in completely describing how the universe worked (say, the motion of the planets dragged through the ether or the chemistry of life). But as physics and chemistry developed, they kept reducing the role of God in the universe until he was nothing more than the clock maker who started things going and then watched them evolve from a distance. Finally, it reached the point where a mathematician like Laplace could quite properly say of such a God, "I have no need of that hypothesis." God was squeezed out of the gaps and out of their universe.

The God of the philosophers had become delaminated from the God of revelation and from the God of one's personal religious experience. The Deist theologians who had based their faith in God on what they saw as his necessary interventions to make Newton's mechanical universe work (reminiscent, I am afraid, of today's proponents of "intelligent design") clung so closely to the God of our first question, the God responsible for the natural universe, that they lost sight of the God who would answer our longings and give us our place in that universe. It's no wonder people became disillusioned with such a vision of God and declared themselves atheists; as science progressed, this God no longer served to satisfy any of the reasons (like our questions in Chapter Two) for belief.

Indeed, forging too close a tie between one's religious or philosophical beliefs and the best science of the day can be problematic. You can't conclude that just because your philosophy is based on the best science of the day, it must be true. And certainly such a philosophy can't be complete, since science itself is never complete (much less completely true).

But you can't even run the argument the other way and try to conclude that since your science is based on a certain philosophical viewpoint, the success of that science proves your viewpoint was correct. It's the inverse problem again: you can arrive at the same scientific explanation from more than one philosophical starting point.

After all, modern science developed precisely because the medievals believed in a creator God, and thus they had the confidence to assume that this apparently chaotic universe ultimately did make sense (and was worthy of study). The fact that science has turned out to be a fruitful endeavor does not, unfortunately, prove that their assumption of a Creator was necessarily correct.

On the other hand, a modern biologist starts with a purely mechanical view of the universe. (Unlike physics, which has been humbled by the oddities of the quantum state, biology still operates in a Newtonian universe.) The fact that the biologist can map the genome and even invent pills that restore your sexual prowess and cure your baldness does not necessarily mean that his or her mechanical viewpoint is correct, either.

Hindu astronomy does not prove Hindu cosmology. Kepler's laws do not prove Kepler's theology. Scientific observations can appear to be consistent with a certain worldview, and some worldviews can even lead to correct scientific descriptions and laws, but the laws don't prove the beliefs. Science can't make that judgment, either way.

PART TWO

Why Would a Techie Join an Organized Religion?

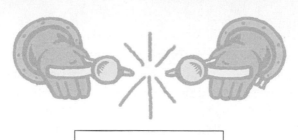

CHAPTER 4

Big Science, Big Religion

≳ Why Religion? ≲

A techie was in a Bible study class, learning the story of the Prodigal Son. "After going through his inheritance," the techie heard, "the Prodigal Son was reduced to feeding the pigs in a far distant land. But when he realized that a welcome awaited him in his father's house, in sorrow and repentance the son returned." The techie listened intently to the whole story. But a puzzled look came across his face.

The leader of the Bible study saw the look and asked him, "What's the problem?"

"After the son went home to his father," the techie wanted to know, "who took care of the pigs?"

As we noted in Part One, techie pragmatism means that scientists and engineers are likely to approach religion with their own peculiar set of expectations and questions. But the very idea of an engineer in church raises its own questions. What opportunities, and what problems, does the technical, pragmatic worldview create for the churchgoing techie? For that matter, why would a techie join an organized religion in the first place?

Indeed, there is a distinction that many techies make between accepting the possible existence of God and actual participation in a church. In Part One, I raised three questions that postulating the existence of God is useful in answering: Why is there something instead of nothing? What is the source and the object of my deepest yearnings? And how do I make sense of my life? If you grant that any one of these questions could be a valid question and that an answer could possibly exist for any of these questions, you have implicitly accepted the possible existence of something bigger than our ordinary, everyday life: a transcendent being. The name we give that transcendent being is God.

But a techie might well ask, is there any evidence that this God, should it exist, wants any interaction with the created universe, with the inhabitants of Earth, or with me in particular? And what is it that we expect of ourselves in relationship to that God? Is there something I'm supposed to be doing here?

And even if there is something I should be doing, why should I need a religion to do it? Why do I need to involve anyone or anything else in order to be in a relationship with the transcendent? Just as we approached the question of God from the pragmatic point of view, we can put our questions about religion in a similar "functional" framework. What is the function of an organized religion? And how well do the ones out there perform that function?

For many techies, religion carries the connotation of an unresponsive hierarchy, a heavy-handed bureaucracy, a stifling set of rules. The costs and dangers of Big Anything are real and familiar to every techie: high overhead, loss of control, a lot of paperwork or other justifications to bosses who you suspect haven't a clue— the Dilbert syndrome. So why would a techie put up with it?

In the high-tech business world, big outfits are often the only show in town or at least the only place that has the opportunities and the tools; they own the sandbox where the techies yearn to play. For the chance to do what they love to do, and get paid to do it, techies will put up with the "suits." The same fact of life holds true in organized religion. To the techie, the preacher in the pulpit might be just another incarnation of Dilbert's pointy-haired boss; but if the benefits are worth it, they'll ignore him just as they ignore their bosses.

So what are the benefits of belonging to a religion? What possible useful functions could a religion provide to us techies? What's the least we should demand from and the most we should expect to get out of a religion? And how can we apply these tests to the religions already out there?

Religions—plural. For when we talk about adopting a religion, we're moving from a generalized, formless theism to something more formal, more explicitly "theological." And unlike the present state of science, at least, where everyone more or less agrees on what the equations for Newton's laws are, in religion we have the problem of choosing not only among many competing religions but among their sects and denominations. How does a technically oriented person judge which, if any, are worth looking into?

(I once heard an interesting alternate universe suggested at a science-fiction convention, where everyone accepted more or less the same religion but followed very distinct sects among the sciences that they practiced. Indeed, in quantum physics, we're already beginning to see schisms into separate and at least partly incompatible schools of thought.)

Even if you reject all organized religions, these are still useful questions to ask. No matter what your faith, or lack of it, we all still face living in a world where organized religions do exist. A lot of them. Nobody expects you to believe in all of them; in this context, it doesn't matter if you believe in any of them. Understanding what a religion is all about is a useful tool in dealing not only with a religion you might believe in but even more in dealing with all the religions that you are certain you do not believe in. Once we know what religion in general is supposed to do, we can have some basis for deciding how well any particular religion performs that function and how we should relate to any other religion outside of the one we've decided to believe in.

As a starting point, it seems safe to say that the general function of a religion is to provide a systematic way for human beings to deal with God. But that assumption immediately raises the first question: Does God want to deal with us? What evidence is there that he (or she or it) wants anything to do with us?

One answer to this central question is a very practical one: if he doesn't want to engage with us, our reasons for believing in him are useless. A God who does not interact with us is not one we can use to define our lives, nor is it a God we can use to help us make sense of our yearnings. Unrequited love is not my idea of heaven (rather, the opposite; it's no fun for either party).

Indeed, even the idea that there is a God who is responsible for the existence of the universe would be an unsatisfactory answer to the question of the why of existence if that God doesn't have anything to do with the universe after having created it. In such a case, the universe would continue to have no reason for being. A God who answers the question of "why is there something" really has to be the answer to "why is there everything?" And everything includes us—all of humanity. I may be only one person out of six billion, on one planet out of six billion planet-bearing stars, in one galaxy out of six hundred billion galaxies, in one of Lord knows how many parallel universes; but nonetheless, I am. I exist. I am unique. And any God who is responsible for the unlikely "accident" of my existence is, by definition, already in some sort of relationship with me.

If that is the case, if there is a relationship, then why am I not aware of it? The theist would answer that I am aware of it—even if only dimly at times. That awareness is what in Chapter Two I called the hunger for the transcendent and the source of our transcendent hungers. And satisfying that hunger is the meaning of my life. The way I do that defines who I am. (The three questions in Chapter Two, about existence, yearnings, and identity, do ultimately tie together.)

But my awareness of that transcendent hunger is not constant. It comes and goes, often coming in an overpowering way that makes me want to run and hide myself, sometimes coming at the most inopportune times, and too often evaporating at the moment when I most want to grasp it. So how do I deal with that elusive yearning?

And the hunger for the transcendent can often be confused with other hungers. How can I tell it apart from my other, more mundane physical desires?

And if and when I do grasp (or am grasped by) that hunger, what in the world can I do about it? I am a material guy (or girl), living in a material world. (Even cheesy pop singers can sometimes stumble onto real insights.) I need a concrete way to deal with that hunger, just as I need a concrete way to deal with my hungers for food or sex.

And dealing with those hungers isn't always easy or safe. We have all learned from painful personal experience that simply giving in to those hungers—be they for food, sex, or religion—isn't always the right answer. Indeed, indigestion of the soul can be the most painful result of such an overindulgence—and the hardest to sleep off.

These, then, are the functions of religion: to record and systematize our collective experience of the transcendent; to help us recognize and make sense of it; and to give us something we can do to participate in it while avoiding its dangers. That's what makes belonging to a religion useful. Following this chain of reasons allows us to become more specific in outlining the various jobs we expect a religion to do.

≳ Why Organized? ≲

If there is an interaction between us and God, is there any benefit in formalizing it as an organized, group activity? Why do we need an organized religion to systematize our relationship with God?

This is not a trivial question. In most of England nowadays, the majority of the population still claim to be believers in God, but they have effectively abandoned any particular denominational ties. In America, there is a long and deep tradition of "finding Jesus on your own." Indeed, the American Congregational movement and many other branches of Protestantism are based on a strong suspicion of any sort of large institutional church. These suspicions were born out of the historical experience of a people who concluded that the medieval institution of the church had become irreformably corrupted and that the corruption of power was an inevitable adjunct of any strong institution. Far safer, they believed, to abandon the institution entirely than to let its power take control of the individual.

Even Thomas Aquinas—that bastion of the medieval church—concluded that any individual could in principle come to learn how to find and recognize the transcendent, and how to respond to it, all alone on his or her own. It's possible. It's also possible that a sufficiently smart person could invent all of mathematics and physics on his or her own. (There is, after all, the example of Srinivasa Ramanujan, the remarkable self-taught Indian mathematician who in the early twentieth century succeeded in reinventing Newton's Calculus by himself.)

But it's not likely to happen too often.

Even a Congregational church has some sort of structure, local though it might be. And even a person who follows the adage to "find Jesus on your own" first heard that adage—and first heard about Jesus—from somebody else. Bibles and other holy scriptures don't spontaneously print themselves.

A key element of techie wisdom, and one might argue the whole secret of human progress, can be summarized by the aphorism "Don't waste your time reinventing the wheel." And an organized community is the first place that an individual goes to begin to learn about either science or religion. Consider this: even those fiercely independent computer programming types who teach themselves out of computer books, away from the formal academic community, are nevertheless relying on the benefits of the community that exists to produce those books, and they seek approval (and employment) from whatever part of the community they decide is forward-thinking and entrepreneurial enough for their tastes. In the same way, the faithful souls who claim to eschew organized religion (not attending church, for instance) but who still read religious books and pay attention to what religious teachers have to say are depending on the very churches that they disdain.

And so you can see that the techie case for organized religion closely parallels the techie experience of organized science. The limitations of each community are very similar, too.

Both science and religion are taught to us at an early age—too early, some might argue: when we're forced to memorize Bible passages or the names of organic chemicals, the experience can stunt our appreciation of either for the rest of our lives. Most teenagers have had enough of both to last a lifetime and often never give either a second chance.

Those who do endure the introductory courses long enough to get to the good stuff know better, of course. Just as there is more to science than working out physics problems to get the answers that appear in the back of the book, so religion is more than parroting set phrases and miming obscure rituals. Yet I don't know of any other way of teaching physics than by starting with those awful first-year physics problems; and likewise, the rules and rituals are generally where you have to begin in order to live a religion and thus learn where and how to experience what that religion can offer. Painful as it may be, following the well-worn paths of a community's accumulated wisdom is still the fastest, easiest, and most reliable way of getting up to speed on the subject.

Once we have gotten up to speed, we still depend on the organized community to develop and extend our knowledge. While the classic Hollywood religious "visionary," like the classic Hollywood mad scientist, is a slightly crazed loner whom nobody understands, with wild hair and a fanatical gleam in the eye, the actual experience of people in both science and religion is quite different. Indeed, the more typical practitioner of science or religion is a far more conservative, far more careful person, a team player, a member of a community, who is all too aware of his or her own fallibility and shortcomings.

In both science and theology, progress is made in tiny incremental stages based on slow, unglamorous work, building on the work of a large body of fellow laborers, past and present, whose ideas have already passed the test of time or who can be available now to check your work and keep you honest. Both science and religion depend on continuity and on community.

Progress in both fields is dependent on tricky judgments constantly subjected to the criticism and revision of one's peers. That means, among other things, that an idea that's "ahead of its time" often does more harm than good to the eventual progress of the field, if all it does is incite skepticism. As the 1920s social commentator and gadfly Charles Fort put it, "A tree cannot find out, as it were, how to blossom until comes blossom time. A social group cannot find out the use of steam engines until comes steam engine time." And likewise, a bright idea in science or religion that can't be fit into the present state of knowledge will have no way of adding itself to the sum of human knowledge; instead, it is certain to be misunderstood and, justifiably at that point, discarded. That kind of prophecy bears no fruit. "And by their fruits you will know them."

That sense of progress, slowly and painfully gained, applies not only to the general advancement of knowledge in a people but also to the growth of knowledge within an individual. It takes a lifetime, and a lot of work, for any given individual to really learn a religion or a science. An organized structure in science or religion helps us develop our understanding, slow though it might be, to support us while we digest our knowledge and turn it into wisdom.

But the community does something even more important in the long run: it allows us to preserve and transmit that hard-won wisdom to future generations.

Both science and religion depend on the accurate communication of difficult and subtle ideas. Yet in spite of the inherent difficulties in expressing these subtle thoughts, the urge to communicate, to propagate, to hand on what we have learned to a new generation is a common thread in both science and religion. (And the opposite urge, to keep our knowledge "secret" and held apart for an elite priesthood, is a sure sign of a science or a religion gone bad—the gnosticism of the crank.) Precisely because these ideas are so hard to communicate, one needs to take special care to make sure they are communicated well.

Even the most modest approach to propagating one's insights requires some degree of structure. If you want to leave your wisdom to those who come after you merely by writing books, you still need publishers and printers—and a populace educated enough to be able to read. If you are going to hand your wisdom down by word of mouth, you still need disciples to receive your petals of wisdom. We are a social people. Only hermits can live without some degree of organization in their lives; and even they derive their power and significance from their contrast with the society they have deliberately turned their backs on.

This urge for a religion to hand on its hard-won insights is what led to the formation of the medieval university. Universities are an interesting link between techiedom and religion, by the way; they were originally founded by the church, and they became the cradle of technology. And they illustrate one reason why both science and religion need organization: ultimately, someone has to run those universities, to pay their bills if nothing else.

More than cash is needed, however. A university needs a structure and an entire culture to prepare new professors, new administrators, and new researchers to maintain the path where seekers of knowledge can progress in an open, understandable, and universally accepted route from apprentice to master to doctor. That's structure; that's organization. Not surprisingly, the structure of a university looks very much like the structure of a religion, even down to the kinds of robes that you wear at special ceremonies like graduation.

And with structure and its attendant hierarchy come all the very real possibilities for abuse that continue to drive many people away from Big Religion (or Big Science). But ultimately some sort of organization is needed. Though the fight against the corruption of that organization is never-ending, it is never in vain.

≷ Comparing Religions ≷

The functions of religion, as noted earlier, are to record and systematize our collective experience of the transcendent, to help us recognize and make sense of it, and to give us something to participate in. We'll examine each of these points in more detail in the next chapter. However, before we get into them, it might be worthwhile here to pause and ask what these functions suggest about the minimum and maximum expectations one should have of any organized religion.

To fulfill its function, a religion needs to have a way of recording and communicating the history of God's interactions with its people. In addition, it needs to have a way of defining what counts—how you can tell which purported transcendental interactions are real, which ones matter, what they mean, whom they apply to, and who's in and who's out. And it should provide some guidance as to what should be done about those intrusions of the transcendent into our lives—some method for responding and worshiping as an individual and as a community.

Notice that some things that we tend to assume would be part of any religion are missing from this list. For instance, there's nothing here about a moral code. We are used to getting our Ten Commandments in Sunday school, but there's nothing inherent in the concept of a religion that demands that it act as a moral guidepost or judge. Discerning true from false messages of the transcendent is not necessarily the same thing as discerning good from evil. Indeed, if you read the scriptures from which we get the Ten Commandments, you realize that the ancient Jews were quite proud of their moral code (and justifiably so) precisely on the grounds that no other god was as good as their God because no other god had given anything like this moral law to other peoples. They recognized it as unique. We now take it for granted.

Likewise, there is nothing here about a cosmology, a definitive system to explain where the universe comes from and how it works. We used the existence of a God as a way of providing a why for the universe, but we also note that there are other reasons for believing in God. If your reason for believing is only to explain your transcendent urges, for instance, then you don't necessarily need a cosmology God. But more to the point, even if you are using God as an explanation for "why is there something instead of nothing," you don't necessarily have to tie that God to any specific answer: as the mathematicians point out, sometimes it's enough just to recognize that a solution exists without being committed to any particular solution.

In that regard, I note once again that there is nothing inherent in a religion that demands some sort of belief in an afterlife or a judgment. (Judgment might be implied if we are using God to provide us with a meaning for our life, but it is not required; as noted before, the God who provides us with a meaning must at least be flexible enough to allow us our free will, and that can include accepting our choices without necessarily judging them.)

My point isn't to argue that there is anything wrong with the idea of judgment or afterlife or cosmology or ethical rules. Rather it's to point out that a religion that does include these things has provided extra features beyond the minimum set one might expect to receive.

And that's a brave thing for a religion to do. As any software author will tell you, the more features you add to your program, the more opportunities you have to introduce bugs and screw things up. Not surprisingly, in the history of religions, one consistently encounters tensions between these two tendencies. You can have a "bare bones" religion that offers simplicity of use but has limited utility. Such a religion could get by without a standard set of ceremonies for births, marriages, and funerals or a detailed set of ethical rules or a Sunday school to teach them to your kids.

Or you can have a "full-featured" religion that provides many services but carries a high overhead: someone's got to define and keep track of those rules; someone's got to run those ceremonies; someone's got to provide milk and cookies for the Sunday school. And belonging to that religion means putting up with those someones even when you disagree with how they're doing things.

From these considerations, we can deduce a few common trends that can make a religion more or less successful.

In general, it looks to me like the old established firms have certain unshakable advantages over new start-ups. (Of course, as I am a representative of one of the major brand names, you may take this opinion with the grain of salt it warrants.) For one thing, ancient religions have the advantage of a longer history on which to draw, giving them more examples of times when God has appeared to have interacted with people, more "raw data" on which to do theology. Likewise, they have more experience coming up with rules for living and dealing with the transcendent that are likely to fit the way that human beings are actually put together (rather than the way we would like to believe we are). And any religion that has succeeded at surviving for a thousand years or more is likely to know well how to play the delicate game of dancing with changing times without surrendering to the fads of the moment.

Indeed, one advantage of a big religion is that it affords the opportunity for many different and coexisting ways to believe or worship. The varieties of ways in which one can establish and nurture a relationship with the transcendent are as varied as humanity itself, and so it is useful for a religion to offer different varieties of spirituality.

For example, the contrast between the stereotypical "feel-good" tree-hugging Franciscan friar and the ultrarational, worldly Jesuit priest has become the basis of a whole class of jokes among Catholics. (A Jesuit and a Franciscan are walking through a garden, silently engaged in prayer, when the Jesuit pulls out and lights up a big cigar. The Franciscan whispers, "My spiritual director says one should not smoke while one prays." The Jesuit replies, "Mine said it's all right if I pray while I smoke.")

Of course, the Franciscans can field some top-notch intellectuals, and the Jesuits provide plenty of empathetic spiritual directors, but the point is, they do each have distinctive styles in the way they approach God, and they come from very different traditions. Yet both are thoroughly Catholic. (And we do greatly appreciate each others' gifts.)

Is one religion "just as good" as the next? I surely don't think so, any more than I would argue that Aristotelian physics is "just as good" as quantum chromodynamics. (And no doubt practitioners of those other religions would agree with me, for their own reasons.) Even speaking only of the major "mainstream" outfits that I seem to be favoring, are they all equally successful at doing what they set out to do? Even there, I would judge not. (And again I suspect that Presbyterians and Sufis and Baha'is would have their own reasons for judging why their particular expression of faith is the most satisfactory.)

All of us would agree that some now-extinct religions probably deserved to fail. One of the experiences of history is that popular heresies generally spend themselves within a generation or so. For instance, even with the implicit support of the Roman emperors and very crafty politicians among the churchmen, the oversimplifications of Arianism (keeping all the trappings of Christianity while fudging the divinity of Christ) in the fourth century are now just a footnote in church history.

But even as religions rise and fall, the same dumb ideas do keep coming back in new guises; gnosticism and its temptations of "secret knowledge" crop up in every generation, and it seems to be a standing trait that every New Age philosophy feels that it must call itself "new" (though by doing so, it makes one suspect that there's nothing new there after all). By contrast, a mainstream twenty-first-century believer in any of the long-established religions is happy to acknowledge that he or she can still read and get a lot out of the writings of a fifth-century forebear.

The basics of our religions do survive and endure, even as new understanding is added to them. It's enough to make you suspect that Someone is keeping an eye on things. But by that same criterion, I have to admit that a thousand years after the Christian church split into east and west and five hundred years after the

Reformation, the fact that all three parties are still flourishing may well be a sign that God wants each of us to learn something from the others. (It's interesting to see how similar our various theologies have become over time.) A similar judgment, I suspect, might be made among the divisions within Judaism or Islam.

Anyone who works in a parish will confirm that often the best parishioners are those whose route to the church has been "nontraditional." They're the ones who have had to think things through, and so they're the ones who know why they believe what they believe. If you've wandered far from the straight and narrow, your route back will no doubt take you over terrain every bit as strange and dangerous as the realms where your wanderings took you in the first place. You'll have seen things that the more timid of us could only imagine; you'll also respect the difficulties of that terrain and appreciate all the more the advantages of the well-trodden path.

Techies are very likely to be prime examples of such nontraditional believers.

CHAPTER 5

The Functions of Religion

≫ The Repository of Religious Data ≪

The first thing organized religion does for us is collect and preserve the combined religious or religious-seeming experiences of an entire people's history. Most religions have some sort of sacred writings to preserve this history; they may also depend on traditions, handed down orally from generation to generation (and usually also recorded eventually in another set of sacred writings). The sacred writings or traditions can contain hymns of praise and rites of worship; they can contain detailed rules, suggestions, or teachings to help the follower keep in touch with genuine religious urges and avoid false ones. But primarily these sacred scriptures serve as a record of the community's history of interactions with the transcendent, a sort of database of possible religious moments that the present generation can look back on.

This database serves to remind people that powerful moments do occur, when God apparently does intervene in our lives. This collection of historical stories also provides a template against which we can compare our own experiences of the transcendent.

It's worth noting that the sacred scriptures of most ancient religions are based on collections of stories and histories, often very literary in style, rather than detailed theological treatises. There's a practical reason for this—stories are easier and more fun to remember than dry theology—but the preponderance of stories speaks to a deeper significance. The point of these sorts of sacred writings is to record, not evaluate. Christian churches refer to this as the "repository of faith," a phrase that reminds me of the repositories of spacecraft images that NASA maintains—and with reason, as they have a similar function. Someday I may understand the religious experience of my ancestors in a new light (as Christians now reinterpret passages of the Jewish scripture), in the same way that some new understanding of planetary processes may make me go back and look at those 1965 Mariner 4 images of Mars and see things I never noticed before.

In both cases, I depend on the repository maintaining a faithful record of what actually happened. But I also recognize that the data are inevitably colored by the expectations of the people recording those events—colored literally, in some cases. We shoot pictures of Mars through a set of colored filters to help reduce the effects of haze or to differentiate between different types of terrain. But knowing what we know today and wanting answers to different questions than we had back then, our space probes now use different filters than the ones we chose in the 1960s.

In science, we say the data are "theory-laden"—and that's meant not as a criticism but merely as an observation. It is inevitable that our perceptions are influenced by our expectations. After all, it's only by having some idea ahead of time of what we expect to see in the data that we can judge what is useful data and what is irrelevant noise. But it may turn out that what is noise to us will be a signal to our grandkids.

That's why a scientist will publish not only the conclusions of his or her work but also the data on which those conclusions are based. Ten, fifty, or a thousand years from now, someone with a different problem to solve may want to use those data in a totally new and unexpected way. The ancient Chinese scholars who recorded the appearance of "guest stars" (which we now recognize as supernovas) never knew that their records would someday help us estimate the Hubble constant, which tells us the size and age of the universe. But they didn't need to know that; they just needed to be complete and honest recorders and reporters of what they saw and how they saw it.

The kind of theological study called "form criticism" is an attempt to make the same sorts of interpretations of scriptures. After all, these holy records were written in a culture and place (and language) far removed from our own. In addition, it's only to be expected that later interactions between God and humanity may give us new ways of understanding what happened earlier. The most common experience in any intellectual work is the eureka moment when one final piece allows us to see in a new way how the whole puzzle fits together.

The need for such continual interpretation is obvious. Obvious, too, is the danger of overinterpreting (or reinterpreting) what we see written in the past and thus imposing our own desires or prejudices on the data. I recall the inscription on the Kirby Hall of Civil Rights at Lafayette College in Pennsylvania, where I used to teach astronomy before I joined the Jesuits. Fred M. Kirby had inscribed over the doorway a quote from the Gospel of Matthew (20:15): "Do I not have the right to do what I will with my own?" It's from the parable of the generous master who pays a full day's wage to workers hired at the end of the day; but Kirby took it as a biblical injunction against income taxes! (He considered taxes to be a violation of his "civil right" to spend all of his own money however he chose.)

The same problem occurs in reducing scientific data. I once heard James Van Allen describe how the belts of high energy particles now known as the Van Allen belts were discovered by the first American satellite, Explorer I, in 1958. Hoping to measure the amount of ionization in the upper atmosphere (which the satellite would encounter during the low points of its orbit), he had installed a detector of energetic particles—essentially, a modified Geiger counter—in the satellite. To his surprise, the strongest readings actually came from the high points in the satellite's orbit. Van Allen recognized that this must be caused by a belt of high-energy particles trapped by Earth's magnetic field. But when he showed the data to a graduate student, the student, knowing that the detector was based on a Geiger counter, came to a completely different conclusion: "Space is radioactive!"

We cannot help but view the world through goggles colored by our own expectations and personal histories. Our hope nonetheless is that—correcting for these known sets of biases—we can let the data speak to us at whatever level of wisdom (religious or scientific) we have attained at any given moment. And we should recognize that future progress, in ourselves as well as in our community, will allow us to see ever deeper than what we can see now.

⟩ Judging the Data ⟨

As noted in Chapter Three, not every outside urge is an urge from God. And not every event that occurs in a people's history is necessarily the specific result of divine intervention. Human free will and perhaps even blind chance also play a role. So how can we have any confidence in the significance of some seemingly transcendent experience?

Indeed, some of those "religious" experiences in the record may turn out to have been false signals. (That's always an appealing thought if you're trying to discredit somebody else's religion!) Or they may have been misrecorded or misremembered, inadvertently or deliberately. It happens. Spacecraft instruments have been known to have glitches, too. But false readings, religious or scientific, happen less often than you might think, especially for events for which there are a lot of witnesses.

That's where the second function of an organized religion comes into play. In cases where we might question the accuracy of the record or the way it's been interpreted, our collective religious wisdom should give us some tools that allow us to recognize each event in its context, to see the general trends and the reasons for the exceptions, and to provide some criteria for throwing out the data points that look suspiciously far from the norm.

We know it's bad theology—and bad science—to hang your whole "Theory of Everything" on one possibly questionable point of datum. (That leads to fundamentalism, both in religion and in science.) And we know from experience that religion, like science, can progress most securely when it is seen and understood from many points of view. To borrow a phrase from the open software community, "Given enough eyeballs, all bugs are shallow"— the more people there are using the product, the more quickly they'll discover its problems . . . and see how to fix them.

Separating the real from the false is a vital function of a religion. This might come as a surprise to those who would accuse religious people of being overly credulous, but in practice, those who have the strongest sense of what they believe and don't believe are often the ones best equipped to resist a spurious philosophical sales pitch. (That's the plot gimmick of nearly all of G. K. Chesterton's Father Brown mystery stories.) Of course, the opposite complaint often heard against religion is that it's never open to new ideas. You can't win.

What are some of the useful rules of thumb most religions use to differentiate the valid from the fraudulent? Nothing startling.

First of all, see if the claim is logical. Logic is a key to theology. Remember, the science of logic was developed by medieval theologians as a way to pin down the otherwise elusive nature of God.

And consistency matters. You have to wonder about a claim that flies in the face of everything else we know about God. Our experience makes us rightly suspicious of the loud and flashy huckster whose wares are too good to be true or the cynic who insists that everything you know is wrong or the purveyor of cheap grace who only tells us what we want to hear, changing with the prevailing wind. (I am reminded of a certain church I saw in Chicago, part of a modern and free-thinking sect, that had replaced the cross on its steeple with a weather vane.)

One common insight of many religions is to realize that the words of God are to be found not in earthquakes or in fires or in a great wind so strong that it splits mountains and breaks rocks in pieces but often only in the sound of a still, small voice. In such cases, it helps to have a lot of ears listening, to be sure that the voice has been heard correctly.

Perhaps the most reliable way of recognizing, in retrospect, the true voice of God is to judge by results. This sort of judgment operates on the presumption—perhaps startling, to some—that God actually wants us to be happy. But happy for the long run, not the momentary pleasure that you later come to regret. There's the rub.

As the recorder of a people's history, religion is in a position to have observed the kinds of behaviors that lead to contentment and those that don't. The logic then runs like this: a transcendental experience that inspires us to lives that are ultimately happy, fulfilled, and content is more likely to be coming from the transcendent being who wants those things for us. An urge that experience tells us ultimately leads to unhappiness for us and misery for others probably doesn't. Again, the trick is to realize that what the world judges to be the source of happiness isn't necessarily so, as seen by the number of rich, successful people who are in psychoanalysis, suffering from the woes of excess.

The general principle on which all of these deliberations are based is that the common religious experience of many people over a long period of time is more likely to have genuine substance than the intense experience, however profound, of a singular mad prophet on his own. (Especially if that mad prophet is *me*.) For if our experience of the universe tells us anything, it's to be skeptical of the guy whose distant drummer has him marching alone off the edge of a cliff.

Yet the occasional prophet who can change history does come along. Though one such person may show up only once a century, every age and field does have its Einstein or Bob Dylan or Martin Luther King Jr. How do you recognize them? At the time, it can be hard. (How many of us who followed pop music in the 1960s knew that Dylan would last and Donovan wouldn't?) In retrospect, it's easy—by their results. Again, having a community to help out in these decisions can be very useful. And singular as they may be, these prophets are nonetheless effective precisely because they are products of their time. They stand on the shoulders of those who have gone before them and say out loud the things that we, the community, had already heard deep in our hearts but were afraid to heed. No revolution, religious or scientific, appears out of nowhere. It succeeds by resonating with something already inside of us.

≋ Religion as Community ≋

Like science, the practice of religion is fundamentally the work of an individual but is guided by a community. I spend most of my scientific working hours at my computer; I am alone, yes, but more often than not, I am responding to observations or inspirations or just the daily e-mail of my colleagues around the world. When I go into some deserted church to pray, I face God alone, but I am surrounded by an edifice that's been built up (figuratively and literally) by countless people before me. Even when I am alone, I am part of a community. It is as a community that we meet in scientific congresses, to hear and report about the work we've done, and it is as a community that we meet to be reminded of, and respond to, those messages from the transcendent.

But how should we respond? Indeed, how can we?

I recall early in my Jesuit life attending a prayer service for the elderly and infirm members of our community at which we were each invited to give a blessing on each man by placing our hands on his head. Afterward, one of the older Jesuits (a sweet, if slightly daffy, fellow) came to me with a gentle smile and said, "You know, you have healing hands."

"Huh?" I asked.

"I could feel the power," he said, "when you put your hands on my head."

I tried not to show my skepticism at this absurd suggestion; but a niggling little voice asked, "My God, what if this were true?" To my surprise, my immediate reaction was one of utter horror. Maybe it came from reading too many Marvel comics with their angst-filled superheroes, but the last thing I wanted was any sort of super powers!

As anyone who has had a strong religious experience can testify, the most common impulse when faced with the transcendent is to run away. "Fear of the Lord" is not just an empty phrase. The experience of realizing that this stuff could be real is enough to unsettle even the most devout believer, forcibly shaking us out of our complacent day-to-day world and making us see things with a clarity that we normally associate with moments of terror, like experiencing a car crash. The most realistic (albeit fictional) prophet in the Old Testament is Jonah, who fled on a boat to get away from God's call—and got tossed overboard for his problems, which is how he met that whale.

One of the reasons we may find it easier to meet God as a community is merely the feeling of strength in numbers. Ritualizing the encounter takes some of the fear out of it. It also introduces an element of repeatability. Even if a mediocre religious service is no better than a fast-food burger, at least it provides a certain minimum of spiritual nourishment. Through a history of trial and error, or perhaps even more remarkably through the instructions of God himself, we can collectively find the rites and rituals that allow us to deal with this intrusive transcendent.

It's important that these rituals appeal to our physical natures to express our spiritual longings. We are creatures with bodies: we experience life with our senses. A baby encountering a shiny new toy wants to see it, hold it, listen to it rattle, smell it, and put it in his mouth until he has experienced it with every possible sense. When I'm at the ocean, I want to jump in and swim around in it, feel the cold wetness on the back of my neck and taste the salt on my lips, or build a boat and sail across it, my nose filled with its salty tang and its wet wind on my cheek. Observing nature is breathtaking, but we also want to participate, get in on the act, take a picture, or make a garden. When a lover sees the object of his love, his desire is to become a part of her by dedicating himself to her, living with her, becoming intimate with her, spiritually, emotionally, physically.

We human beings can't just stand there; we have to do something. (And wisdom is knowing when it is time to do and when it is time to refrain from doing.) We want a physical outlet for our transcendent urges.

Sacraments, both in the general sense that you'd find in any religion and in the sense of specific rites defined by certain Christian churches, are a concrete "thing," a service, a function, that only a church can provide. Sacraments provide the touchstones with the transcendent at life's critical moments (birth, coming of age, marriage, death). They provide the function of institutionalizing acceptance, forgiveness, and communion with community and with God.

Recall the importance that the technical person attaches to function: oneself, one's institutions, and indeed all of one's experiences are defined for a techie in terms of what is done and how it happens. A techie can see sacraments as the proper function of a church. Ultimately, more even than for its collective history and wisdom, it should be for the sacraments that a techie would truly embrace a church. Sacraments can be, to the technical mind-set, a unique and irrefutable reason to belong. It is a service, a function, that only a church can provide; no other institution does it or at least does it as well. (But alas, as you will see, it doesn't work out that way in practice for most techies in most churches.)

Sacraments involve things for us to do: kneeling or dancing, lighting candles or burning incense, singing or keeping silent, pouring water, daubing with oils, eating bread and wine. In other times and other cultures, religions have gone for more extreme activities—drinking poisons and handling serpents, sacrificing animals (or people), visiting the temple prostitute. Not every way of ritually trying to encounter God is necessarily a good idea. Sometimes the acts turn into superstitions; sometimes they become so obscure they lose all meaning. Sometimes they're just aesthetically questionable. But be it messy or uptight, every culture practices some kind of ritual that enhances its connection with the ineffable. Even atheists want poetry and flowers at a wake.

The rites and rituals can have an added significance if they are seen as coming from God. To the Jews, for instance, the Torah, the Law, is important precisely because it is from God, and its very existence is a tangible reminder of God's presence in the universe. Likewise, to a Muslim, the Koran is a physical manifestation of God's presence. The Eucharist serves that role for the Christian.

With law come the people whose job it is to preserve and teach the law— those who know it best and know best how to apply it. With books come scribes and readers and teachers and the diligents who authenticate the reliability of the copies. The more heavily sacramental Christian religions—Roman Catholics and Orthodox, Anglicans and Lutherans—likewise have of necessity established rules to determine what constitutes a valid sacrament. And with rites there are different activities that one person or another must be designated to perform ("Only an ordained priest can consecrate Communion hosts") and someone whose business it is to make those designations ("Only a bishop, himself ordained by three other bishops, can ordain a priest"). Out of such interests of preservation, a hierarchy of sorts arises naturally in any religion.

But even if our rites are entirely of our own creation and represent our free response to the transcendent, it's only reasonable to have someone in the community set apart to decide which songs we'll sing, to see to it that we're at least all singing at the same time and from the same hymnbook. Even Congregational churches have ministers; even the Amish take the time to designate someone by lot.

It's nice (though, alas, sometimes more than we can hope for) if the person choosing the hymns has a reasonable sense of taste in these matters. But then, complaining about the organist seems to be a part of the unifying ritual in many churches.

CHAPTER 6

The Dangers of Organized Religion

⧓ The Finite Universe ⧓

Dangers? To be sure. The better something is, the worse it becomes when it gets corrupted. What we recognize as the greatest evils are great goods that have turned bad: art turning into pornography; love turning into obsession; patriotism turning into fascism. If religion is a great good, as I believe, then it carries with it the possibilities of great evil. The alternative to accepting the risks of religion is to reject both the good with the bad. The world of John Lennon's "Imagine" is without hell but also without heaven, a world without war, yes, but also one without anything worth fighting for.

That said, it's worth taking a look at the risks that techies are particularly susceptible to when they get involved with organized religion. I don't mean the obvious ones that everyone knows about, like a religion's temptation to rigidity, bureaucracy, intolerance, and abuses of its power. In many ways, those are the easiest (or at least the most familiar) to deal with; after all, the same abuses can all be found in any bureaucracy. They are a part of every nation's history, and yet that doesn't stop us from being citizens and patriots. Every religion is an institution of humans with all their human flaws, like a typical computer operating system that ships with a long list of known bugs (and workarounds).

However, those are all problems that the *religions* might pick up, and we'll talk all about them in a later chapter. What I am interested in here are the traps that an individual, and especially a techie, might fall into by joining a church. Most of us will never have the opportunity to abuse the power of an organized religion, but we'll certainly all have the chance to make any number of mistakes inherent in belonging to one.

Again, let's analyze this from a functional point of view. Recall that the function of a religion is to get close to God, and the function of God is to address the kinds of fundamental questions of meaning and purpose described in the first chapters. So the risks can be seen in the light of those same functions. We want God as the explanation of our cosmos; our religion fails us if we let it limit our view of the cosmos. We want God as the meaning of our lives; our religion fails us if it substitutes itself in the place of God as the source of our meaning. And we want God as the context in which we find our own identity; but our religion certainly fails us when we use it to warp or deny our identities.

Note how I speak of "our" religion. The failures here are only in part the fault of the religion itself. They are just as much, if not more, the faults of how a technically oriented person can grasp that religion, of how we make it "ours."

One obvious way we can let a religion limit our view of the universe is by insisting that its doctrines are a complete and final description of nature and God. This is a particularly common trap for a techie because it reflects a similar kind of mistake we are prone to make in our technical lives. Every day, for example, scientists (and the engineers who use science to design things) work not with nature itself but with mathematical representations of nature, and after a while, we conflate the one with the other—forgetting that sometimes nature is more complicated than our computer models. In the same way, when a techie adopts a religious orientation, the temptation is to not look farther than that religion's neatly packaged approximation of God.

No matter how deeply we believe God is involved in our religion, its tenets are expressed in human words by human teachers and fall on our own undeniably limited human ears. Our understanding of God is always incomplete; even Saint Paul insisted he saw only "through a glass, darkly." Indeed, Catholic theology carefully notes that all doctrine, no matter how authoritative, embodying divine truth, still requires interpretation because our understanding of that truth is expressed in a given time and in a historically conditioned language and culture.

There are some literalist, fundamentalist versions of religion that don't make that distinction and insist that their take on God is the ultimate and only word. It's an obvious fallacy, and once recognized, it is easy enough to avoid. Almost always, these are churches with a strong emphasis on the individual congregation and its preacher. One advantage of belonging to a larger, more organized hierarchical sect is that the leaders of long-lived, successful religions are not fools, and so they are not so foolish as to insist on that kind of literalism.

There's no such guarantee about the foolishness of the *followers* of a religion, however. And as any techie should remember, great technical ability alone is no proof against being a fool.

Indeed, the scientist's or engineer's mind-set can be susceptible to a particular and subtle kind of narrow-mindedness. Given their "how does it work?" functional mind-set, what a religion is can become equated with what a religion does. And if the only thing we see religion doing is presenting a set of rules and regulations, then a technically oriented person might think that the sum total of belonging to a religion is learning the rules and then following them. Thus Judaism is reduced to Sabbath and dietary laws and Catholicism is equated with avoiding meat on Fridays in Lent. (I know a Jesuit whose mother was a convert from Judaism; she used to keep separate silverware and plates for meatless Fridays, as if it were a Catholic version of keeping kosher.)

For most nontechies, the problem comes when they realize that an arbitrary set of rules makes for an inadequate religion, and then they reject religion simply because they are never able to see beyond its set of rules. But the problem for some engineers can be the opposite. Many techies are themselves rule followers to the extreme. After all, a computer is completely unforgiving of the slightest misstroke of a key; the laws of nature make no exceptions for scientists with pure hearts or good intentions; rules, in the techie experience, must be obeyed exactly. Thus they are liable to latch onto the rules of a religion and never look any further. They wind up living in a finite universe of rules.

Someone with this way of thinking may then assume that salvation can be earned just by strictly following the rules, like directions in a cookbook. Rule-following appeals to the deterministic streak in the techie mind-set; it gives you a pleasant sense of control over your own destiny. By wrapping yourself up in the minutiae of religious practices, you can close your eyes to the real, scary God of the transcendent urges. In its place you've substituted a trained seal that applauds when you ring the right bells.

The embrace of legalism in turn can lead to a terrible intolerance—not only of the faults of others but, to a worse extent, your own faults as well. From there, it is a short path to either denial ("I'm still here, so I must not have made any mistakes yet—I am not a sinner!") or despair ("I've got to follow the rules, but I keep screwing up. I'll never get it right; it's hopeless. . . ."). Even the sacramental role of a church is not immune to this understanding, when sacraments are understood only in terms of rites and requirements that are codified as law.

I do not mean to deny the existence and importance of rules. A techie understands the value of rules; any attempt to reduce religion to a set of "feel-good" emotions, besides being dishonest, would imply to a scientist or an engineer that religion is without substance and thus devoid of worth. And though a typical techie would love to be an expert in everything, the more realistic among us realize that there are times when we're forced to rely on the expertise of others. For many of us, religion is one of those times. That's when we depend on rules to guide us.

But a technically oriented person should also know that following rules is not enough. (At the very least, a Christian techie should read Saint Paul, whose constant theme—one might say, his prime rule—is that following the Law is not enough.) Depending on a cookbook is a sign that you don't understand all the chemistry behind the cooking. That's OK; the cookbook will let you turn out an edible meal. But you have to understand that it's a crutch, not the sum total of the science behind the stew.

Likewise, that trust in the cookbook should not come easily to a techie. The intellectual content behind a theology ought to count a lot to a techie; we are people whose lives are primarily lives of the intellect. And so one would hope that a techie would choose to join a religious community only if it had a sufficiently rigorous, time-tested intellectual base. Our religious cookbook, our set of rules, comes to us from the community of our organized religion. We trust that organized community to have the experience and the intellectual depth to have come up with rules that are based on a deeper understanding than we might have ourselves. But we rely on the traditions of a community only because we know that there's a deeper substance to the religion than just the rules.

If nothing else, one obvious problem with a religion reduced to nothing but rules is that even the best set of rules can only cover situations that have already been encountered. There's no ability to deal with anything new.

Worse, a religion of rules alone can imply faith in a God who only punishes, not a God who creates. Rather than a religion leading its followers to the God who gives them what the universe is for, they wind up with the religion of a God who can only give them what-for.

There's another way this trap can manifest itself among techies, in which our very strengths can trip us up. We scientists and engineers are easily tempted to think of ourselves as smarter than the rest of the world. We techies are too often confident to the point of arrogance about our intellectual ability, our ability to work things out on our own. We are, after all, highly trained at our own work, and we can sometimes extend belief in our own abilities in science or engineering to all subjects. Scientists are prone to this temptation, but engineers are especially vulnerable. Whereas scientists are valued by how much their ideas are accepted by other scientists and so tend to be more sensitive to what other people think of them, the engineers' worth depends solely on the widgets they make: if they make a good widget, they'll find work, regardless of their politics. Furthermore, engineers in particular can often be surrounded at work by "suits," executives who don't really understand what the engineers do. Engineers are used to being the smartest guys in the room—in their own eyes, at least.

What this means for religion is that engineers are often not inhibited by social pressures from adopting beliefs that the rest of the world would find absurd. Ironically, this often makes techies easy prey for the peddlers of modern forms of gnosticism, from UFOs and the "face on Mars" to faddish diets and strange new religions—the kinds of arbitrary rules that are presented as "secret knowledge" known only to a select few. The fact that nobody else seems to share the engineer's quirky ideas doesn't surprise the techie; it's perfectly reasonable to the techie that everyone else could be wrong.

One place where this is especially evident is in "creationist" sects that demand what they call a "literal" interpretation of the Bible. This whole "literalist" mentality is actually a modern phenomenon of our technical age, an age that spends its days reading technical manuals and is no longer comfortable with the fact that some subtle truths can be expressed only in poetry and myth. By contrast, they should read Saint Augustine's *On the Literal Meaning of Genesis*. Writing fifteen hundred years ago, he put a creative spin on biblical passages that at times seems highly inventive to modern ears, as when he argues (in chapter 9) that the words "Let there be light" actually refer to instilling rationality into intellectual creatures.

Augustine also goes on to say, in chapter 19 of that work:*

> It is a disgraceful and dangerous thing for an infidel to hear a Christian, presumably giving the meaning of Holy Scripture, talking nonsense on these topics [of cosmology]. . . . If [non-Christians] find a Christian mistaken in a field which they themselves know well and hear him maintaining his foolish opinions about our books, how are they going to believe those books in matters concerning the resurrection of the dead, the hope of eternal life, and the kingdom of heaven, when they think their pages are full of falsehoods on facts which they themselves have learnt from experience and the light of reason? Reckless and incompetent expounders of Holy Scripture bring untold trouble and sorrow on their wiser brethren when they are caught in one of their mischievous false opinions and are taken to task by those who are not bound by the authority of our sacred books.

---

*Saint Augustine, *The Literal Meaning of Genesis*, Vol. 1 (trans. John Hammond Taylor, S.J.). New York: Paulist Press, 1982, pp. 42–43.

Many of the proponents of creationism are themselves engineers who, for instance, try to force a one-to-one mapping between this year's latest theory of cosmology and the seven days of creation found in Genesis. The fact that the history of interpreting the Bible, from Origen to Saint Gregory of Nyssa, from Saint Augustine to Saint Aquinas, and on and on, shows a far broader range than such historical fundamentalism cuts no slack with them. It's a part of the techie mind-set's all-too-common fallacy to dismiss the wisdom of the past, as if knowing how to program a computer has somehow made us smarter than anyone else who ever lived.

≳ Loving the Torah More Than God ≲

To a techie, one of the most appealing reasons to search for God is that this God could be the foundation of the elaborate physical world, whose laws are our delight and provide the structure of our work and our lives. But if we are not careful, we can let our religions define and limit our universe and eclipse the God it is supposed to be leading us toward.

The major religions themselves recognize the dangers of literalism and excessive rule-following. An old Jewish folktale warns against "loving the Torah more than God," and Jesus reminded his followers that "the Sabbath was made for Man, not Man for the Sabbath." But still, we can get so wrapped up in beautiful liturgies and eloquent prayers and following the rubrics exactly that somehow we lose sight of God.

Religion is supposed to serve as a guide, a pointer, a help to God. When it becomes the source or goal of our entire universe, it usurps the role of God. It fails to resolve the questions of the universe's existence because it has become a universe unto itself. And it cannot lead us to the source of our meaning if it makes itself our "meaning of life."

A Jewish friend once described perfectly the sort of thing I'm thinking of; there were some Jews, he complained, who lived so entirely inside a mental Jewish ghetto that they would attend lectures with titles like "Thermonuclear War: Bad for Jews?" This same narrow mind-set drives born-again Christians to shop exclusively at stores run by other born-again Christians or cause

Catholics to root for certain college teams based only on whether or not the school is (nominally) Catholic. In many parts of the world—Northern Ireland, the Balkans, and the Middle East come to mind—this sense of total or exclusive identification with one's religion carries a much more serious cost.

From the outside it may look like this sort of religious cultural hegemony is imposed by some tyrannical hierarchy, but in fact, more often than not, it is just the opposite; it's something thought up by the rank and file and supported (if at all) only reluctantly by an authority that, truth be known, would much rather not be bothered with such things.

We find the same sort of provincialism in science, of course; you're much more likely to cite the work of your colleague down the hall than the fellow across the continent who may actually have done the work first. But when it arises from a religious worldview, it can be harder to identify and harder to resist.

This total identification with religion is an attitude like that of a hopelessly unrequited lover. A person obsessed with the object of love winds up having no life. He makes all sorts of sacrifices for what he thinks is love. But all he's in love with is an image of his own imagination's creation. And in the process, he's given that loved one nothing, not even someone to love in return; he has made himself into an utter bore who's not in the least appealing or lovable.

This sort of behavior is an especially strong temptation to the techie—and not just in our romantic misadventures! After all, what could be more important than God? And if religion is my route to God, doesn't it make sense to subordinate everything else to it?

Well, no, it doesn't. We may think our religion is our best and surest route to God, but our religion is not God. Religion has its due, but we are reminded (in the Bible, even!) that Caesar has his due, too. The clearest evidence that this kind of exclusive single-mindedness is wrong is seen in watching how the lives—and religions—of those who follow such a path become constricted and shallow until they wither and die.

(Not to mention the self-contradictions that are sure to arise of out this sort of mind-set. In a small Michigan village where

I once lived, a fellow who'd recently moved into town was negotiating to rent a storefront from a longtime resident who came from such a religious bent. When asked what rent he wanted, the devout landlord replied, "I'll have to ask the Lord about that; come back tomorrow." The next day, the landlord told his potential tenant, "Last night, the Lord told me to ask for $500 a month." The prospective tenant didn't miss a beat. "That's funny," he said. "I was talking to the Lord last night, too, and he told me I shouldn't pay more than $250.")

This sense of viewing the world entirely through the filter of one's religion can arise when the faithful are an embattled minority in a culture perceived to be essentially hostile. If people view their religion as making them "a people set apart," that will color how they view everything they think they are set apart from. (Atheists are just as prone to this as any other religious group, by the way. I once overheard a group of self-proclaimed "secular humanists" complaining how hard it was to be a good atheist in an America dominated by religion, using the exact same terms that my born-again friends use to complain about the problems of raising kids in an America dominated by secular humanists!) But the opposite condition, when the religion is part of the dominant majority culture, can produce the same bad effect. In that case, God and country become one indivisible concept, and to question one is regarded as rebellion against both.

In either situation, religion can become so choked by its tight intertwining with culture and history that eventually it is no longer free to live or grow or function.

This narrow-mindedness has another odd effect. People outside of a church sometimes think of churchgoers as snobs or hypocrites who think they're better than anyone else, and in fact, all too often this accusation is true. But it doesn't manifest itself in the way you might suspect. It's not the person outside my church whom I scorn; it's the guy in the pew in front of me. I have almost never heard a fellow Catholic speak ill of Hindus or Jews (or even Protestants). But all the time I hear conservative Catholics bashing liberal Catholics in the most apocalyptic terms, while liberal Catholics seem to be willing to shower tolerance on almost anyone or anything except their more conservative coreligionists.

In such cases, our universe has become limited to our own religion; the outside doesn't even rate a second thought. And in that lack of context, we find heresy in the thought that God might actually understand and forgive the manifest sins of "those people," forgetting that "those people," too, reflect the image of God.

Fun with Your New Head

We're all familiar with the term *born-again* that evangelical Christians use to describe the moment of actually choosing to follow Christ, giving in prayer one's life to Jesus, an event very often precipitated by a life-transforming experience. The symbolism of the rite of baptism is heavy with the notion that this is a new birth. True and powerful as these images can be, they can be read falsely by the unwary. While it's a new you being symbolized, it's still you. Or at least it ought to be.

Recall that one of the useful features of a belief in God is that he serves as an external measure against which you can gauge yourself, for good or bad, to see who you are and where you are succeeding or failing. The obvious fear is that a false image of God would give you a false reading of where you stand. But there's a more subtle problem: as quantum physics has emphasized, any attempt to make a measurement invariably alters the thing being measured. If, by presenting yourself to be judged by the standards of your religion, you try to twist yourself into a shape that perhaps is easier to measure but is no longer you, you've defeated the reason to have a religion.

The idea of changing one's life is not to replace an "old" you with a different, "new" one. It's to fix what's wrong—to remove the things that aren't really you but some sort of affectation and to build up what's right in you, what makes you unique and especially good. What religions have traditionally called sin can be thought of as all the bits in your life, your deeds and actions and opinions and prejudices, that get in the way of your being all the you that you can be. They're the bad habits that you have accreted like barnacles and now deflect you from what you really want to be doing, the posturing that smudges over the characteristics that really make you different from everyone else, the actions that erode your skills or your wisdom or your patience, or your unique blend of all of these things.

To enhance those traits that make you special should be your goal; when you've done that, you will be even more different and special, more uniquely yourself. The opposite tack, to squeeze yourself into some prefabricated shape, destroys your individuality and thus robs you of your claim to uniqueness. On the mathematical coordinate system of life, you've stuck yourself at zero in every direction. It's an easy spot to find, but it's not particularly interesting.

But to "be all you can be," you have to have an idea of what you ought to be. That clarity should be one of the functions of a religion: to hold up examples of people who got it right so that you can see what getting it right looks like. The trick, of course, is that those saints were all unique individuals, too. You can't just take someone else's example and slavishly copy it. The best you can do is take a look at those whose examples resonate most with you and try to figure out how to generalize and apply those lessons to your own situation. (Sounds like the classic problem-solving technique from freshman physics.)

But a big problem is that in our culture, technically oriented people don't have a whole lot of worked-out examples to follow. Given how over the past hundred years or so the myth of a war between science and religion has been built up (beginning with popular books in the late 1800s, back when both science and religion were equally arrogant in thinking they had a unique lock on the truth), the very thing we are striving for is too often held up to us as being an impossible self-contradiction.

The popular picture most of us have for what an engineer or a scientist ought to look like might include a lot of things we would aspire to ourselves: self-reliance, cleverness, fearlessness in the face of challenge. And it might include a lot of things we know to try to avoid: ill-fitting clothes, geeky haircuts, pocket protectors. But our image of a typical techie doesn't include anything about getting up for church on Sunday. Meanwhile, modern-day saints (we're told) are only people like Mother Teresa or Desmond Tutu; unless your goal in life is to care for the poor on the other side of the world or lead mass movements against racism and injustice (fine things, indeed, but not everyone's calling), you're likely to lack a role model.

We've already discussed one of the classic traps that can befall a techie joining a religion: excessive legalism in attempting to conform to some rigid ideal. It was pointed out that this kind of behavior contains the fallacy that you can somehow buy salvation by the way you behave. What I want to emphasize here is that real people in the real world can't possibly live the kind of life implied by a simple following of rules.

If engineering were just following rules, it would be the most boring life imaginable. If a "holy" life could be attained just by following rules, saints would be the most boring people in the universe. This kind of holiness may be what you were taught in Sunday school, but it sure isn't reality. And almost certainly, it misses all the wrinkles and complications in our lives and our personal situations that make us the very people we are. By forcing ourselves to fit into any kind of cookie-cutter mold, religious or otherwise, we cease being ourselves.

Saints are never made of plaster, formed in a mold. And a faith that forces you into such a mold is probably going to squash something essential. Such faith is like a jazz ensemble that plays every note by rote memory—or like the German roommate I had briefly at MIT back in the days of bell-bottomed jeans who, sadly, embodied all the negative stereotypes of rigid German orderliness: wanting to fit into the '60s Cambridge ambiance, he intoned, "I vill be ein hippie, ja!" and made himself a schedule of "hippie things" that he felt required to perform every day. Alas, you can't memorize Zen.

≳ Superstition ≲

The difference between a dog and a cat, so the story goes, is that if you feed a dog, the dog thinks that *you* are God; but if you feed a cat, the cat thinks that *he* is God. The joke, besides being a commentary on dogs and cats, is also a commentary on God.

Earlier I noted that among the reasons to believe in God or practice a religion, some of the most common rationales are conspicuously absent. Among these is using God as a source of comfort: God as Santa Claus. If you have a dog's-eye understanding of God, then for you God is a source of goodies. If you have a cat's-eye view, religion is a mechanism designed to stroke your own ego; like Peter O'Toole's character in *The Ruling Class,* you notice that every time you pray, you're talking to yourself, and from that you conclude that you must be God.

I do know some techies who think that goodies or egoism is what God and religion are all about. It's no surprise that they are the techies who are most likely to be atheists. If that were my idea of God, I'd be an atheist, too.

Believing in a "pie in the sky" God is dangerous. The classic example is the little boy who prays to God for a red bicycle, and when it doesn't magically appear under the Christmas tree the next morning, he decides that God, like Santa Claus, must be a fake. Even more dangerous, however, is the false faith that arises when the little brat actually gets the red bicycle and concludes that his prayer is what caused it to appear. A faith based on a lie is worse than no faith at all.

Such a faith is nothing more than superstition—mistaking chance for cause. Pope John Paul II once endorsed science by saying that it can protect religion from superstition; alas, techies can be as prone as anyone, or even more so, to being superstitious themselves. In the techie world, superstition is a constant companion, friend and foe.

When an engineer is trying to debug a complex system or a scientist studies a complex process in nature, the first thing the person tries to do is establish the order in which things occur. A fundamental assumption is that the cause always comes before the effect, so you can line up potential causes and rule out other possibilities by seeing which bits occur before the effect that you're trying to understand.

But that kind of reasoning can be very misleading. Just because event A occurs before event B does not by any means prove that A causes B; it merely shows that B cannot be the cause of A, which may be useful information, but it's not at all the same thing. The logicians refer to this fallacy using the Latin phrase *post hoc, ergo propter hoc*—"after that, therefore because of that." Unfortunately, most techies have never studied formal logic (or Latin).

This post hoc assumption provides endless opportunities for practical jokes. There was a VIP visitor to Milwaukee a few years ago who was shown the new baseball stadium with its retractable roof. His host, knowing that the roof was going to be opened at a certain time for a baseball game, had brought along his television remote clicker, and seconds before the scheduled opening, he handed it to his guest, saying, "Here, we're going to let you open the roof tonight! Just push this button."

Here's another example, from my own field of planetary astronomy: the nineteenth-century Italian astronomer Giovanni Schiaparelli (the guy who saw *canali* on Mars) first noticed that certain meteor showers—"shooting stars" caused when space dust plunges into Earth's atmosphere—were associated with the orbits of certain comets. The dust traveled around the sun in the same orbits the comets followed. Did the dust come from the comets? Schiaparelli proposed just the opposite: that the comets were being formed out of the streams of dust!

But then people saw a comet break apart completely; the meteor showers continued anyway, brighter than ever for a while, not dying away until a hundred years after the comet was gone. Death of the comet occurred before the death of the meteor stream; therefore, meteor streams come from comets, not the other way around. So far, so good—except that recently, we've been able to send spacecraft to sample dust from comets and view dust bands spiraling off asteroids, and we're learning that it's actually a whole lot more complicated, with both comets and asteroids providing a confusing array of different dust types. Our nineteenth-century view of meteors as comet dust was a bit oversimplified.

B. F. Skinner, the famous behavioral psychologist, performed a classic experiment describing "superstition in pigeons" in the late 1940s. He had developed a method of training pigeons by making them hungry (starving them to 75 percent of their normal weight) and then putting them in a box that would provide food whenever they did whatever he wanted them to do—stepping in a certain pattern, say, or pecking at a certain image. But as he describes in a paper in the *Journal of Experimental Psychology* in 1948, he also put some hungry pigeons in boxes that would feed them at regular intervals with no reference at all to what they were doing. He reported that the pigeons would train themselves to do whatever it was they were doing the first few times they were fed, as if their behavior—walking in circles, pecking at the left side of the food dish, or whatever—was the cause of their feeding. This, Skinner said, was an example of how superstitions arise among people. More aggressive skeptics have used his result as an explanation for why people are so foolish as to believe in religion itself.

My point here is to emphasize that the skeptics have a valid point: a religion that is adopted just for the goodies it provides can indeed very easily descend into superstition, even if it truly does provide those goodies. I know people who insist that you can sell your house more quickly if you bury a statue of Saint Joseph, upside down, in the backyard; when they finally sell their house, it confirms both their faith in the superstition and their faith in Saint Joseph!

(Needless to say, it doesn't always work out. "Alas, Saint Joe failed me miserably in my most recent home-selling attempt," a friend confided after reading this section. "I buried him at the urging of some 'true believer' friends. When the house didn't sell and I went to dig him up, the automatic sprinklers came on, and I couldn't get to him. A few weeks later, I noticed that the trees near where he was buried had died. I'm getting the feeling that some superstitions can do more harm than good!")

In its own way, superstitious faith is as bad as modern satanist wanna-be's who think you can command and control the devil by painting pentagrams on the floor. I don't know what's more pernicious about these beliefs: that they show a desire to control and manipulate God (or the devil) or that these people actually think God (or the devil) can be controlled in this way.

Superstition is faith based on quicksand. And when it fails, as inevitably it will, it can at the very least destroy your capacity to believe in better things and at worst pull you down and destroy you, the way that trusting in a quack medicine can kill you if it prevents you from taking a real cure.

On the other hand, I also think fondly of those poor pigeons.

Consider their theological system from their point of view. If a pigeon walks in a circle and then gets fed, causing it to think that there's a connection between its walk and its food, what is it really believing in? It believes that there exists a Big Food Server (we'll call him BFS for short) who lives outside of its cage—which is true. It believes that this BFS, who has the power to feed it, is actually watching it, to see what it is doing—which is also true. And it believes that the BFS is delighted every time that it does its meaningless little dance—which, I am sure, is true again, as I can imagine B. F. Skinner chortling and pointing out the behavior of those silly pigeons to his friends and colleagues and planning how he would write up his paper exposing their superstitious behavior. So in what way was this pigeon theology false?

I do have faith (and I pray, fervently) that the God I believe in is a nicer fellow than B. F. Skinner. But I have no reason to doubt that he is any less real.

PART THREE

What Is the Techie Experience of Religion?

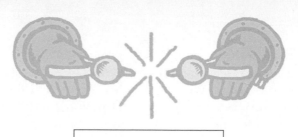

CHAPTER 7

Talking to Techies

⩔ Jesus Was a Techie ⩕

During the French Revolution, a bishop was led to the guillotine for execution. The crowd jeered, the drums rolled, the blade of the guillotine was drawn upward; then it was released, and it plummeted toward the poor bishop's neck. But as the blade flew down, it suddenly shuddered and came to a stop a bare inch above the bishop. A cry went up from the crowd: "It's a miracle! It's the hand of God!" And the bishop was released. Next, an atheist philosopher was brought forth; once again, the drums rolled and the blade was drawn up; but when it dropped, once again it stopped one inch before decapitation. "Another miracle!" cried the crowd, and they released the philosopher. Then an engineer was brought forth. Again they strapped him down, rolled the drums, and pulled up the blade. But just before it was released, the engineer glanced at the mechanism drawing the blade into place and cried out, "Wait a minute! I think I see the problem!"

Several years ago, I was invited to lead a certain "Bible study" group (I thought to myself, no way—Catholics don't do Bible studies) in Houston (especially not in Texas!) for a bunch of astronauts (astronauts? Oh, well, that's different). And of course, it turned out that half the astronauts in the group were Catholic. But one of the other half, active in a small Protestant church, wanted to make it very clear to me that he was a strict seven-day creationist: he was unwavering in his belief that the universe was created exactly, word for word, as described at the start of Genesis. I wondered to myself if he had ever actually read Genesis—

especially the part that describes the world as a flat plane, topped by a dome, with waters above and below (Genesis 1:6–10). Where did he think the space shuttle went? How come it didn't get wet?

Then he told me what he'd done for a living before he became an astronaut, and I began to understand a little better where he was coming from. He'd been a test pilot. And of course, you don't really want a test pilot who is in the habit of "creatively interpreting" his written instructions!

For a lot of occupations, especially technical occupations, a rigid literalism is part of the job description. Just don't ask people in those vocations to be comfortable in a museum of modern art. But there's a bigger issue underlying this "literal" mind-set than not being able to puzzle out the more subtle meanings of scripture. It speaks to the serious misfit between the typical techie and the typical church.

In 2004, chatting with a Jesuit friend of mine who worked for the weekly religious magazine *America,* I was invited to submit an article on how techies and Catholicism get along. They ran my short piece in January 2005 under the title "Talking to Techies." It was my first attempt to publish some of the ideas that I've written about in the first two parts of this book. The things I had to say at that time were written from a particularly Catholic perspective, though now I realize they can be applied to the experience of techies in any church.

What had struck me then was the contrast between the Catholic church of my immigrant ancestors and the places where I saw Catholics living today. A hundred years ago, the Catholic church in America was a blue-collar church, a church of laborers and factory workers. But nowadays, the economy of our world has become dominated by high-tech business: computers, information processing, and other fields of engineering. And thanks to all those Jesuit (and other) Catholic universities, many of the laborers in those white-collar jobs are the children and grandchildren of Irish and Polish and Italian immigrants. Yet I saw no evidence that my church was responding at all to the needs of these modern working techies.

I was inspired as well by a couple of incidents that had occurred to techie friends of mine. One friend once told me about a preached religious retreat he'd gone to where the director encouraged her listeners to "image yourself as a rosebush!" I guess the artists in the group were supposed to contemplate the ways that their lives could be compared to tangled, thorny branches that bring forth fragrant, beautiful flowers. My techie friend spent his time wondering, what kind of camera would he use to "image" his rosebush? What exposure would be appropriate?

Another case seemed like something straight out of Evelyn Waugh's tragicomic novel *Brideshead Revisited*. An engineer who wanted to marry a Catholic (he's a much nicer fellow than the Rex Mottram character from the novel, but he was in much the same situation) had decided to become a convert himself, and he had asked me to be his sponsor. For two months, we went together to "RCIA class"—Rite of Christian Initiation for Adults sessions intended for the religious education of aspiring adult converts— and week after week, the nun who taught the class expounded on ways that we could learn to experience God's love. It all sounded good to me; but my convert friend was growing more baffled every week. "What's with all this stuff about God and love?" he finally broke down and asked me. "When are they ever going to get around to telling me the rules? What I am supposed to *do*?"

Religious instructors and retreat directors spend a lot of time trying to develop the "affective" side of our personalities, the part that speaks to our hearts and innermost desires, and that's challenging enough for most people in our culture. For techies who have no idea what those people are talking about, such preaching sounds like gibberish.

Meanwhile, other aspects of religion that would be especially appealing to a techie are commonly downplayed nowadays. For example, the church can claim a historical connection to Jesus Christ and his immediate followers, but "apostolic succession" is a phrase rarely mentioned in a pulpit nowadays; it smacks of a kind of nineteenth-century triumphalism that does not play well in our multicultural society. Yet when a scientist friend of mine visited me in Rome and I took him to see Saint Peter's, I discovered that he was fascinated with the posters for sale in tourist shops around Vatican City that list the name and dates of every pope going back to Peter. The simple fact of a traceable line of succession going that far back was amazing to him. (Indeed, to some skeptics, it is so frighteningly powerful that they devote an inordinate amount of energy into trying to debunk its historical credibility.)

Indeed, the magnificence of Saint Peter's Basilica itself—often an embarrassment to American Catholics of a bent toward modest self-reflection—incited a real religious conversion experience in another visiting scientist whom I was showing around Rome. He'd walked into Saint Peter's an avowed skeptic (a "fallen-away Unitarian" was the way he'd described himself), but halfway around the church, he turned to me with a stunned look on his face and whispered, "The people who built this place—they actually believed all that stuff, didn't they?" Not long afterward, he became very active in a church—a Protestant church, as it happens—back in America.

The power expressed in the immensity of Saint Peter's, like the idea of apostolic succession, is tied into the greater issue of authority. Ministers of the church are often afraid of coming across as "too authoritarian"; they tend to want to project humility and downplay their own training or ordained status. But this "we're just one of you" attitude can be exactly the wrong tack to take with a techie.

Authority has enormous importance and respect in the technological world. Every techie is an expert in his or her own field. Like the Centurion of the Gospels, techies understand what authority means because in their own fields, they exercise it themselves. A techie knows to respect expertise. But it is also typical for techies, who have a high opinion of themselves and their own education, to wonder why they should listen to some "guy in a dress" up in the pulpit who doesn't even know how to make the microphone work. Ministers who do not assert their own credentials not only give the techie no reason to respect or listen to them; they also implicitly disrespect the techie, whose own sense of worth is directly tied to his or her own sense of authority.

That education, however, is another source of conflict for techies belonging to a parish. For many technical people, the years of study and work that have gone into developing their professional abilities mean that they have delayed or even abandoned the idea of participating in the traditional lifestyle of marriage and family. But there is rarely any scope for activity given to single adults in a typical parish; parishes are oriented around families.

And for techies, that's part of an old story. From the time they were kids, most technically oriented people have been systematically excluded from the communities of their peers. Pegged with abusive labels like "geek" and "nerd" and facing hostility born of being different (academically more successful, for instance, but often physically less adept), many technical people simply assume that the world at large may lust after their technological goodies but no one is interested in them as people. Alienation is a powerful, and universal, techie experience.

Thus all too often, typical church responses to the problems and concerns of techies can range from the unhelpful to the downright repellent.

The irony is that it should not be so. Jesus himself was a techie.

It's not just that he was male, single, and smarter than everyone around him, and when he tried improving the world ("I think I see the problem!"), he got crucified for his efforts. The term technology comes from the Greek technē, "art" or "skill," which to the ancients represented the mere mechanical refashioning of the physical world, as opposed to the more exalted vocation of philosopher or priest. No wonder Jesus the carpenter was as welcome among the Scribes and Pharisees as a plumber is at a philosophers' convention.

What's more, in today's world, technology is a social justice issue. Curiosity about the world is a basic human trait; denying it denies one's humanity. The ability to understand the world in a scientific sense empowers an individual, providing a habit of mind that looks for cause and effect (a worldview often lacking among the poor). It gives people the power to understand the difference between forces they can do something about and those beyond their immediate control. And it shows how "impossibly big" problems can be broken down into smaller, solvable ones.

Yes, the "mechanical" view of the world is clearly incomplete; what worldview isn't? But seeing the universe in terms of cause and effect is what gives us the courage to attack problems like poverty, disease, and social injustice with the expectation that solutions do exist.

And yes, many techies have a woefully underdeveloped affectivity. But how can a church expect to reach them, except to meet them where they live? And even a spiritual guru could maybe benefit from the discipline of learning how to manage a computer. Or how to get the microphone to work.

≷ The Science of Amateur Ethnography ≶

I expressed a lot of these thoughts in my *America* article. However, after rereading it when it was published and reviewing the notes for some recent talks I had given (at Loyola University of Chicago and the University of Detroit Mercy, early versions of what's become the first two parts of this book), I began to suspect that perhaps my analysis at times had been just a little, um, glib. Once I'd published that article on techies, it dawned on me that maybe it was time for me to start doing the research for it. It was time to stop listening to myself and my own take on things and ask the techies themselves. How do real engineers and scientists actually make their religion work?

So in April and May 2005, as a part of a Jesuit program called Tertianship (a sort of spiritual sabbatical that Jesuits take after they've been in the order for a dozen years), I moved to Santa Clara University, the Jesuit university in California's famous Silicon Valley, and spent six weeks driving up and down the U.S. 101 freeway between San Jose and San Francisco doing interviews with scientists and engineers in the area who had expressed a willingness to talk to me about their religious beliefs.

My questions to them were simple and basic. Why do they go (or not go) to a church? What are they looking for in their religion, and what are they getting from it?

In addition, out of curiosity, I added one more specific question: How do they deal with the issue of multiple religions? Intellectually, how do they understand the differences between one religion and another? Do they believe (or expect) that one religion is right and all the others are wrong? Or do they believe that all religions are equal? And in a practical way, how do they choose one religion over another?

As you can tell from my first six chapters, which were mostly written before I did these interviews, I already had a pretty clear idea of the answers I expected to hear—the classic answers of the philosophers and theologians whom I was quoting (if not always citing) in those chapters. But as you will see from what follows, though I (and the scholars I was stealing from) did get a number of things right, there was more than one instance where I found out that my idealized view of techie religion was pretty far from the mark!

Before presenting the results of these interviews and my reactions to them, which I do in Chapters Eight and Nine, I want to emphasize a couple of things I learned, things that are important to keep in mind when you read these notes.

First of all, I learned that conducting interviews like these is a very tricky business. People spend years earning doctorates learning how to do this stuff. I haven't, and I didn't. I am a rank amateur at understanding how to interview people or even just how to listen to them and hear what they are actually trying to say.

I am an astronomer, not an ethnographer. As an astronomer, I deal quite often with amateur astronomers; I know what the amateur can offer, in terms of time and enthusiasm and even the occasional bright idea. But I also know the distance between the amateur and the professional. What I am presenting here is nothing like a professional job. The best I can hope is that I irritate some professionals enough to get them to go back and do what I tried to do, only do it right.

The other thing I learned is how hard it is to hear the truth. I knew going in that there is a great gap between what people will tell a total stranger about their religious life and what they'll tell someone they have reason to trust. That, if nothing else, was my justification for trying to play interviewer: as a fellow techie, I had reason to believe that I could establish a certain level of trust when talking to other scientists and engineers about a topic as personal as religion.

Furthermore, as I know well, techies are not always able to communicate their ideas (especially deeply personal, emotion-laden thoughts) in a manner that nontechies can easily interpret. I assumed I could read, sympathetically, the meaning behind typical techie circumlocutions.

I still think that's true. The value in my interviews comes from my being able to translate what the techies said into words that communicate what the techies really wanted to say. But I also learned early on that my presence in the interview, as a Jesuit as well as a scientist, profoundly colored what the interviewees were willing to say to me and how they were willing to say it.

Some of these interviewees were essentially strangers to me, at best, friends of friends; others were longtime friends with a history between us going back as much as thirty years. It made a difference, clearly. I learned to appreciate that there is a great gulf between what a person will say to a stranger, no matter how trustworthy, compared to what they will say to a friend.

But more, there's a gulf between what one will say to a friend and what one will say to family. Another gulf yawns between what you'll tell your family and what you say to yourself. And most of all, there is an immeasurable gap between what you tell yourself and what is actually the truth.

In the interviews that follow, I have changed the names of the people I talked to (the names I've invented here are alphabetical, reflecting the order in which I spoke to them), and I have done my best to preserve their privacy. If I have done this right, they should be able to recognize themselves but no one else will know who they are.

This is not a complete set of my interviews. Some were redundant, and others went off on tangents not relevant to the things that I wanted to talk about in this book. The interviews presented here are based on detailed notes written, from memory, within a few hours after each interview. I didn't want to inhibit my subjects by the presence of notebooks or tape recorders.

Rather than organize their comments by theme, I've kept them in the order in which I heard them. Interspersed on occasion are my own comments, my own ponderings and explorations, paralleling my thoughts at the time I was talking to them.

CHAPTER 8

Listening to Techies

≽ The Church Shoppers ≼

It's a Tuesday in mid-April, and I've taken the Caltrain commuter train into San Francisco and then the BART subway under the bay to Berkeley. I am sitting with Alan and Beth, an astronomer and a medical doctor, in a genteelly decaying hundred-year-old house, perched on lumpy furniture amid an explosion of toys and books, only some of which belong to their kids.

They're in the process of shopping for a religion for their family. The needs and desires of their children are driving the issue, and the kids are growing up quickly, making their decision one that cannot be put off much longer.

Alan was raised a Unitarian, Beth a Catholic; she had a bad experience with her church growing up but still has strong feelings both for and against it. After they were married (by a justice of the peace), they attended Quaker meetings for a little over a year. Now they are sending their children to a Jewish school, which they chose partly because of its high academic rigor but also out of respect for Alan's ethnic background. It seems that Alan's mother, who still lived in New York City and was ethnically Jewish, had become very active in her local synagogue after Alan's father died, though she had kept this activity secret from the rest of her family. At her death, Alan discovered this connection and became aware of how important Judaism was to her; he also saw how supportive the synagogue was to the family at the time of her death. It got him thinking, and he became much more interested in his own Jewish background.

Talking about choosing a religion for his family now, it is the intellectual content of a religion that is most important to him, Alan says. Beth, for her part, says that she is looking more for an emotional content to liturgies—chants and drums, that sort of thing. But it is clear that Alan would be repelled by bad liturgies and Beth by fraudulent theology. Beth is looking for a sense of mystery, which she feels is lacking in Unitarianism, and Alan also describes the Unitarians as "sterile." On the other hand, Alan was put off by the Quakers, calling them "too flaky," though Beth notes that it might just have been the variety of Quakers found in their part of Northern California.

Yet even with Alan's desire for an intellectual foundation to his religion, the core beliefs of any given religion are not so much things to be believed as to be "not disbelieved" or unbelievable. They are not looking for the church that is closest to being "right." They don't feel that they could ever make such a fine distinction among the different churches. But they wouldn't belong to a church that was, in Alan's words, "obviously wrong."

What do they mean by "unbelievable"? What churches would a techie think are "obviously wrong"? I asked them; and since that interview, I've posed the same question to a number of other techies. Without exception, every person I have asked has named the same two religions that Alan and Beth specifically rejected: Scientology and Mormonism. Indeed, no scientist of my acquaintance has ever had anything good to say about Scientology— rather ironic, given its name. But as it happens, I know a number of techies who are Mormons, including my thesis adviser at MIT. Outside the fold, however, Mormonism does appear to have a reputation for being slightly odd.

Alan and Beth each see an advantage to any church with a long history and, to a lesser extent, to a religion that had a large geographical spread. Catholicism, Lutheranism, and Judaism are cited as positive examples in this regard; these are religions that are seen as having a well-tested philosophy and content and so are more likely to be "true" because they have been seen to work in a wide variety of times and circumstances. But they also want a church that shows a certain openness to new developments, not tied to a closed interpretation of the truth. On that account, they rule out Islam.

By sending their children to a Jewish school, they appear to be leaning toward Judaism. But even so, they are worried about which variety of Judaism and which synagogue would be most appropriate. They have not made any decision; to a large extent, the decision may well be determined by what setting the children feel most comfortable in. If nothing else, their older daughter is looking for a rabbi she can have a good argument with!

Wednesday evening, the week after my trip to Berkeley, I'm sitting in the Mountain View, California, home of Carol and David, two scientists at the NASA Ames Research Center. They are older than Alan and Beth, and their house is more sparsely furnished. On the mantle over the fireplace are two framed pictures, two sets of families: her adult children and his.

Carol describes herself as a liberal Methodist, David as a nonbeliever. Carol uses belief as a way of orienting and structuring her life; as she says, "Believing in God makes me a better person. That is why I continue to believe." But to them both, the most compelling attraction of religion is the way it addresses the internal urge that makes one look for the transcendent. Even David admits that he can be "moved in uncomfortable ways" when he's attending church with Carol at Christmas and New Year's.

But David is still an atheist. "I was raised a Presbyterian," David tells me, "and in my early twenties, I was active in our young adults group. One day our minister brought in a rabbi and a Catholic priest to speak to us about their religions. They were both very good. So was our minister, for that matter. But I realized then that they couldn't all be right. It seemed to me that the only logical possibility was that none of them were."

I can see how logically fallacious this argument is, and from the twinkle in his eye as he tells this story, I am pretty sure David can, too. But I am struck by how, at a certain emotional level, it still seems compelling to him, especially since, in a funny way that I can't articulate myself, it almost feels reasonable to me, too. It's a comment, and a reaction, that I will keep pondering.

Carol finds other scientists to be hostile to religion, and it bothers her. She talked about a conversation at work where some of her fellow scientists had criticized the noted cosmologist George Ellis, whom they felt had lowered his status as an astronomer because he had accepted the Templeton Prize for science and religion. Her story is striking to me precisely because I have never encountered anything like that myself—not among astronomers, anyway. And that makes me wonder, how much do my friends and associates censor themselves when they talk about science and religion issues in my presence?

Saturday evening the following weekend, I'm being driven up the winding roads above San Jose into a luxurious gated community that looks out over the valley. (I'm told that the two biggest building booms in California over the past ten years have been gated communities and prisons.) I've been invited for coffee and dessert with Edwin, Fred, George, and Harry. They're all Silicon Valley engineers, some of them (like my host) pretty far up the food chain. Three of them work at big multinational outfits; the fourth is with a small start-up company. All were raised Catholic and all but George are still Catholic. Ethnic identity is a part of the equation; one of them is Filipino, and one of the others is married to a Filipina.

They talk a lot about religion as a "set of rules." Edwin, noting how techies can become rule-bound, describes a former engineer he knows who has become a Catholic priest and who is now quite a stickler for the rubrics. Fred and George speak out against rules in the church that seem to be self-contradictory and rules that they feel do not follow the teachings of Jesus.

George in particular says that he wants "a thinner book of rules." Now the sole non-Catholic in the group, he says he left the church at an early age precisely because he thought it had too many rules. Though he left Catholicism, he continued to believe in God, and when he married, he joined his wife's church. For someone opposed to so many rules, he now notes wryly that he's become a Seventh-day Adventist! Still, his take on his new religion is strongly colored both by his techie background and his early Catholic training. He says he sees the Bible as a "manual" for life, yes, but it is a manual that needs to be interpreted. He describes himself as still something of a seeker. Nobody, he says, and no religion, has all the answers.

Edwin tells us that he became an atheist in college; but as he grew to know the limits of science and then began seeing what he called "too many coincidences" in the universe, his atheism slipped to agnosticism. Then, he recalls, a professor showed him that you could find truth in poetry and once said to him that "an agnostic is an atheist with no courage." That clearly shook Edwin's easy agnosticism. After graduation, he married a divorced Catholic who herself had issues with the church. But with the birth of their first child, they went back to attending Sunday Mass. The biggest impetus to belonging to a church, he says, is the community he found there.

Harry, too, was raised Catholic, fell away during college, and then after being married—but in this case before they had children—he started going back to church. He's active now in his parish.

Fred's route was slightly different; raised Catholic, he never left. He married a non-Catholic who converted, despite family pressure not to do so. He also sees "too many rules" in the church, but he says he has a very relaxed attitude toward them. Community and relationships, not rules, are what he says are most important.

All four express the impression that religion is a very private matter among their coworkers. At times, each of them may think that they're the only believers among their fellow engineers and that no one else shares their set of opinions. And then, as Fred notes, they'll be surprised at a wedding or a funeral to see how many people from work are there, participating and taking communion.

Why do they believe in God? "Just look up at the stars at night," says Edwin. Fred echoes Edwin's comment about there being too many coincidences in nature to be explained purely by chance. Edwin and Harry also think the question "Why is there something instead of nothing?" is an important reason for them to believe.

Why do they belong to a religion? This is my first big surprise. Contrary to the alienation from church communities that I thought I had heard from many of my techie friends before I did these interviews, these four engineers all cite "community" as the primary reason they belong to a church. (Of course, all four of them are married with children, unlike many of my alienated, single techie friends.) And also contrary to my theorizing and expectations of how the unique sacramental "functions" of a church might be attractive to a techie, none of them cite the role or availability of sacraments or ritual as a reason for believing. Only Fred sees them as a part of the community, and even to him, it is still the community, not the liturgy, that matters.

In fact, they all agree that the things that go on during church services on Sunday are largely incomprehensible to them. They can't follow the function of the ceremonies or the logic of the liturgy. And that very incomprehensibility is itself distracting, given their techie mind-set. As George puts it, "I keep asking myself, why are they doing it this way instead of that?"

Harry says he sees religion as a system designed to address "problems to be solved." But as George notes, "The difference between a computer program and a human is that a program stays debugged; the problems stay fixed, once you've fixed them. Human problems keep coming back." They all agree that religion is a source of community; but to these engineers, how community actually works is a great mystery.

The fact that parishes even exist and function is a source of some amazement to them. Harry takes note of the wide diversity of people within his own parish and wonders how you could come up with a religion or a parish that could deal at the same time with cradle Catholics and converts, recent immigrants and longtime residents, Hispanics and Filipinos. And yet somehow, it all seems to work.

This theme keeps coming back even as the conversation drifts to other issues. I ask, What are the things that keep you awake at night? Edwin mentions the problem of evil: Why does God allow bad things in a good universe? George agrees, but then he turns it back to the previous concern: "Why would a God make human beings so ornery?"

≋ Many Religions ≋

After my first set of interviews, I have a phone chat with a Jesuit friend of mine, a philosopher teaching in a seminary. What has struck me the most about these early interviews is how little these techies seemed interested in finding the truth. "They only want a community of like-minded people, in a church that is merely 'not obviously wrong,'" I complain. "They don't look to the church to be a source of truth." I had expected techies to be drawn to churches as a source of religious authority, but the only techie I had met who even seemed to worry about truth was David, the atheist who'd concluded that no religion had it.

My Jesuit friend asks in reply, "Is this perhaps an example of postmodern thinking? Are they saying that there is no truth?"

I ponder for a minute. "No," I finally admit, "I don't think that's it at all. These are engineers, after all, not English literature professors. They may think they already have the truth, just like they think they already have a good enough idea of morality. It's like most people already have their own ideas of what's right and wrong; they don't want to hear anyone else's opinions on the matter. In the same way, these guys aren't interested in learning the truth from someone else. They don't want to be challenged. They just want someone who will confirm for them what they have already decided to believe."

Of course, it occurs to me, what I am complaining about in "most people" is just as much a good description of what I am seeing in myself. I don't like it that I haven't always been hearing what I expected or wanted to believe about my fellow techies. I had assumed that most techies would see religion as a place to go to learn things about God and to find ways of relating to God. Instead, it sounds like they are only experiencing religion as a bunch of rules about how to behave in a community that serves mostly to organize potluck dinners and classes for the kids.

After I hang up, though, I decide that my response to my friend was a little too cynical—or at least incomplete. After all, precisely by asking for a church with "fewer rules," these techies are implicitly acknowledging that the church has something else besides rules, something more important than rules, some vague, undefined thing that, for lack of a better word, I'm labeling "truth."

What I also see in these early interviews, though, is a despair of ever being able to know the truth. Tied in with this despair of knowing the truth (the cause of this despair or its effect?) is the fact that there are so many different religions in our society. If there is any truth to be found in religion, why should there be more than one religion? Given a universe that is seen as a series of problems to be solved, techies are used to there being only one truth, only one right answer.

The comment that my interviewee David had made—"They can't all be right, so they must all be wrong"—brings two very different kinds of reactions when I tell that story to other people. To most people, especially the nontechie Jesuit academics I am staying with at Santa Clara University, the lack of logic in it is laughably absurd. But to most techies, including me, the power of the argument seems somehow compelling.

Why? Maybe the attraction of this patently illogical argument results from the way that techies instinctively look for the "ring of truth" in their work. When we're faced with a practical problem, there is usually a full suite of possible answers, a number far too huge for us to go through them all, logically, one by one. Instead, a techie uses his or her experience and instincts to guess at the most likely solution and then uses the tools of logic and the scientific method to confirm—or disprove—that hunch. You save lots of time and effort—and earn kudos from your friends and colleagues—if you're good at hunches and can get close to a workable answer the first or second time out.

One way to work these hunches is to examine not individual solutions but "families" of solutions. If you can show that one or two members of a family fail, then you are more likely to rule out wasting your time chasing down all the other members of the family, and instead you'll go looking for your answers in another direction. You learn to do fast, back-of-the-envelope calculations on simplified or extreme examples of a family of solutions, examples that you don't expect to be perfect but that you can calculate quickly to get a feel for how the solutions behave. If none of the examples comes close to solving the problem, you conclude that you're barking up the wrong tree and look elsewhere.

For instance, people once postulated that the moon came from someplace else in the solar system and was captured by Earth. We can run computer models to test the celestial dynamics of how the moon might have been captured; but the easiest examples that we can try out don't do a very good job of ending up with the actual orbit that the moon has today, and there's no obvious improvement when you vary the parameters. Rather than keep chugging through an infinite number of such models, it seems much more likely to assume that the whole capture idea needs to be abandoned and that maybe the moon was formed in a completely different way.

Hence the logic of my friend David. If there is no immediately obvious reason to choose one religion over another, if moving from one to the other doesn't provide any immediate and visible advantage or bring you any closer to the truth, then you might suspect that there's nothing that *any* religion can contribute to, well, whatever it is that religion is supposed to contribute to. (Note the peculiar lack of definition for the basis on which one is supposed to actually rate religions or find significant differences.)

But you could run the argument in a different direction: if there really is a significant improvement from, say, Scientology to any of the more mainstream religions, this ought to imply that there is good content to the mainstream sects that makes them more worth looking into. However, I've never heard any techie make this case.

There are many other flaws, some subtle and others obvious, in David's logic. The biggest flaw of all, of course, is shown up by the insight that the engineer George had about "problem solving" in general: human issues are different from problems in the physical world, and it's not at all clear what counts as a "solution."

The physical world is not intelligent. That's one reason why techies are peculiarly vulnerable to philosophical charlatans and snake oil salesmen. They are accustomed to dealing with a universe that plays fair. Unlike pesky human beings, the physical universe is not trying to figure you out and adapt to you at the same time that you are trying to adapt to it. It does not have its own agendas, nor does it deliberately try to mislead you. It is not driven by emotions, by the things that it loves or fears; nor does it try to play on your loves and fears. And once it is "solved," it stays solved.

And so all in all, there's no reason to expect that the tools that work well in finding the truth of the physical world will necessarily be of much help in human situations. But when you've got a really good hammer, especially if it is all you've got in your toolbox, it's hard not to see nails everywhere.

⧽ The Tools of Techiedom ⧼

This temptation to use the tools of techiedom on problems of religion comes into play many times in my interviews, especially in dealing with the "many religions" issue.

Ian is an Eastern Orthodox engineering professor whom I visit at a local university. He has a very techie analogy for explaining why so many different religions coexist. Religions, to him, are different "series approximations" to the truth. "Some religions converge on the truth faster than others" is how he puts it. "And some only get close but then diverge entirely." If you don't know what a "series approximation" is, this will take some time to describe—be patient here, because I do think it will be worthwhile.

One of the great advances of scientific revolutionaries like Galileo and Newton was to use equations and mathematics to describe what nature does. In some cases, you can guess the proper equation to describe nature from first principles: I know that the orbit of a planet depends on the gravity of its star, and I know the fundamental equation that describes the force of gravity in terms of the star and planet masses and separation, so it's just a simple matter of filling in the appropriate values for a given star and planet. But in other cases, nature is complicated enough that you can't immediately see which, if any, simple sets of equations could describe it.

In such a situation, one way to proceed is to add together lots of different equations, each of them describing one of the many forces controlling the phenomenon you're trying to describe, in the hope that the whole can be described as the sum of the pieces. For example, the gravity field controlling a planet in a triple-star system is just the sum of the equations for gravity due to each star. There are times, though, when even this doesn't work; there are so many millions of particles in Saturn's rings, not to mention all the little moons in the area, that it's just not practical to add up each of their contributions individually. Even worse is when the forces interfere with each other (the temperature of a fluid depends on how fast it convects, which depends on its viscosity, which depends on its temperature) so that you can't simply treat each factor separately without reference to the others. And of course, there are plenty of cases where we don't know enough about the forces controlling things to let us know what equations to add into the mix.

But there's another way to match an equation to a phenomenon, a more brute-force method. The mathematicians in the nineteenth century showed that you can arbitrarily match any regular curve by adding together a long string of terms made of periodic functions, each one with a smaller period, making each term bigger or smaller so as to match the finer details of the curve. In principle, you should get closer to the curve you're trying to model with each term you add to the string. You need an infinite number of such terms to match the curve perfectly, of course, but with luck, you won't need too many terms to get "close enough" to the true answer.

Sometimes your infinite series only gets close to the curve you want and then starts diverging away from what you want—"going to infinity" they say, or "blowing up"—as you keep adding more terms. At other times, you do get to the truth, but it takes an inordinately large number of terms. But occasionally, if you're lucky or clever in your choice of functions, the series will "converge" to something very close to your goal very quickly, after adding only a few terms to the series.

But don't forget, this is a purely mechanical way of getting a mathematical function to fit reality. Unlike the first method, there's no reason to think that each individual term has any physical meaning (although sometimes it turns out that they do). And there are any number of functions to use in the infinite series— sines, cosines, Bessel functions, Legendre polynomials, and so on. There is not just one, and only one, infinite series that will work. But there usually is one infinite series that works better than the others in that it converges on the answer—the truth— the quickest.

This was Ian's way of thinking about different religions. They all attempt to "converge" on the same truth; some just do it better than others. Notice the hidden techie assumption in this formulation: it is assumed that a religion can be described as a "solution" to a "problem," a "tool" to match a particular human "function."

Not all techies are as nerdy as Ian, however. On a Tuesday morning in late April, I sign out a Jesuit community car and drive up Route 101 almost to San Francisco and then peel off into the rather ordinary suburban neighborhood of South San Francisco. The only thing that tells me I am not back in suburban Detroit, where I grew up, is the smell of saltwater only a few blocks away. Driving down a street of cookie-cutter houses, in front of one I see a Volkswagen microbus up on blocks, slowly rusting in the sea breeze. This is the place.

Waiting at the house is Jules, a Caltech graduate who now makes his living as a professional photographer. He combines an artistic talent with his techie abilities in the darkroom (he still doesn't trust digital cameras to give him the resolution or color quality he's looking for) to produce some astonishingly beautiful images of nature. They're all around us as we sip tea in his living room. As I settle in, he offers me a choice from twenty different kinds of teas, all kept loose in little glass jars in his kitchen cabinet. We're also surrounded by a thousand vinyl record albums, dozens of paintings, and a couple of original cartoons signed by the artists. Seeing him sitting there, dressed in a wide Hawaiian shirt with a peace symbol on a cord peeking out from behind his unkempt beard, I am almost transported back in time, except the beard is gray now, and the shirt a bit wider than it would have been thirty-five years ago.

I describe my project to him, and we chat about it for awhile. Like me, he sees himself as a "techie-plus," someone who's part of that community yet still able to step out of it and look it over from the outside.

Jules suggests to me that as many as 80 percent of techies are religious but that this number is highly uncertain because the subject matter is taboo among most techies; it's not something we talk about in our daily working lives. The experience of most techies is that discussion about religion is acrimonious and pointless. It's my clerical collar (worn or not) that gives them permission to talk to me, even if it also colors what they are willing to tell me.

When I describe to him my idea that the typical techie is an engineer looking for the rules of the universe, he laughs. "Engineers are strong on content but weak on process," he reminds me. "They don't see that the process of how one arrives at a solution can be as important as the solution itself."

He also gets a laugh out of David's "they can't all be right" statement and asks, "Why can't they?" But then, in true techie fashion, he and I start to outline and enumerate the different ways that we see techies approach the "many religions" question:

1. They can't all be true, so they must all be false. (That was David's answer.)

2. They are all true, just different descriptions of the same truth. All churches must be equally true, because they all essentially teach the same thing. This is especially obvious if you view religion as essentially a source of ethical rules for human behavior rather than theological truths about God and make the techie assumption that content equals rules; then, if all your churches come up with the same rules, they must all be based on the same content, and thus ultimately they must all be the same. (I think I saw this in George, the Seventh-day Adventist.)

3. Different religions are like different computer operating systems adapted to different computer platforms; which one is right for you depends on how you are "wired." In other words, the choice of which religion you should follow depends on your personal history, your internal needs, your genetics, or the general question of what you're trying to get out of that religion. This is not quite the same as answer number 2, because it suggests that for a given person, one religion might be better than the others; but for different people with different histories and different needs, different religions might be more appropriate. And like computer systems, some religions have more features than others, but at the cost of a higher overhead and the greater possibility of bugs. Again, the unspoken assumption is that what is important in the differences between religions has nothing to do with how close their theological descriptions of God correspond to reality, either because those differences don't exist or because they are impossible for us to judge, differences too subtle to be detected by us, lost in the "noise" of our human limitations, personal history, genetics, and so on. (This sounds like Alan and Beth, the church shoppers.)

4. Different religions are different approximations of the truth, but some approximations converge on the truth faster than

others (Ian's solution). This is different from numbers 2 and 3 because it suggests that there is one religion, the one that converges the fastest, that really is "better" than the others, at least in a functional sense, if not necessarily "truer" in the long run.

5. Different religions are like different levels of physics. We know that Aristotelian physics, though a perfect example of "common sense," is actually less accurate (and much less useful or powerful) than Newtonian physics. But likewise, at a certain point, Newtonian physics fails, and we can see that it is less accurate than quantum physics. Only the last comes closest to the truth. For many people, and for much of the time, the less true versions of religion (which may be easier to grasp) can be adequate, just as most human beings happily live in the common-sense world of Aristotle without even realizing it, and most engineers can do most of their work using merely Newtonian physics. But at the end of the day, and especially evident in the hardest and most extreme cases, those other versions of physics will fail to give an accurate description of the truth.

Note that of the five, this last model is ultimately the only one that suggests that one religion really does more closely match the truth than any of the others. We can argue about which one!

Armed with this fivefold model for techie approaches to religion, I continue my interviews. The next day I visit Karen, a biologist in her mid-forties. She calls herself an atheist. "Religion is just a behavior modification system to get people to act good. But if you don't need a religion in order to have ethical standards, then what's the point?" Listening to her, I try to pigeonhole where her response fits in the scheme Jules and I devised. I see a bit of process number 1 and process number 2: they're all the same, and they're all wrong, or at least unnecessary. Only long after the interview is over does it occur to me to wonder, where does she get *her* ethical standards from?

Larry is a software engineer originally trained as a chemist, also in his mid-forties. Though raised a Methodist, he now attends a local evangelical Baptist church with his wife. Why that church? It is located conveniently close to their house. And, he concedes, the theology preached there agrees with what they already believe.

What does "theology" mean to him? Well, for example, he tells me he would reject a church that did not teach the reality of Jesus' miracles, but that doesn't mean he agrees with the six-thousand-year-old Earth of the strict creationists. Fortunately, he says, that's not an issue that comes up in his church very often.

When I ask, he concedes that the lack of a sacramental life in his Baptist church does bother him; he misses not having a Eucharist like he did when he was a Methodist. But that's not important enough to make him leave his congregation. Indeed, although he says that the theological content of a church is what's most important to him, he concludes that all Christian churches must be equally true because "they all essentially teach the same thing." Process number 2: content equals rules, and if all your churches come up with the same rules, they must all be based on the same content.

Maybe it's because I'm a Catholic, but I've always been confused at the easy way some of my Protestant friends, like Larry, hop from Baptist to Presbyterian to Methodist to any of the other numerous branches of Protestantism. Are their theological differences that trivial?

But I have to remember that this isn't a dissertation I'm dissecting here, just a conversation between friends over coffee at Starbucks. A good part of the fuzziness in his comments that downplay the differences between denominations are the deliberate ambiguity that we've all learned to introduce into any discussion of religion: we don't want to offend anyone by pointing out where we think other people are wrong, especially on an issue as touchy as church. And as Larry made clear at the start, there is a limit to how much fuzziness he will tolerate.

Mike, an engineering professor in his early forties, understands religion according to process number 3: to him it depends on personal history and taste. He was raised a mixture of Congregational and Catholic, he tells me. When he was in college, he called himself a "semiatheist;" but he had a strong interest in social justice issues and attended Quaker meetings at that time. Then he married a Catholic woman with a degree in theology. After college, they worked together with Catholic religious groups in the Third World and later with poor communities in the rural United States.

Today, active in his local Catholic parish, he says to me, "I can believe about half of what's in the Apostles' Creed." Instead of a list of items to believe, what provides a central image of God for him is what he calls "the web of life." It is his attempt to make sense of this nonrational intuition of spirituality, he says, that leads him to belief.

Belonging to a church is a good way for him to challenge and expand his faith, he says, but he does not see it as the source of that faith. Ritual is definitely not a plus for him. Holidays leave him cold. But a sense of community is very important; so is a theology—a description of who God is and how we relate to him—that matches his own experience of God. Unlike Larry, Mike and his wife travel a long distance every Sunday to a parish where the pastor is "prophetic." By that he means that he sees in his pastor a stronger than average contact with that mysterious transcendent, that "something out there" we're all searching for, the source of the desire that makes us want to believe in God in the first place—the answer to my second question back in Chapter Two.

He says he would be happy in any church that had a sense of mystery and "room to evolve," one that is free to admit that its description of God could never be the complete and final word on the subject. In Catholicism, he has seen both a mixture of much that is rich and good, and a lot of stuff—from decrees out of the Vatican to the prayers used in the Mass—that is so poorly thought out and so poorly written, that it makes him wonder, did people who've been to college actually write this junk? Still, he has stayed with Catholicism both at the urging of his wife and out of a sense of his familiarity with it all.

I spend another evening with a group of six couples; all of them, both the husbands and the wives, were trained either as scientists or as engineers, and all of them are working scientists today. They come with a variety of religious beliefs, including atheist, Methodist, Lutheran, and Catholic.

What is the role of faith in their lives? The atheist in the group says that it is "unscientific" to accept things on faith; he says he needs evidence before believing. This immediately inspires a lively debate among the others. (I keep silent, just listening.) What kind of evidence is he looking for? He admits that he can't describe the kind of evidence that would convince him. That's a telling point against his argument, in the eyes of the other scientists present. They point out that there are a lot of assumptions that go into being a scientist, items that must be accepted "on faith." He concedes the point, but he does not see that it contradicts his original stand.

I bring up my five processes for describing the multiplicity of religions. A Lutheran and a Methodist both agree that they preferred a "minimum feature set" religion. "Faster convergence" gets a favorable nod from others as a model for explaining the difference between different religions.

Rituals and rites are not important or particularly valued by those present; more than anything else, they emphasize that they value a sense of community in their churches. The Catholics comment that to them, the sermons they hear at Sunday Mass are usually nothing more than "white noise"; the homily is a time for them to tune out and meditate on their own. (Exceptions to this rule, though rare, are very welcome, they say.) The preacher in the pulpit, in their opinion, is generally out of touch with real life. Worse, the odds are that he is probably less educated than the people in his congregation and so has little to teach them. (They're techies; education and personal worth are synonymous.)

A few days later I visit Norris, a geologist. He was raised an atheist, as a child brought up among the radical students at Berkeley in the 1960s. Norris still calls himself an atheist, but he takes the content of religion seriously. Given the "they can't all be true" argument, he too responds with an immediate "Why not?" He criticizes the attitude I'd been hearing that seems to use religion merely as a source of community without a commitment to truth: "What a cop-out!" he sniffs. Listening to him, I am reminded of a comment I'd read in an e-mail from another techie: "If God has not spoken clearly, how can man improve upon his meaning? Thus I reject the authority of any religion while continuing to respect and learn from them whenever possible."

⟫ Interviews at a Catholic Engineering School ⟪

In early May, I have the opportunity to spend a few days meeting engineering students and faculty at one of the two Jesuit Catholic universities in the San Francisco Bay Area. In this one setting, I find a surprising array of backgrounds and attitudes.

Oren is an engineering professor who came to academia out of a successful career as an engineer in industry. He's Jewish and active in his faith. But he notes that in Silicon Valley, unlike back east, there is no center of Jewish culture except maybe in Palo Alto, around Stanford University. He confirms to me an insight I first heard from a Jewish friend who teaches at another Jesuit institution: Jews who have left their faith feel very uncomfortable in a Jesuit school, but practicing Jews feel right at home in the Jesuit milieu of faith and academic rigor.

I ask him about the "different religions" question, and I trot out our five processes to explain the multiplicity of religions. "How can one religion 'converge faster' than another?" he scoffs. "Religion is not a process but a single point. How does it 'converge'?" (I hear echoes of what Jules had said: to an engineer, what counts is content, not process!)

He speaks at length of his lifetime history of involvement with Judaism. His own parents were not believers, and partly as a result, he is not close to them today; but he is very close to his wife's parents, who are observant and who passed their faith down to their daughter. It was through her, and thus through them, that he was brought back into the faith.

For him, there is a tremendous grace to be found in the religious services, especially in the music, but he also deeply values the teaching he hears. He does not see his attendance at the weekly services to be a source of challenge to him but rather as a source of emotional fulfillment. I sense in him both a joy that comes from being in touch with the transcendent through his religion and the more immediate way that the practice of his faith brings him closer to his wife and children.

It is clear to me that for him, community and culture, faith and family are all woven together. Each strand is individual, and one is not confused or mistaken for the other, but the web of his life is fashioned by all of them together, and the whole is given strength by the way each thread supports the others. On reflection, I realize that that's true for many of the people whom I have interviewed, but it is especially clear in him as a Jew living in a very non-Jewish milieu.

Elsewhere on campus I chat with Peter, an undergraduate computer science student. He tells me, "I was raised a strict Christian. I guess I'm a theist in practice, but I call myself an agnostic." In other words, I take it, he'll concede to himself that he believes in God but won't admit it to his friends! I have to smile at the typical teenager's desire to have it both ways. But it also makes me appreciate the ancient distinction between a private belief and a public *confession* of that belief.

For all of his public indecision, Peter says that religion is very important to him and that he dislikes glib answers. He names C. S. Lewis as a strong influence, especially his book *Mere Christianity*. Truth is what matters to him; he rejects an attitude that would suggest "even if it isn't true, I want to believe it." And he does see religion as a source of truth; indeed, he sees it as more important than science, and so he holds it to a higher standard. Science is allowed to correct itself when it realizes it is wrong; religion is not allowed that luxury.

Quentin and Roger are two professors from the physics department. Quentin is active in the local chapter of the Campus Crusade for Christ; Roger is an ex-Catholic who was married in a Unitarian church and has since divorced.

Quentin describes having had a sense of a personal call to religion while he was a teenager, even before getting into physics. He was raised Episcopalian, but he notes that even then he tended to react strongly against authority; he'd argue with his pastor on all sorts of issues. Today he belongs to a large, modern Protestant megachurch. He attends primarily because of the relationships he has developed with others in that church, though in fact his wife wanted to belong to a smaller church.

The truth content of a church is not an issue with him. I mention my finding that older techies do not look for truth in church; he suggests that this is not only because they already have the truth they're looking for but also because older folks are too occupied with other concerns; they don't feel they can afford the time or the effort to be continually challenged on issues that they've already decided on and moved past.

When I trot out my five models for the multiplicity of religions, he says he rejects any such technology "parables" to describe religion. On the other hand, he admits he uses similar mechanical "parables" when he teaches and uses physics, but that's because, he says, "that kind of mechanical thinking more closely reflects the reality of physics."

What does he use instead to describe his religion? He never says; questions about how he describes what he actually believes, himself, soon run off into different directions.

Quentin is concerned that Protestantism can appear to be anti-intellectual. Most of his Christian reading, he notes, comes from Catholic writers. He also wonders why there is so little intellectual writing coming from the Eastern Orthodox churches. Where are their thinkers or popularizers? Where is their missionary effort? Is this just evidence of how little we know about that church, he asks, or is it a symptom of a religion gone sterile?

Roger, by contrast, is convinced that all religions are equal. He admits that he is afraid of making a wrong choice, and so he cannot choose. He objects to what he sees as "emotional manipulation" in the Catholicism in which he was raised, and he says he felt liberated when he stopped considering himself a Catholic. "I realized, from outside the church, how ridiculous it looks for the pope to be saying Mass over a bunch of bones in the catacombs." Still, he admits to having strong emotional ties to certain Catholic teachings—"especially the sanctity of marriage," he admits wryly, an attitude that, he suggests, his ex-wife did not share.

He also finds it ironic that he will come across students who are willing to believe in UFOs but not in God.

One physics student who clearly does believe in God is Sam, a junior. He wants to talk to me about becoming a Jesuit himself. I pick up immediately that he is driven by his understanding of the Roman Catholic Church's detailed theology about the nature of God, but coupled with that intellectual drive is a sense of both his own failings and sinfulness and God's forgiving love.

It's a very Jesuit attitude. I can't tell if he has a vocation or not, but he certainly has the right spirituality for the job. The sense of God's immanence, which he says he finds lacking in other religions, reinforces his commitment to Catholicism. He sees God most clearly in his inner desire for the transcendent.

By contrast, another physics student, Timothy, a sophomore, sees much less content in theology. "There are four major religions," he patiently explains to me. "Judaism, Christianity, Islam, and Buddhism. But they're all the same. Or at least, they all have the same ethical teachings and stuff. That's because they're all responses to the same human needs."

This delightfully naïve formulation reminds me again of the contrast between the generations. Forget the fact that Timothy would probably have a hard time passing World Religions 101 and instead notice that he is judging religions on their teachings alone—not their liturgies, their cultural history, or the nature of their communities. He doesn't even recognize any of the aspects of religion that my older interviewees cite as their reasons for choosing and attending a church. The older techies I've been talking to use religion primarily as a source of community; it seems to be only the students who expect religion to be a source of truth.

Truth or community? Is that the way it divides?

I have a chance to talk about this again during a second visit to Jules, the photographer. He ponders awhile and then comes up with a new idea. Isn't there really another reason for techies to belong to a church, one that no one had voiced? "Do you think techies aren't looking for comfort in their religion, or is it just that they don't admit that they do?"

But what kind of comfort? I wonder. What is the source of discomfort? Is it the same as that inner urge for the transcendent? Is "comfort" the transcendent good that we're looking for? When we say we're looking for truth or community, is this just a different way of expressing (or hiding) our real desire, a desire for comfort?

And yet I recall a conversation I had years ago, when I was still at MIT. One of my friends there, a nonbeliever, was trying to understand why I went to church. He too had said, "I suppose your religion must be a source of comfort to you." But when I described this to another MIT friend, a fellow Catholic, she just gave me a dirty look and said, "Comfort? Hell!"

She made an interesting point. It can be comforting to be assured of God's boundless love, but a religion that also makes you realize that your choices have eternal consequences can in fact be highly unsettling.

CHAPTER 9

The Rule of Rules

≥ The Generation Cusp ≤

In Silicon Valley there is a local chain of coffee and dessert restaurants that, I am told, is a prime hangout for techies. It's a Friday evening; though I am a stranger, my first time here, when I look around I see familiar-looking faces at every table. From one, I can hear a heated discussion about the latest Neal Stephenson science-fiction novel. From another, a small group of young people are hunched over a piece of paper that one of them is scribbling on madly while the others chime in with bright ideas.

This is the new millennium; half the parties at these table are female, and a good proportion are minorities. But still, techies look like techies. They tend to long hair, comfortable loose-fitting clothes, and body shapes that tell me that a lot of coffee and pie has been consumed in places like this. This could be just another science-fiction convention or a scene from thirty years earlier, when I was still a student at MIT. I feel incredibly at home.

At our table, my host is Uri, a young software engineer in his late twenties. With him is his wife, Vicky, an accountant, around Uri's age, and Will, a thirtyish friend of theirs. Will's also an accountant, versed in computers, who works with Vicky and spends his weekends with Uri; they hang out with a gang who are into very elaborate role-playing games: think Dungeons and Dragons on steroids.

All three of these techies were raised Catholic; all of them have left the church; all of them have horror stories of dysfunctional families involving divorces, in some cases abuse by family members, and a too-strict Catholic upbringing that never made much sense to them. They are hostile to organized religion but not to the point of having a deep passion against it. Their attitude is summed up by a bumper sticker that Will quotes to me: "I DON'T MIND GOD—IT'S HIS FAN CLUB I COULD DO WITHOUT."

Indeed, the professional ministers of organized religion in their stories were all good people, understanding people, people who were willing to recognize that religion cannot be forced on anyone. But as Uri puts it, the "amateurs" who tried to teach them their faith (including strict but poorly educated nuns from the Philippines whom he encountered in his grade school) were not so understanding.

On the job, Uri handles sensitive data, data that he could illicitly sell to others or use himself to make a fast buck. The idea of abusing that trust is so deeply repugnant to him that he's convinced he could never do it, not without violating something deep within himself. And he sees his Catholic upbringing as a source of that strong ethical center. Indeed, all three of these people are proud of their strong ethical standards—a touchy point especially for the two accountants.

Will was raised by his divorced father in what he considers a warm, loving Irish family. By contrast, he relates a conversation with his mother, now a member of a very conservative Protestant sect, that ended with his finally telling her, "You have a string of rules that you believe you must follow in order to gain salvation. But what if I obey the same set of rules, just because I want to obey them, without any thought of gaining a goal? Isn't that more virtuous?" Uri and Vicky, hearing this story, nod their heads in agreement.

Much like the strict rules in their role-playing games, Uri and Will are looking for a comprehensive set of rules to live by. But they express a great hostility toward rules they do not understand, such as the hoops you have to jump through in order to get married within the Catholic church. Uri notes the irony that in fact he lives a very "clean" life in terms of the traditional standards of right and wrong: he has been highly moral in his work; he's married to his high school sweetheart, to whom he has been faithful; he doesn't drink, smoke, or do drugs. He says his life is cleaner than many of those he calls "the hypocrites who are found in churches."

Vicky and Uri assert that those who are ultrareligious (like the "Bible Belters" that Vicky describes meeting when she was in college) are so out of a sense of inferiority or lack of control. Such people need to feel superior to everyone else, they say. When I comment in reply, "Unlike those of us who really are superior and thus feel no such need," they laugh at the irony, but they do not dispute the characterization.

All three note that although they do not practice any religion, they all still remember the rites and could probably start practicing again. They all say that religion is something they would want to take more time to learn about, but in the future and on their own. They have picked up things about religion and history in the science-fiction books they've been reading (Neal Stephenson again) that have piqued their curiosity to learn more. They are techies and hence voracious readers, and they believe that reading a book will teach them what they want to know and what they need to know.

I see Uri and Vicky living on the cusp between the undergraduate students I've been speaking with earlier, who are looking for truth, and the middle-aged engineers who belong to a church mostly for the sense of community. They have no children, not yet. But Uri in particular values the sense of ethics he feels he learned in childhood from his religion (from those very nuns, he admits, that he had just scorned). And he worries that if he and Vicky start a family, how will their children learn right and wrong?

The next week, I talk at a Catholic college to an undergraduate English class, mostly freshmen and sophomores, all non-techies, about my "talking to techies" project. Their general reactions to the questions I am raising are interesting. Some of them remark that the reasons they see their parents participating in a church are exactly what I have found, a desire for community and a way of educating their children.

"How is going to church different from joining a bowling league?" I challenge them.

"It's different, because in a church there is a common set of values."

Actually, I think to myself, what can be more common than the shared value of knocking down bowling pins and drinking beer?

Still, I see the point. Their parents aren't coming to church to find their values or truth or meaning in their lives. They feel they already have their sets of values and meaning, and they're probably just as happy not having either set challenged. They just want to be in a place where they are confirmed in those values, a place that will help them pass those values on to the next generation.

The students themselves, however, see different reasons for belonging to a religion. They feel they don't need to join a religion to find a sense of community (though a campus church group can be a good place to meet members of the opposite sex); they have a ready-made community of their classmates at school. But they are still looking to find meaning in their lives and still trying to discover what they are supposed to be doing with those lives—my third question in Chapter Two. They are still dealing with issues of self-identity. Faced with the question "What do I care about, and why do I care?" they see the "What do I care about?" as the more important aspect to be resolved. At their stage of life, that's the question they are more worried about finding an answer for. If they do turn to God or religion, it is to help them find that answer.

This insight is confirmed in an interview I have a few days later. Xavier, a twenty-eight-year-old self-described atheist, is no stranger to evangelical sales pitches; he works at Apple Computer. It strikes him that most people use membership in a church for the sense of community, just as I have found; at his age, though he lives alone, he does not yet see a need for a church to provide that sense of community for himself. But when I lament, "What people go to church for is not what we are selling," he throws me yet another techie-religion parallel: "You think you are selling truth," he tells me, "but your audience has already brought their own truth with them to church. All you are selling them is tech support."

Church as tech support? Once-a-week scheduled maintenance?

≋ Zen and the Art of Xerox Copier Maintenance ≋

Through the generous help of the scholars at Santa Clara University's Center for Science, Technology, and Society, I am put in contact with Dr. Julian Orr, a retired ethnologist. (Since I am about to quote his book, I am not hiding his identity behind a false name.) Orr worked for Xerox in the late 1980s studying the subcultures of corporate offices, and in 1990, he wrote a doctoral thesis at Cornell, published in 1996 as a book titled *Talking About Machines*, that describes the peculiar subculture of Xerox copier repairmen. Now in retirement, today he raises sheep in the hills above Half Moon Bay, California. We arrange to meet for lunch at a favorite Middle Eastern sandwich shop in Palo Alto to chat about techics and religion before he heads off to see his acupuncturist. (At this point, I have been staying in Northern California long enough that this all sounds very normal.)

Over couscous and falafel, we chat about my very amateur work with these interviews. He is supportive and encouraging, but between our conversation and reading some of the literature he recommends to me, I appreciate all over again the gap between what I am trying to do and how a professional would do things.

But the most important result of this meeting is to set me up for the insight that hits me upon finishing his book, *Talking About Machines*. For me, the key passage is on page 149, and I quote it here:

> The work done by the [Xerox copier repair] technicians I studied . . . is often very different from the methods specified by their management in the machine documentation. There is clearly a disparity between the tasks that they are told to accomplish and the means that are said to be adequate to the task. The . . . technicians choose to give accomplishing the task priority over use of the prescribed means, and so they resolve problems in the field any way they can, apparently believing that management really wants accomplishment more than strict observation of the prescriptions for work. The technicians pay more attention to other messages from management which address the goals of service, giving the technicians

a general mandate to solve problems. Managers do say, for example, that customer satisfaction is the primary goal of the corporation, and such messages can be interpreted to warrant a wide range of activities. However, the need to choose from conflicting definitions of the work and the means thereto also opens the way for continuing disputes about the very nature of the job, the legitimacy of different activities, or the adequacy of one's compensation, since it is not clear which activities require compensation as being part of one's work.

The copier repairmen are given thick manuals about how to fix their machines, but in practice, the manuals are often of little help. Machines don't always break the way they expect back at the factory; there's no documentation about what to do when a baloney sandwich gets caught in the paper feed! Instead, the repairmen use those manuals to try to deduce how the machines work, and then, from those deductions, they invent their own ways of fixing the kinds of problems they see in the field. These solutions are passed around in an oral tradition of stories recounted over endless cups of coffee at the local Denny's as the repairmen hang out waiting for their beepers to go off.

And then it hit me: Isn't this also the way that religion-practicing, rule-following techies deal with the rules of their religion? They agree with the overall general goals that they hear from their churches, but they don't have a particularly high opinion of the "documentation" that describes how to reach those goals. And just like with the Xerox copier repairmen, there is among at least some techies an unspoken contempt of those who merely follow the documentation literally—and even more of the "suits" in management who insist on such behavior. Blindly following the edicts from on high implies that you don't really understand the underlying technology.

So while they still have a strong devotion to following rules, the rules they follow aren't always exactly what you find in the catechisms. Instead, they take those rules apart and try to deduce what the underlying principle is that their religion is trying to support. Then they create for themselves a new set of rules, a set that fits their own situations—and their own prejudices and predispositions as well, needless to say. Those self-created rules are the ones they follow religiously.

I find exactly the perfect illustration just a few days later, talking to Yaz, a scientist in his early forties who works near Palo Alto. For the most part, what he has to tell me is a good summary of what I have heard, again and again, from most of my older techie interviewees. Yaz is a devout, active Lutheran. In trying to describe his reasons for believing, he tells a now familiar tale: he relates strongly to the "Why is there something instead of nothing?" issue, but he is also motivated by the desire for something "out there." The sense of using religion as a way of looking for meaning for his own life is much less strong now that he's older; but he describes going through a period of atheism in his college years when science seemed to preclude the need for God, until eventually he learned enough about science to see its limitations and its inability to answer the "why" questions. Since then he has been associated with liberal, university-affiliated congregations.

He feels that all religions have some truth, but he rejects the idea that all religions are equal. On the other hand, as he tells me, his spouse is Jewish, and he respects and admires that, even as he himself remains committed to his Lutheranism. He expresses the difference among religions by analogy to different languages or different kinds of music. In general, his church's theological content—Jesus Christ as Lord and Savior, who calls us to repentance—is important to him; by contrast, when he returns home to his mother's Lutheran parish, he finds what he hears there to be too watered down: "Jesus as partner," with no challenge of confronting one's sinfulness.

Indeed, he values all he has learned in his church, not only its intellectual content but also its sense of community. He finds the presence of liturgy and Sunday communion important, but he doesn't wax ecstatic about ritual, except in one instance: he describes his own wedding as "incredibly moving."

But that was a civil ceremony performed by the mayor of San Francisco during a brief interlude when such marriages carried legal weight. He is an active and committed Lutheran who is also living in a permanent, committed gay relationship.

I could see the way the gears mesh in his thinking. His church does not recognize relationships like the one he is living in.

But his church does teach that sexual relationships should be monogamous and committed. He is attempting to live in such a relationship. Therefore, as far as he can see, he is following the spirit of the rules, even if they're rules that he has invented for himself. He's just like the Xerox repairman who provides customer satisfaction by following a repair procedure that would never make it into the official Xerox documentation.

At my last interview, a dinner with six more techies, I share this insight: We techies invent rules for ourselves from the principles we derive from the rules we are given. Zenna, one of the techies at the dinner table, is surprised that I am surprised. "But of course," she says to me. "That's how everything is always done."

≥ Where Do We Go from Here? ≤

I started the project of this book thinking that I could outline the shape of techie religiosity with simple, clear, and logical strokes, by putting the insights of great thinkers like Kant and Rahner into a techie setting. But the techies fooled me by being much more complex than I thought. They especially fooled me by not always thinking the way I think. This gave me pause on more than one level. Perhaps I didn't know them as well as I had imagined. (No surprise there.) And perhaps I was not such a techie myself but rather some kind of guest or interloper into the techie world.

But upon rereading my notes and thinking about all of my friends, I believe the real situation is much simpler, if much fuzzier. The truth is that techies—like most humans—fail badly at being successfully pigeonholed. We're just too varied. There are not very many generalizations that survive exposure to the data.

Consider this: from what I have written here, you might certainly assume that a "typical" techie is a guy who leaves his religion when he is a teenager searching for truth; spends his twenties without religion; eventually gets married and starts a family; and then, in search of a community in which to raise that family, he joins his wife's church. Now go back and read over the two dozen people I've described here. You'll find that nearly all of them match one part or another of my "typical" outline, sure, but how many of them actually fit that stereotype in every detail? I'd say one or maybe two.

Of course, for my younger interviewees, it's too soon to tell. We do change with age; that's one generalization that I learned from these interviews. Techies at age twenty are at a different place in their religious life than techies in their fifties. I have no idea why such an obvious fact of life should have come as such a revelation to me, but it did.

Some truly life-altering things happen to us, or at least some of us, as we get older. The classic ones include falling in love and getting married; having and raising children; suffering the death of a parent, a spouse, or a child; and coming face to face with our own death.

As it happens, as of this writing, I haven't gone through any of those experiences myself, which may explain why even though I may know I'm not a kid anymore, sometimes I don't feel like a grown-up, either. Of course, since techies are more likely than most people to be unmarried and unattached, perhaps that's something else I share with them. Also, for whatever reasons, I myself never experienced either the teenage rebellion against religion or the adult return that seems to be a common pattern among techies—and many nontechies as well, of course. It still surprises me to hear about other people going through those stages.

Another thing I see in my fellow techies' lives is that we all have only so many hours in the day. One way we deal with this lack of time is to multitask our lives. Sharing books, playing games, listening to music, and going to movies are social moments for techies, times when we can relax while hanging out with friends. (By contrast, many of the other more mainstream recreations, like cocktail parties or sporting events, involve an act of "socializing" that is very much *not* the same thing as relaxing, to an introverted techie!) But at the same time, these are the moments when we contemplate the big questions of life. Techies gravitate toward exactly those forms of games and literature—role-playing games, fantasy, science fiction—that are also conducive to self-reflection, that call on us to examine our own goals and identities and allow us the distance to feel comfortable in doing all of these things. Becoming immersed in a fantasy novel, struggling with the hero's conflicts of good and evil; listening to atmospheric music on a high-tech sound system; or imagining the life of an itinerant monk (with an appropriately high number of hit points) in a role-playing game—these are the techie versions of meditation and prayer.

But meditation and prayer are aspects of *spirituality;* what is the role of *religion* in the life of a techie? Is it just another "life-style choice"—Presbyterian or Methodist, Peet's coffee or Starbucks? I think that may be how the nonreligious techies view it. I recall, when I was thinking of joining the Jesuits, showing some of their literature to a techie friend of mine. Though an atheist, she was into Renaissance art and music, and from that standpoint, she could see why the Jesuit lifestyle was attractive. "This looks pretty cool," she admitted, looking over the vocation pamphlets, "except for all this God stuff they talk about."

But reading over my interviews again and reading between the lines, I have a hunch that for those techies who do belong to a church, it's more than lifestyles or communities. Techies do have a religious life. And when they go to church, it is for something more than what they'd get out of a bowling league. It is precisely for the "God stuff."

Think back to Carol's comment, "Believing in God makes me a better person. That is why I continue to believe." I took that at first as simply a pragmatic expression: going to church was useful to her because she liked the kind of person it made her. But couldn't it be taken in a deeper sense? The fact that believing in God "works" in that it makes her a better person is, if not a proof, at least strongly consistent with the notion that there's something true about this God she believes in; the fact that it "works" is why she has the confidence to continue to believe in it.

Even the strong negative reactions I got from techies about the rites and rituals at their churches doesn't necessarily mean that they don't want or need those rituals. It could very well imply just the opposite, that for all the reasons I discussed in Part Two, they want them very much but just aren't satisfied with what they're getting. In fact, the problem in the typical parish might well be that there aren't enough real liturgists—the rule-bound types who are usually scorned by the other members of the parish. ("What's the difference between a liturgist and a terrorist? You can negotiate with a terrorist.") Instead, most parishes use a sloppy mix of bits and pieces of different liturgies that were never designed to work together—assuming that there was any design to them in the first place. Liturgists are the techies of religion; I suspect that techies would respond well to a well-crafted liturgy if they were told why they are doing what they're doing.

The other thing many techies lack are the philosophical and linguistic tools it takes to describe the religious experience. A number of times in these interviews, I had to puzzle out from the context what it was they were actually trying to tell me. An experience of God is hard enough for a poet to express. Engineers rarely develop new metaphors and rarely go beyond the clichés that they and their workmates always rely on. Furthermore, they are still trapped in a culture that tells them that "real techies don't do church," so they imagine a very strong social pressure against expressing these ideas.

And so they do believe in God, and they do find God in their churches. But they have a deep reticence when it comes to talking about it, even to a trusted friend, even to a family member, even to themselves. Except in the anonymity of Web logs, techies rarely have the opportunity or permission to express themselves on these issues. (And those blogs, far different from a face-to-face conversation with a trusted friend, tend to an odd dynamic of naïve philosophy and self-conscious posturing where their lack of the tools to express themselves becomes painfully evident.) But there wasn't one techie in all my interviews who looked blankly at me when I asked my questions or sought their opinions. They all knew what I was getting at; I wasn't raising anything new that they hadn't already thought about before, on their own.

It so happens that unlike them, I find myself in a job and a life where I have the time, the training, and the encouragement to think about religion, especially my own religion. This doesn't mean that my thoughts are deeper than my fellow techies'. But what my religious formation as a Jesuit brother has given me is the vocabulary and categories—and the cultural permission—to talk about the sorts of transcendental things that everyone experiences but that not everyone has the tools to describe.

And it has given me the time to put those reflections into some sort of order. My daily prayer and those luxurious long uninterrupted days of contemplation that I get every year during my eight-day silent retreats are reinforced by the easy availability in our Jesuit communities of extensive libraries of theology and philosophy, which build on the several years of formal study that the Jesuits have given me in those topics, not to mention the joy of the kinds of conversations I get to hear at the dinner table, daily, in my Jesuit community. There would be something wrong if I didn't have a more elaborated understanding of religion, of the "hows" and the "whys," than most of my fellow techies are able to achieve.

And so that suggests to me where I am to go next. In the first two parts of this book, I attempted to summarize, in an abstract way and borrowing heavily from the established tradition of theology and philosophy, how a religious techie might justify a general sort of belief in God and religion. In this third part of the book, I have tried to generalize from the experience of a large number of individual techies about how in reality they live their religions. From here it gets more specific and more personal.

The whole point of this book is to illustrate how techies live with religion. With that as its goal, what follows is my specific confession of how I, a techie, make my own Christian and Catholic beliefs work.

PART FOUR

Why Would a Techie Be a Christian?

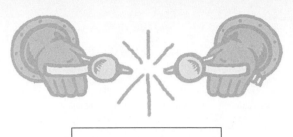

CHAPTER 10

What Does the Truth Look Like?

≷ Would I Know It If I Saw It? ≷

A preacher brought his flock down to the river and stood before them in flowing robes. "If you have faith," he told them, "then your faith can do the impossible. The question is, do you believe?"

"We all believe!" they shouted.

"Do you believe that I can walk upon this water?"

"We believe!" they shouted again.

"Will your faith support me as I step onto the river?"

"It will! It will!"

"Are you certain that the power of your faith can sustain me and stop me from sinking when I stride upon the waves?"

"We are certain! We believe," they insisted once again.

"Well, then," said the preacher, "if your faith is that strong, if you truly believe, then there's no need for me to actually do it."

Faith is a fine thing, but I must admit that I have my share of techie skepticism. And certainly, in the face of the uncertain and some would say unanswerable questions raised by the possibility of the existence of a God, the easiest path would be to retreat into a kind of noncommittal agnosticism. But to me that's not a satisfying answer, either rationally or emotionally.

There are reasons, as we have seen, for belonging to a religion. It provides a community, it offers a setting for weddings and funerals, and it serves as a place to teach morality to the next generation. But I want more. I want reasons to have faith in my faith, to have a reasonable confidence that there is actually truth in what my religion teaches me about God and my relation to God. And that faith has to be based on something within myself that I already trust: it has to be consonant with my experience of the universe and my abilities to reason about that universe.

And perhaps here is one place where I disagree with many of my fellow techies whom I interviewed in Chapters Eight and Nine. I admit that I still have a strong desire to find truth in my faith. And I still have a perhaps naïve faith that I can actually find it, or at least get closer to it.

But how does one find truth?

The question "Where is the true religion to be found?" is too much to swallow all at once. I have to start with a simpler question, bite off a smaller piece to chew on. It's enough for now to ask merely "What does truth look like? How would I know it if I saw it?"

Recall our discussion in Part One about how a scientist goes about solving the thorny problem of trying to ferret out truths in the natural universe. The first tool we start with is a hunch— which is to say, we are constantly bootstrapping on our previous experiences of natural truths to guess what the next step looks like. We can't get anywhere without some idea of where we are going and what it's going to look like when we get there; that's the only way to know when we've arrived. So that means we have to have some idea of what the truth is going to look like. And the only way we can do that is to have some bits of truth already in mind that we can use as models.

We use the bits of science we already trust to help suggest where to find new bits of science that will also turn out to be trustworthy. In the same way, a techie who knows what truth in the physical world looks like will probably use his or her experience with recognizing that truth to guess what truth in the spiritual world should look like.

So what can I say about truth? What does my experience of finding truth in the physical world tell me that perhaps can be generalized to other kinds of truth?

We scientists and engineers start with the assumption that truth is logical, self-consistent, and not arbitrary. Furthermore, truth follows patterns whose "flavor" we learn to recognize—what is often called the "ring" of truth. For example, I have seen over and over again in the physical universe that a true description of what's going on is neither stupidly simple nor hopelessly complicated. Instead, rather like a Bach fugue, it achieves a complex beauty from the interplay of a few simple principles. I see that the force of gravity and the force of magnetism can both be described by simple equations, yet the path of a charged grain of dust in a planet's ring subjected to both laws at the same time is so complicated that it is all but impossible to predict. The growth of crystals in a rock, the swirl of cream in a cup of coffee: the laws of physics governing them are straightforward, but the results remarkably complex—and incidentally, quite beautiful.

Beauty is worth looking for. Often a true description of nature can be recognized by its simplicity and economy of style, as when Isaac Newton showed that the same simple equation for gravity can explain both the orbits of the planets and the fall of an apple from a tree. Scientists call such theories "elegant." Elegance is not a surefire replacement for experimental confirmation, but it's a surprisingly good indicator that a theory that is "so beautiful that it has to be true" often actually is, or at least it is close enough to the truth that it's worth spending time with because it will eventually point you to wherever the truth really is to be found.

It is useful to have such a theory, one that can describe the essential truths that we already think we know, because we can extend it to make predictions about where to find the next bit of truth. That's not enough for the techie, however. A theory may tell us where to look, but it only directs us to the starting point. We may trust the predictions of the theory, but we also want to see them actually confirmed. We won't believe until we see the guy standing on the water.

As scientists, we are all acutely aware that our expectations can color what we think we're seeing. And so we want to see the truth from more than one angle. The more different, independent lines of evidence we have, the more we trust our results. (Maybe the guy on the water is standing on a post in the river that we can't see from our first vantage point.)

Another thing I know about finding truth in my science is that it's hard work. Most of the time, you feel like a complete idiot trying to understand not just what you're seeing in your own results but even simply trying to understand what the other scientists have seen before you. I recall a foreign professor of geophysics at MIT who, rumor had it, knew only two phrases in English: "What? You didn't know that?" and "Bah! You're so stupid!" He had plenty of opportunity to use both phrases on the rest of us. But his comments show the other side of the coin: once the truth is understood, when the eureka moment is achieved and all the pieces fall into place, it suddenly becomes so obvious that you wonder why you ever had a hard time seeing it in the first place. (And everyone else who can't see it is, bah, so stupid!)

So to summarize: each bit of truth must be consistent with all the other bits. It should be supported by many different lines of evidence, which is to say that it can (and must) be approached from more than one direction. And it's hard work getting there. (Everything that is true is hard; alas, not everything that is hard is true!)

So given this sense of how one finds truth, the next question is, Is there a true religion? And if there is such an animal, how do we recognize it?

We can start by reminding ourselves what we wanted a religion to do for us: to help us get in touch with God. And we should remember what kind of God we decided was worth looking for, back in Part One: a God who could explain why the universe exists and why we're a part of it and why we yearn for that God.

If the God we're looking for is responsible for the universe, then in some sense that God has to be bigger than the universe. And so a religion that would give me anything useful about dealing with such a big God would also have to be, well, big.

Big in a lot of different ways. "Big" to me means big in space and time. The truth, I believe, is the same at every place and at every time in the universe. It can't be limited to my own time or my own culture, my own species or my own planet. I recognize that my particular time and culture demand that this truth be expressed in words that make sense to me where I am, but I insist that one should be able to find versions of the same truth that demonstrably work in other times and cultures and that there should be some flexibility to allow that truth to be further translated to accommodate whatever intelligent aliens we discover in the future—including those far-future aliens who are our own descendants!

If it's also supposed to lead me to the God who is the source and goal of my transcendent urges, it has to be capable of showing me, at least "through a glass, darkly," some glimmer of the transcendent. It should be able to give me those little unexpected jolts of joy that C. S. Lewis talked about in his autobiography, *Surprised by Joy*.

A true religion must be capable of showing me truth that, once recognized, can at the very least not be disproved. In this I find myself echoing an attitude of my fellow techies: I do demand that my religion be "not obviously wrong." But beyond that, I insist that it must be capable of telling me things I didn't already know but things that, once grasped, resonate within me with the ring of truth, things that I can independently confirm.

And if it is going to help me find the God who gives meaning to my life, it would have to have the capability of surprising me and challenging me and my comfortable worldview. It should be able to hit close to home at times. I'm not satisfied with mere "tech support" for a religion that just lets me feel good about myself and where I am. I know my limitations, and a religion that does not push against those limitations is a waste of my time and can't possibly be big enough to be true. Which is to say, such a limited religion is "obviously wrong."

Likewise, a true religion must be capable of performing the functions that I am using a religion to achieve, the things I talked about in Part Two. It should be able to remind me of what an experience of God is like, help me discern the real thing from the false leads, and give me something to do about it, once I recognize God's presence in my life.

Every scientific paper starts with a listing of the authors and their institutions. Knowing where an idea is coming from is an important tool that lets the scientist-reader know both how to approach and make sense of what the authors are trying to say and to make allowances for the systematic biases that inevitably color every human being's work. In the same way, I want to know where my religion is coming from. Are these the thoughts of a huckster out to make money? A school of wise people relying on their own wisdom while contemplating the universe? A lone mystic who really believes he or she is in touch with the transcendent?

Of those three alternatives, gravitating toward the philosophy of a school of wise people would seem to be the safest path. But would such a path be big enough to really show me something I didn't already know? I am a techie, thoroughly imbued with techie arrogance; I think that I am as smart as anyone else out there. Why should I follow a religion invented by some other human being (much less a committee) who's probably no smarter than I am? I could just as easily invent my own religion, couldn't I? But I know that I can't even pretend to match a line of prophets who really are in touch with God—not if they can convince me that it's really God they're hearing, anyway.

I have to believe in the possibility that such true mystics exist. If I am going to believe in God and believe that God does want to have something to do with us humans, I have to believe that at least someplace, at some time, in some way, he really did make his presence known to somebody. He must really have told someone, somewhere, something that he wants us to pay attention to.

What would convince me that that "somebody" was actually hearing from God? Two things come to mind.

If that encounter with God happened some time in the past, I should be able to see the results of that encounter; there should be an obvious change in how those people who were presumably touched by God and those who listened to them and followed them behaved afterward. If what they were taught was true, and truly from God, then it should have made (on balance at least) a difference for the good. That would be an external sign of something that comes from a good God.

But the other sign is subjective, internal, but probably in the long run more powerful: whatever that mystic tells me about God and God's message itself must have the ring of truth. It must produce in me a eureka moment, fitting pieces together in a way I never noticed before, producing the same effect of transcendent delight in its rightness that I know I have experienced (all too rarely!) in my scientific life.

So this is what a true religion would look like to me. It would have roots as old as human history but be capable of growing as the human race has grown, in space and time and in wisdom and experience. It should be big enough to embrace all cultures and peoples but specific enough to show me particular instances, in a particular time and place, where this God really did have some specific interaction with that person. The reality of that interaction should be visible in its results; a functioning religion should be able to show me a series of interactions in specific times and places that have visibly changed, and continue to change, human history.

And a true religion can't be just a Hollywood movie that entertains me. I know that I have found truth in my science only through hard work and mortification. In the same way, this true religion must be a stern teacher who makes me work hard. But it should also, like my scientific work, reward me with moments of transcendent joy.

A Naïve Introduction to World Religions

Remember Timothy, the sophomore techie whom I interviewed? He's the one who had explained to me, "There are four major religions: Judaism, Christianity, Islam, Buddhism. But they're all the same, or at least they all have the same ethical teachings and stuff." I had winced at his naïveté, but in fact his attempt to sort out, classify, and thus explain away world religions was a classic techie tactic, one that I am about to use here. However, rather than pigeonholing individual religions, I'm going to start by defining different classes of religion.

Some religions are in fact not religions at all in the sense I am talking about here; they are not institutions that would attempt to facilitate communication between God and human. Rather, they are philosophies that attempt to explain what the universe is all about and how we should live in it. They attempt to satisfy the third question from Part One, "How do I make sense of my life, and what am I supposed to be doing here?" while implicitly throwing up their hands on answering the first two questions, "Why is there something instead of nothing?" and "What do I want, and why do I want it?"

They are the products of the "schools of the wise" that I was talking about earlier. To my mind, the various Chinese philosophies like Taoism and Confucianism fit into this category. So do various classical philosophies, like Stoicism, or modern philosophies, like that followed by those people in the United Kingdom who listed their religion on the census form as "Jedi Knight." The point is that while the central philosopher can be greatly revered, no one really insists that Obi-Wan Kenobi was personally responsible for the creation of the universe.

It's not that the followers of these philosophies don't believe in God but that for them God plays a different role. Their philosophy is not defined by the nature of a divinity. Indeed, there are plenty of examples of people who follow one of these philosophies while also belonging to a more God-centered religion—think of the early Jesuit missionaries to China who incorporated Confucian beliefs into their explanation of Catholicism. (Oddly enough, both the famous Native American mystic Black Elk and the actor who played Obi-Wan Kenobi, Sir Alec Guinness, were also practicing Catholics.)

A very different class of religions posits gods who inhabit nature, who are responsible for its functioning. In most versions, these gods may also play some role in determining the fates of individual humans. These religions tend to have multiple gods who divide their functions among themselves and who may have some sort of ever-changing hierarchy. The variety of such religions in human culture range from African animism to Indian Hinduism; this sort of religion was prevalent in ancient Egypt and Greece and Rome and from the Incas to the Vikings to the Japanese. It's a way of looking at the universe that can be found in virtually every human culture, and the similarities from place to place and time to time speak to some possible common and very ancient origins. It was the prevailing way of looking at the world in the Tigris and Euphrates region four thousand years ago, from which we are told Abram (the founder of the third type of religion) and his family came.

The God of Abraham is significantly different from these other gods. This difference is emphasized over and over again in the Hebrew holy scriptures. The God of Abraham existed before the universe, he was responsible for its creation, and indeed he created it from nothing (unlike the pagan creation myths, which either have the universe happening by accident or shaped by the nature gods out of a preexisting chaos). And this God insists on being different from the nature gods by refusing to be represented in golden statues but rather appearing in subtle if unmistakable ways—as a burning bush whose flames do not consume it or as a still, soft wind rather than as thunder and lightning.

By existing outside the universe, this God is not a part of nature but rather beyond nature: supernatural. Such a God does indeed possess the bigness that I'm looking for.

This God takes a direct interest in humanity. According to the Jewish scriptures and traditions, God gave humans laws that not only show people how they are to worship him but also how they are to govern themselves in their daily affairs. As noted in Part One, this moral and ethical code is unusual; the Jews proudly boasted that no other god ever handed down such laws before. Indeed, these laws contain in them the kinds of truths that were a surprise to those who heard them but that once apprehended seem so obvious that one wonders why they were ever a surprise. (Another ring of truth: the teachings of Buddha and Confucius, the only ethical philosophies that even come close to the Mosaic Law, were the products of mature, well-developed, well-established cultures. By contrast, the Law of Moses appeared in a most unlikely manner among a squabbling, ragtag bunch of exiles.)

This is a God who is capable of explaining the universe and who gives us some markers about who we are supposed to be and what we are supposed to be doing. He teaches us things that we didn't know but that resonate with the truth we intuit within ourselves, once we know what to look for. He's beginning to sound like the kind of God I was looking to believe in back in Part One.

And notice another thing. Curiously, we find that the plurality of religions is not actually as big an issue as it might seem. In all of human history, there's really only one contender for the role of the supernatural cause of the universe, the one who gives meaning and direction to our life. It's only the God of Abraham, as recorded in the Jewish scriptures.

One God, yes; but three branches of religion. The Jewish scriptures are the record of the times and ways in which that One God first attempted to get us stubborn humans to pay attention. Jewish faith is based on that book. But so are Christianity and Islam.

So how do I choose among those three branches? I'm not even going to pretend that my answer is impartial (as I have been pretending up to now). I'm a Christian.

And why am I a Christian? I could state the obvious, that I'm a Christian because I was born into a Christian family living in a Christian society, was educated by Christians, and have been surrounded by Christians all my life. But I have a lot of friends born and raised in identical circumstances who have completely rejected Christianity, so there must be more to it than that.

I can't say that I approach this question without bias. This isn't a mathematical proof I am coming up with here; none of this has been. Remember, the point of this exercise is not to somehow prove that I'm right—that's fatuous and in any event impossible—but rather to demonstrate how I reconcile the choice I've already made with my techie, rationalistic view of the universe. To put it another way, I am not trying to convince you; I am trying to convince myself.

Why bother even doing that if I have already made up my mind? Because I am not satisfied with being self-satisfied. I want some assurance (admittedly, far less than a proof) that my choice is not "obviously wrong." And I want to know that there is in fact a basis for that choice, slim as it may seem.

Christianity as a religion does, at least in theory, fit my carefully contrived definition of what I am looking for in a religion. (But weren't these criteria of mine biased by the fact that I am already a Christian? Of course they were. This isn't a proof, just a consistency check.) It describes a God who does all the things I want a God to do; it provides as a religion all the features I was looking for in a religion. And only in Christianity, unique among world religions, do I find a most explicit description of a God who, in the person of Jesus, makes absolutely and unmistakably clear who he is, what he wants of us, and why we want him. As a solution, it works.

But is it the only solution? Or the best solution? I can rationalize my choice for Christianity over Judaism or Islam to some degree, though I recognize that these are mere rationalizations and not proofs.

I can rule out Judaism for myself on the simple grounds that I was not born Jewish, not born into the Chosen People. There are plenty of examples in human history of peoples who considered themselves "chosen," but oddly, Christians are the only group I know of who believe that there is a Chosen People, and it's someone else. This does raise the whole issue of what "a Chosen People" means to the rest of us; suffice it to say that traditional Christian theology has plenty of room for accepting good people who haven't had the opportunity to know God through no fault of their own, so the idea that one group of people has been chosen doesn't necessarily mean that everyone else is out of luck.

As for Islam, I haven't made any kind of serious study of it; how can I reasonably dismiss it without knowing more about it? It's a large unknown. But my techie experience teaches me how to handle unknowns like that. Techies like to describe any process in which we can observe what goes in and what comes out without knowing at all what goes on inside as a "black box," and we are used to making judgments on those black boxes simply on the basis of their inputs and outputs. It's no different from following the biblical tenet "by their fruits ye shall know them."

And what are the fruits of Islam? Frankly, none of the Islamic-based cultures around the world are places where I would want to live. That does seem to be a telling point to me. The millions of emigrants from those countries to the West would seem to indicate that I am not alone in this judgment. Of course, there are obviously many more factors besides religion that determine how a society develops and flourishes or why people would want to leave it. Still, without knowing anything more about the cultural and economic histories of those countries, this observation nonetheless means that Islam does not intuitively seem very attractive to me.

But obviously, this is hardly an ironclad proof against the religion. After all, a hundred years ago, my ancestors emigrated from Catholic Italy and Catholic Ireland to come to what was then a very Protestant America, yet we all stayed Catholic. And today both Ireland and Italy have become very attractive places to live indeed. Maybe in a hundred years, Islamic countries will be a lot more attractive.

And so obviously, this is not a proof that Christianity is the one true religion. For one thing, I invented all that list of what I wanted God and religion to be from the point of view of someone who was already a practicing Christian. It would be impossible for me to forget my religious history and false to pretend that my own religious background didn't color my expectations. Once again, as I argued in Part One, this could be merely another case of recovering the assumptions I made at the beginning of the argument.

But I am not interested in coming up with such a proof. I don't want to prove that everyone else is wrong. The justification of this whole argument is merely to show how a techie like me lives with a belief in religion, in my case Christianity. In choosing Christianity because it "works," I can at least demonstrate what "works" means to me.

And the fact that I don't go looking any further into the other religions is actually another typical techie trait: once you find an answer that works, it's hard to justify wasting any more time looking further. Either the other solutions are not going to be as good, or else they are in practice no different from the one I've already found.

Logical? Strictly speaking, no. Practical? You bet.

Having said all that, I will end by pointing out one key issue that I do see Christianity emphasizing, something that I trust (or at least hope) is present in Judaism and Islam but that I don't see being given nearly as prominent a role there: love. That God is love is a point made everywhere in the New Testament, especially in John's Gospel, and explicitly with those words in John's First Epistle. Merely having a God who is responsible for the universe and who tells us how to govern ourselves in it matches the God we decided was needed to resolve the first and third questions of Part One ("Why is there something instead of nothing?" and "How do I make sense of my life?"). But only a God of love is capable of resolving the second question: only a God of love is the answer to what it is we are desiring, and why we desire it.

CHAPTER 11

The Root of Christianity

≷ What Is Christianity? The Observational Evidence ≶

Some fundamentalists have done their best to turn the term *Christian* into a dirty word, signifying all that is narrow-minded and bigoted and self-righteous. But then, a hundred years ago, the sloppy liberals at the other end of the philosophical spectrum tried to turn it into a formless generic term, where a "Christian" was anyone who had ever had an occasional urge to be a nice guy.

Let us begin by putting those two straw men behind us.

A Christian is a person who belongs to a religion founded on the historical person Jesus. Jesus' earliest followers termed him "the Christ" (Greek for "the anointed one"), so one who follows Jesus Christ is "Christian." Luke's book *The Acts of the Apostles,* which was written around A.D. 70, mentions that the term *Christian* was first used to identify the people in the city of Antioch who professed to follow Jesus, about twenty years after his crucifixion (which occurred about A.D. 30).

Nicely documented, yes? Or is it? Though you probably won't want to challenge the accuracy of that simple historical statement—there's no reason to think Luke is lying about where the name *Christian* came from, and nothing particularly important is at stake about whether his story about it is true or not—in general, there is a certain problem using Christian texts to find out about Christianity. One might challenge them, quite reasonably, as being less than objective.

Still, there should be no controversy over the factual existence of a person named Jesus. He's mentioned by several non-Christian contemporary historians, most notably the Jewish historian Josephus. He is even mentioned briefly (as "Chrestus") by the Roman historian Tacitus. Of course, if you are a severe skeptic, you could insist that these histories were somehow forged or at least heavily edited by the Christian monks who preserved and copied them. (There is a variant copy of Josephus that is so blatantly pro-Christian that it almost certainly was doctored in this way.)

Indeed, since virtually all our history has been passed through the hands of religious believers, can we trust any of it? Is it possible to get an unbiased assessment of Christianity?

Actually, that's both a profound and a foolish ambition. It reflects the greater truth that no data are pure. At the very least all data are, in the words of the philosophers of science, "theory-laden." Before you can even design an experiment, you have to have in mind some sort of idea of what the answer is going to look like; how else will you distinguish the answer from the noise? But it does mean that anyone else using those data later on has to be aware of the expectations, if not the biases, of the researchers who recorded the data.

Furthermore, we scientists are used to the fact that we're always working with a limited and "biased" set of observational evidence. For one thing, it is inevitable that the data we have the most of are the data that are easiest to obtain, and not necessarily the data that are most representative of the way nature actually works. For example, all our samples of the moon brought back by the Apollo astronauts came from a set of sites on the moon chosen primarily for the ease of safely landing the Lunar Excursion Module. Thus the Apollo rocks are mostly basalts from the flat "mare" regions with only a few rare chips from the "highlands" regions in the soils collected by the astronauts. There is no reason to believe that these proportions are typical of the lunar surface in general.

But we know how to correct for such biased data sets. Wouldn't it be an interesting exercise to apply such techniques to examining the Christian religion?

Essentially, the way you correct a large but biased set of data is to try to find some subset of the data, no matter how small, that you can be confident is unbiased. Then you can scale the rest of the biased data against it, checking for consistency and correcting accordingly. For instance, spectra taken by satellites orbiting the lunar surface can only tell us the abundances of a few elements, but that's enough to calibrate what fraction of the whole lunar surface is highlands and how much is mare. Given those fractions, we can scale the rest of the chemical abundances, as measured in the lab on Earth from the detailed chemistry of the rocks and the soil chips, to come up with a more realistic idea of what the chemistry of the whole lunar surface is like.

Thus the first step of such an exercise is to assemble what little we know from unbiased sources. We admit that past historical records may have an innate Christian bias. So let's ask ourselves, from merely what anyone alive today could observe, what can we deduce about Christianity?

You can infer the existence of some sort of person named Jesus simply by noting the large number of Christian churches in your town. Where did they come from? (For that matter, you might also ask where all those monks came from who supposedly doctored all those ancient documents that tell us what little we know about that Jesus.)

Christianity must have come from someplace. It wasn't invented last year; the art and literature of the past two thousand years testify to its antiquity. Those paintings in every art museum; those churches that date back five hundred years, a thousand years, fifteen hundred years, or more; those monks you would blame for forging the documents—they did not spontaneously generate themselves. There must have been someone, somewhere, responsible for getting it all started.

And more than just churches and artwork show evidence of its existence. Virtually every university founded before 1800 and many established since then were the product of Christian religious groups. (Take a look at old versions of the Harvard emblem, as carved on the side of some of its older buildings, and you'll see a reference to God that our present-day preppies pretend isn't there.) The names of the major hospitals in any American city also reveal their religious origins. For that matter, so do the city names themselves—Los Angeles, Corpus Christi, Saint

Louis, San and Santa Everybody. Even Newark is short for New Ark of the Covenant.

It is instructive to see just who earns the right to have cities named for them. Los Angeles, California, indicates angels, messengers of God; in fact, the original full name of the town actually honored Mary as Queen of the Angels (*El Pueblo de la Reyna de los Ángeles,* "the village of the queen of the angels"). According to Christian legend, this Mary herself was a poor country girl noted for bearing a certain child in defiance of certain societal expectations. Corpus Christi, Texas, is named for the body, battered and pierced, of that child, grown to a man, killed as a criminal for preaching love. San Jose is named for Joseph, the carpenter who helped raise Mary's child. San Francisco (Saint Francis) was a young Italian nobleman from the town of Assisi who turned his back on his noble birth to preach a love of God and God's creation while living a life of stark poverty, and Santa Clara (Saint Clare), also of Assisi, was one of the first women to follow his example and found an order of like-minded nuns. Saint Louis was the one French king of the many named Louis who did not try to conquer his neighbors or put on ostentatious displays of wealth and power but ruled justly and wisely while living a simple life.

By contrast, ask yourself who gets airports and stadiums and public buildings named for themselves nowadays?

Indeed, one of the hardest things about getting an objective take on Christianity is that our own culture is so thoroughly saturated with it, it is essentially impossible to separate ourselves and our attitudes from it, no matter how skeptical or anticlerical we may personally be. Even our skepticism, even our anticlericalism, even our very desire for unbiased external evidence are all cultural attitudes that have their roots intermingled with Christianity.

Think of any of the characteristics of our culture that are commonly called "Christian." All those hospitals imply that someplace in Christianity there must be an emphasis on care for the poor and the sick and the elderly. The universities suggest an emphasis on education. Using a Bible in the courtroom implies a religious source for our sense of what constitutes justice and truth, as does our stated ideal of all people being equal before God and law.

But to what degree are those ideals the hallmarks specifically of Christianity, and how much of it is actually a flow in the other direction, with cultural ideals becoming adopted by the religion? Other religions also preach these ideals (and build hospitals and schools)—do all religions preach the same ideals ("they're all the same, or at least they have all the same ethical teachings and stuff"), or have they all just been influenced by the dominant religion in Western culture, Christianity, in doing so?

And what about the times in our history when those ideals were forgotten—sometimes in the name of religion? Can we blame Christianity for those lapses? Or would we have recognized them as lapses if there had been no Christianity to preach what has, alas, so rarely been practiced?

Those are all impossible judgments to make. Christianity as it is practiced today is so completely interwoven into our way of life, even for those of us who are not Christian, that it is very hard to point to any aspect of the church and identify it, independent of its culture, as being specifically Christian.

Still, we can draw some pretty basic conclusions. Christianity has existed for a very long time. It has a connection with someone named Jesus, called by his followers "the Christ." It has a strong interest in education, in ministry to the sick and poor, and in defining (if not always following) an ethical code. And judging from the heroes for whom Christians have tended to name their cities and institutions, its saints are people noted for excellence in service and scholarship and ethics, rather than those with wealth or power or military prowess.

≳ The Historical Setting ≲

Another way to get a handle on Christianity is to look into what we can tell about its origins from nonbiblical sources—contemporary histories, letters, and the like, materials written or at least preserved by the Christians in their monasteries and universities. Even if you dispute the accuracy of the history, these books are at the very least evidence of the attitudes that Christians hold up as ideals. Even if they were all fakes, they would still be interesting for what they indicate about the kind of history that Christians would want you to believe.

It is clear from non-Christian historical sources that Christianity started out as a sect of Judaism. In the Roman Empire at the time of Christ, the majority of Jews already lived far from Jerusalem and prayed and worked in Greek. They were a significant presence in the empire, making up some 10 percent of its population—comparable to the proportion of Jews that you would find living in New York City today.

The members of this Jewish "Diaspora" were in many ways alienated from the Hebrew-speaking Jews of Judea, who along with their language clung more closely to their original culture. In Palestine, Judaism was a cultural touchstone that set the people apart from their oppressors; elsewhere in the empire, it was a religion to be shared and proselytized among those same oppressors. The Jews in Palestine fought the Romans; those elsewhere had learned to come into accommodation with them.

Christianity upset both groups. It opened itself to the Gentiles (non-Jews), horrifying the Palestinian contingent. But it refused to go along with the compromises that many Hellenistic Jews had made to coexist with the other gods of the empire.

As a result, for its first three hundred years, Christians lived under intense persecution from the Roman Empire while at the same time suffering bitter attacks from their Jewish coreligionists. Being thrown out of the synagogue was a terrible punishment to those Christians who thought of themselves as first and foremost Jewish. On the other hand, the Gentile converts could not have cared less. As they came to dominate Christianity by their sheer numbers, within a hundred years the religion had all but forgotten its Jewish roots.

Even after it was admitted as a state religion by the emperor Constantine in A.D. 313, the Christian church still maintained a separate line of authority. More often than not, the Christian hierarchy found itself in conflict with the policy from the emperor's palace. Constantine himself, for example, flirted with the Arian heresy (the Arians, in a convoluted way, denied the divinity of Jesus) and didn't get along at all with the popes of his time.

Once the Roman Empire fell apart, the bishop of Rome—known as the pope—filled the power vacuum locally around the city of Rome, but everywhere else his temporal power extended only to setting the crown on the head of whoever was Holy Roman Emperor that week. (And said Holy Roman Emperor, more often than not, had very limited power compared to local kings and nobles.)

Indeed, it is interesting to note that as much as it is an intimate part of our culture, one of the essential features of Christianity in the West is that even when the local ruler could rule on clerical appointments, the church maintained a stubborn independence on matters ranging from doctrine to the independent rights of the clergy. The most famous Thomases in English history, Thomas Becket and Thomas More, earned their fame as able bureaucrats who were forced to choose between king and church, a choice that both of them recognized had no room for compromise. Both Thomases chose the church; both were killed.

Indeed, Western Christianity appears to have functioned best when it was independent of secular authority, acting as a counterbalance—and itself being counterbalanced—with the power of the king or party or pop stars or whoever else would otherwise set the dominant tone of the culture.

For example, recall that the universities, founded by the church, flourished most wherever they were independent of the local government. Even today, town-gown tensions are an accepted and expected fact of university life; in the Middle Ages, town versus gown meant state versus church. The universities needed (as they continue to need) their independence from the established order. However, they have also always had to have their feet held to the ground, and at times to the fire, by the practical needs of the society in which they exist (and which pays their bills). Hence the tension. It is interesting to note that of all the medieval universities, the one in Rome—where, by accident of history, the church was also the government—never achieved anything like the status or reputation of those in Paris, Padua, or Oxford.

Even after the Protestant revolution and the compromise that "whoever rules gets to choose the religion," the long tradition of independence more often than not still held in practice for the local religion. Meanwhile, Catholicism in nominally Catholic countries like France, Spain, and Italy often faced governments that were overtly hostile to it. (As a result, for instance, the church buildings in Italy today are actually state property, confiscated as "works of art" by the anticlerical Italian governments of the late nineteenth century.) Moderate religious-left "Christian Socialist" parties like the one developed in Germany during Bismarck's time stood in opposition to the reigning governments of the day while enjoying only limited support from the structural church.

And even when the anticlerical governments fell, the church would often find itself in an uneasy relationship with political parties of the far right who tried to use religion as a cover for their own agenda. In the 1920s, Pope Pius XI directly condemned one such supposedly prochurch but in fact protofascist movement in France. When he informed the head of a certain religious order that his members were forbidden to belong to that group, the head of the order replied, "I'll see what I can do." At that, the pope grabbed the priest's beard and shouted in his face, "You won't 'see what you can do'—you'll do it!"

In the twentieth century, the churches in Europe were the strongest where they were most strongly opposed. While religion languished in the West, where it had complete freedom, the Catholic church in Poland and the Evangelical church in East Germany were key players in the toppling of communism (after which, having won, their popularity in both countries waned significantly).

The result of this independence is that the interplay between church and culture for two thousand years has been a very intricate dance. And it's hard to tell at times who was leading. It also makes it effectively impossible to determine what was cause and what was effect in tracing the development of Western culture under the influence of Christianity.

For example, it is clear that in most places at most times (with exceptions that are both well known and quite exceptional), Christian cultures have valued things like the role of the individual, freedom of conscience, and the freedom to explore new ideas and speak about them in public.

This emphasis stands in stark contrast to the prevailing attitudes in the cultures of the East. Notice the virtues that are honored with palaces in Beijing's Forbidden City: earthly peace, unity, heavenly purity, benevolent tranquillity. Conspicuously absent are such virtues as justice, truth, and love—virtues highly regarded in the West, even though pursuing them more likely than not will disrupt any society's peace, unity, or tranquillity.

But is this a result of the West's theology? Or is it an accident of the historical separation between church and government that also led to the tradition of an independent university? Or perhaps this is a legacy of the independent-minded ancient Greek philosophy that also underpins the West? It's hard to make that judgment. But individual freedom is definitely a part of Christian culture, wherever it comes from. One need only read the theological writings of Thomas Aquinas to see it specifically outlined and defended.

Even bogeymen like the infamous Spanish Inquisition actually fit this pattern. The Inquisition, after all, developed many of the basic rights of trials we now take for granted. According to the rules of the Inquisition, there could be no secret evidence; the accused had the right to confront and reply to the accusers; and even if you were found guilty, you had the right to recant at the end of the trial and escape punishment. More than 90 percent of the people brought before the Inquisition were found innocent and set free. (Compare that to how the American system treated Japanese internees during World War II or suspected terrorists after the September 11, 2001, attacks.) And even so, the Inquisition was ultimately abandoned as an unworkable and unjustifiable intrusion on personal freedom, a hundred-year aberration of the tradition of free inquiry. The Inquisition (especially its anti-Semitic aspects) remains a shameful blot on the church to this day.

So far, then, the evidence of history is quite consistent with the slim unbiased evidence of our present-day observations. This religion is one whose ideals concern ethics, education, and helping the poor and weak, even if it, and the culture in which it is embedded, have rarely lived up to its ideals.

What we cannot deduce from history or observation alone, however, is why this church holds the ideals it teaches. What is the logic behind its teachings?

≷ Christianity on Christ ≶

To learn the distinctive characteristics of Christianity and the logic behind them, we have to go back to its origins, read its published creeds, and follow its history. To begin with, what do we know about its founding figure? Our oldest source material for who Jesus was and what he taught is both remarkably extensive and frustratingly vague.

The oldest are a series of letters from a particular follower, Paul of Tarsus, who clearly had some significant Jewish theological training before joining up with the Christians. They were written some fifteen to twenty-five years after Jesus died. But what they have to say about Jesus is mostly theological, not historical, except when his theological reflections make reference to the events of Jesus' life—such as the institution of the Eucharist and the fact that Jesus died and rose from the dead. Written slightly later than these letters are four well-established works of varying degrees of independence (they clearly borrow from each other, in a complicated way that makes it hard to be sure which version came first) called the Gospels: the books of Matthew, Mark, Luke, and John. They were produced over a period ranging from thirty to eighty years after the death of Jesus. We also have a few letters by contemporaries of Paul and the evangelists, written at about the same time as the Gospels: the books of James, John, Peter, and Jude.

In addition, we have letters and commentaries written by people in the century following Jesus' death who recorded stories they'd heard from the original apostles and their understandings of how the church evolved.

We also have a large body of "apocryphal" documents such as the "Gospel According to Saint James" and the "Gospel According to Saint Thomas" whose origins are open to question but are, at least from our perspective, undeniably antique. Anyone hoping to find in them evidence of some secret suppressed truth will be disappointed; even to the untrained eye, they're pretty awful.

Characteristics of these books are absurdly magical stories with no edifying purpose, along with sayings of Jesus reported out of context or with no context at all, in a style that has been described as "tasteless and bombastic." Trusting them to give you a picture of Jesus is probably less reliable than trying to derive a history of World War II from watching John Wayne movies. When I read them, I felt like somebody was saying to me, "You don't think the Gospels were divinely inspired? Take a look at what an uninspired gospel looks like by comparison!" One interesting trait is that individual copies of the four canonical Gospels stick pretty rigidly to the same text from copy to copy, from library to library around the world, and even in quotations in letters written from the era; whereas the various copies of the Apocrypha vary wildly from version to version, as though the people doing the copying realized that these books didn't matter enough to keep them canonical.

To complain that the canonical Christian scriptures are somehow "contaminated" by the fact that they have been selected and transmitted to us via the Christian community is fatuous for our purposes here. Of course, all who wrote after Jesus was gone were influenced by what they believed about him; but since it is the Christian *religion* that we're trying to evaluate, that's precisely what we're interested in here: in finding out what the Christian community believed about Jesus. That's a different question from trying to derive a historically accurate biography of Jesus himself (in which case one does have a legitimate complaint that the biographical details in the Gospels are too heavily influenced by hindsight). Such a biography might be fascinating to read, but it would clearly be separate from the issue at hand: defining the essence of Christianity as a religion as seen by the original Christians themselves.

All these sources tell of a miracle worker named Jesus who, against significant opposition, taught an unpopular doctrine of love and forgiveness for one's enemies, preached to a conquered people who had no reason to love or forgive their conquerors. According to all these books, his ultimate miracle was to suffer a humiliating execution—ironically, at the hands of the conquerors whom he loved and forgave—only to rise from the dead and continue teaching the same message of forgiveness and peace that got him killed in the first place.

Improbable as the stories in these writings seem to be, it is clear that they were ultimately based on eyewitness accounts by people who knew what they saw and truly believed what they were reporting. Matthew and John were traditionally identified with the apostles named in the Gospels themselves (though scholars have long debated how many different Johns there were, whether the Gospel, the Epistle, and the Apocalypse all attributed to "John" came from the same author, and if any of them were the apostle of that name). According to the Acts of the Apostles and Paul's letters, Mark was a companion of Peter and Luke a companion of Paul. Assuming that we have the authors right, one thing we do know is that they were sincerely writing what they believed to be true: rather than recant, all but one died horrible deaths under the rule of the Roman Empire that made cruelty in executions its specialty. (The exception is the apostle John, who died of old age around A.D. 100.)

You can tell from reading these books, even in translation (as most of us must), that they were written by different people with different backgrounds, different levels of education, and different assumptions about their audience. Luke is quite literary, written in educated Greek. Matthew was apparently first written in Aramaic and later translated into Greek. John expresses some pretty subtle theology with a remarkably accessible and uncomplicated vocabulary. Mark is copying down stories he must have heard somebody tell out loud; his is the breathless style of the spoken, not written, word—every sentence begins with *and*.

At least that's the traditional description of the authorship of the Gospels, based mostly on fragments of writings from fifty to a hundred years after the books were written. There's probably not a statement in the description I've just given, though, that hasn't been seriously questioned by some scholar somewhere. But *somebody* wrote these books. And these traditional names and attributions are the only written evidence we have for their authorship.

With four different sources, there are inevitably contradictions from source to source; that's typical of any story based on eyewitness accounts. Some people argue that the "older" books are closer to the truth; however, it seems just as likely to me that

John, for instance, may well be correcting mistakes in the earlier books that particularly bothered him (such as the citing of the wrong date for the Passover when the crucifixion occurred).

But the most remarkable thing to me is that, first of all, for a bunch of books written by nonprofessionals—as stylists, the Evangelists never pretend to be in the same league as Tacitus or Virgil or the other literary greats of Rome—these Epistles and Gospels have enough profound content that you can still write academic tomes about their theology two thousand years later without ever fearing that you'll run out of things to say. And perhaps even more remarkable, though they may disagree on the details of their stories or the order in which things happened, from a theological standpoint, these very different works from very different authors, written over a long span of time, are remarkably coherent in their content. They all stay on message; and it's the *same* message—and a very unlikely message at that. Anyone who's ever tried to coordinate the output of any kind of committee or club can attest to what a supernatural accomplishment that is.

We have heard so much about Jesus in our popular culture that it can be startling for some of us to actually read what the Gospels actually say—and don't say—about him. Rather than looking for a summary of them here, go read some of them for yourself. By all means, choose a modern translation (the King James Version is, alas, a foreign language to our modern ears). John's Gospel is the last and most theologically developed, but for that reason it's also the hardest to understand at a first go. Matthew is straightforward, but it assumes its audience is Jewish and familiar with Jewish customs and laws. Luke's Gospel is the most literary in style and probably the most complete, but that also means it's the longest (and, sorry to say, it does drag at times). The Gospel of Mark is as good a place to start as any; it's simple and it's short.

⧽ But Is It True? ⧼

"For this was I born, for this I have come into the world, to bear witness to the truth. Every one who is of the truth hears my voice," says Jesus at his trial (John 19:37). To which Pilate responds, "What is truth?"

A large chunk of Christianity depends on how you understand the descriptions of Jesus found in the New Testament. Indeed, according to some Protestants, all of Christianity is based on the New Testament, a point on which I disagree; but even in the Catholic tradition of honoring "tradition," scripture emerged out of that tradition and is a part of tradition. But how much can we trust what we read in the Gospels?

In studying scripture, you can employ any number of techniques whose goals range from finding the most accurate rendition of the words to understanding the intent of the authors given the social setting in which they worked. All of this work, besides being fascinating in its own right, is but a necessary prelude to the final, ultimate question: Is it true? But the answer you find often sounds like we're echoing Pilate's question. What is truth?

So much of our impression of the Bible is prejudged. Our faith (or its lack), our own social prejudices, and our own hopes and expectations inevitably control the direction and usually the outcome of our inquiries. We just have too much at stake in the answers, and so we shade our judgments to match our desires—or our fears.

It would be convenient if we could transport ourselves back to the time of, say, Saint Mark, knowing all about the culture that produced the man—and nothing about the effect that his book will have on history—and watch him write, see what he was trying to say, and try to understand what compromises he felt he had to make to communicate his truth.

We can't do that. However, twenty years ago, I had a privileged seat at the construction of another book. Back in the late 1980s, a friend of mine, Cliff Stoll, was an astronomer-turned-computer manager at the Lawrence Berkeley Laboratory at the University of California, Berkeley, when he found an intruder, operating out of West Germany in the pay of East German and KGB agents, tapping into his computer system. From there, the hacker would systematically break into military and other sensitive computer installations around the world. The story of how Cliff found this intruder and what he learned about computer security, national security, and his own personal attitudes toward these questions (Cliff is probably the longest-haired male ever to receive an award from the CIA) made for fascinating reading in his book, *The Cuckoo's Egg*.

Cliff wrote the book in the first person, based on notes he took as the events were unfolding. It purports to be a historically accurate chronicle of events. It also attempts to instruct the reader in the details of computer operations necessary to the story. And it tries to be entertaining enough to be readable. Its success as entertainment can be judged to some extent by the fact that it spent three months on the *New York Times* best-seller list in the fall of 1989 (and again made the list of best-selling paperbacks a year later). It is in print even today, years after publication—a rare event in the book world. And its success at describing computer operations and computer security can be seen by its impact in the computer security field since its publication.

But was it true?

The position we wish we could have watching Mark write his Gospel is the position that I was actually in with Cliff writing *The Cuckoo's Egg*.

The events that Cliff wrote about took place in 1986–1988, and for a lot of that time he couldn't talk about them, which must have been a trial to someone who loves telling stories as much as he does. Then the actual nabbing of the hacker made the front page of the *New York Times,* and his book contract followed soon afterward. Once the information became public, he wrote up a technical article and started giving what turned into ten years of public talks on the issues of computer security and his own adventures capturing spies. Remember, this would have been in the early 1990s, when public awareness of the Internet was dawning. One reason his talks, and his book, were in such great demand was that his story not only entertained people but also helped them understand how the Internet worked.

Cliff himself has explained how he wrote his book to various Usenet groups (the 1990s predecessors to blogs). While writing the book, he was still working at the Lawrence Berkeley Labs and later at the Harvard-Smithsonian Center for Astrophysics—his publisher's advance wasn't enough for him to quit his day job, and besides, as a scientist, he wanted to stay engaged in his science.

So while he spent half of his time giving talks and writing about computers and spies, he spent the other half of his life compiling a catalogue of the X-ray-emitting objects in space observed by the orbiting Einstein X-Ray Telescope.

He worked on the book from his personal diaries and the logbooks that he had kept at work as the events in his story evolved. As a scientist, he understands well the rule that if you don't write it down, it didn't happen. These notes let him keep the timeline straight. However, he has said, "I did slide the dates [of some events] by a few days to remove jogs from the story."

His main adviser and editor was not his official editor at the publishing company but his sister Jeannie. He admits that she suggested some of the main structural points of the book and even wrote part of one chapter. I had a small role in the writing of the book, too—mostly just reading early drafts for consistency and listening to Cliff deal with the problems and challenges associated with preparing the manuscript.

One interesting point in these discussions was that very early on, he started referring to "the Cliff character" in the book in the third person, independent from himself. It was quite clear to him that the person depicted in the book was a very separate entity from the flesh-and-blood Cliff who had lived through those events and who was writing about them at a later time.

So what can this tell us about how Jesus was portrayed in the Gospels?

First, recall that Cliff the storyteller and scientific lecturer was already on the road with his tale even while he was writing the book. The events and dialogues in Cliff's book are clearly reconstructions, based to a large extent on his memories of the last time he told someone the story. Something of this same effect undoubtedly operates in the Gospels. The stories must have been told and retold so often that they took on a life of their own. And yet as with Cliff's book, many of the other principals of that story, and plenty of other eyewitnesses, were still alive when Mark's Gospel was written to confirm the essential truth of the story. (Or to complain. To give some local color, Cliff described bicycling home from work while hearing the Grateful Dead play at a nearby outdoor stadium; this prompted dozens of complaints from loyal

Deadheads, who knew that their band was on the other side of the country during the time in question.) Seeing how these checks operated in Cliff's book gives me confidence that the events in Mark's Gospel are likewise not too different from the ways that Mark's contemporaries remembered the stories.

In addition, Cliff has said that he did not write some parts of his book, parts where he had no firsthand knowledge or where he was advised to round out the story. Also, the paperback edition of the book has an extra chapter at the end, updating some of the things that happened after the first edition came out. The changes in style and alternate endings you can find in the most ancient versions of Mark's Gospel may be equally contemporaneous with the writing and have similar causes. Did Mark (who, judging from his Greek style, was not a highly tutored writer) have friends, advisers, and editors read and suggest changes to his manuscript while he was writing it? That's what the biblical scholars of the Redaction Criticism school suggest, and it certainly makes sense to me, given how I saw Cliff's book being written.

Note also that the historical Cliff is indeed very different from the Cliff of *The Cuckoo's Egg*. My real friend Cliff is a complex person with a very complicated history. For instance, in the book, he writes about himself as "an ex-hippie." He deliberately identifies himself with a stereotype from the 1960s to help develop the story of his own personal growth—a "coming of age" theme in the book, which his sister suggested—that is one of the threads that keeps the book interesting to read. It's not a particularly accurate description of Cliff, however. The stereotype "hippie" was supposedly deep into radical politics, rock music, and drugs, but I know that Cliff was never particularly committed to far-left causes, his taste in music runs more to Dixieland jazz, and he didn't even drink beer, much less do drugs. Furthermore, the stereotypical hippie was a child of privilege who dropped out of the system; Cliff, a Buffalo bartender's son, was hardly a dropout from a system he never took part in. (Incidentally, having grown up in the 1960s and gone to college in Boston in the early 1970s, I must say I knew darn few people who actually fit the hippie stereotype anyway.)

This tells me to be wary of any attempts to see Jesus or John the Baptist as simply "another Essene"—a member of the Jewish sect thought to be responsible for the Dead Sea Scrolls—or an example of any other common "type" or a member of any extant movement. Jesus was not "another Essene." But it may well be that for people who knew Essenes but who did not know Jesus, the easiest way to give them an understanding of what he was like might well have been to draw parallels. The parallels, however, might be only a literary device; too much should not be read into them.

In the book, Cliff portrays himself as an astronomer who didn't know much about computers. But in fact, Cliff's jobs in astronomy since he began his doctoral program have involved computer programming for big projects. Cliff's value was that he was a competent programmer who, unlike most programmers, understood astronomy and what the astronomers wanted his programs to do. However, for the purposes of the book, he deliberately made himself seem ignorant of computers (and many other topics) so that he could explain concepts to his readers as if they were new to him. He made himself look stupid so that anyone reading the book might say, "Even I knew that!" and thus feel more friendly toward the Cliff character, rather than being distanced and in awe.

In the same way, the foolishness of the apostles as portrayed in the Gospels (especially Mark) may well be another literary device. From our vantage point, we might be tempted to read Mark's description of them as evidence that he was hostile to the established apostles. But I would say, rather, drawing parallels with Cliff's book, that this argues strongly for the authenticity of Mark as coming from the apostolic community. The modesty with which they are portrayed can be seen as a literary device, to encourage readers of weak faith not to be discouraged. (Self-effacement was in fact a characteristic style of that community, if Saint Paul's letters are any indication.)

Third and finally, we return to the original question: Is it true?

Is Cliff's book true? By his own admission, we know that dialogue is rewritten, facts and dates are rearranged, and much has been left out. But in the sense that matters most, Cliff's book is true. Not only did the story happen essentially the way he described it, but the message he wanted to tell, about the needs and problems of computer security, were spot on.

One way to evaluate a book's truth is to look at the impact it has had on its audience. Cliff's book founded a whole genre of "computer hacker" books, and to this day, it serves as a textbook in college courses about the Internet and how it works, even though the technology has gone far beyond what he dealt with in the 1980s. In the same way, the essential truth of the Gospels is proved by the way in which they have unquestionably changed the world. The endurance of the church itself can be cited as testimony to the hand of God being present in the books of the Gospels (in spite of the failings of the writers of those books) and present in the church itself (in spite of the failings of the members of that church!).

But on even a more microscopic level, the Gospels are probably about as true as Cliff's book. In both books, I am sure that some of the stories have been polished, some of the facts rearranged, and everything is recast through the lens of hindsight. Written without notebooks and much longer after the event than in Cliff's case, the stories in the Gospels must have certainly taken on a life of their own. But just as with Cliff's book, I can easily believe that every episode in Mark is based on something that actually did take place.

And on a more personal level, if anyone asked me what my friend Cliff was like, I would hand them a copy of *The Cuckoo's Egg* and tell them to start there. Likewise, the Gospels are the place to start when trying to figure out what Jesus was like. But they are only places to start. I can tell you plenty of stories about Cliff that never made it into the book because they didn't fit the theme or the time frame or simply because they got left out by accident.

Cliff's book ran to one hundred thousand words and had the luxury of being written with a word processor by the main character himself, based on written notes, only a few years after the events. The Gospel of Mark runs to only fifteen thousand words, was written in longhand by someone who knew Jesus perhaps only by hearsay, some twenty years after the event. And I suspect that Jesus was a more complicated person than Cliff! Hard to explain, hard to describe, the Gospels of necessity can be only a beginning.

Cliff has been changed by the fact of the book's existence. The stories that his friends tell about him are now woven into a tapestry that includes the book but go beyond the book. And that's how the traditions of Jesus and the books about him interact. The Gospels form a point of reference. But our own unique interactions with Jesus and the history of his interactions with all those people who have gone before us or who are living with us today—the church—are precisely what changes the flat literary character of the written word into a multidimensional, complex human being present in our lives in this instant.

CHAPTER 12

A Techie's Contemplation on the Trinity

≷ Essential Christianity ≶

What did those early Christians decide was the essence of their own religion? We could try to summarize the theology of the Gospels, but in fact that work has already been done for us.

In letters from around A.D. 140 by Bishop Polycarp, who as a young man had studied under the aged Apostle John, we can find fragments of the statement that the church in Rome asked new Christians to say they believed (in Latin, *credo,* "I believe") before they would be baptized. Other books and letters from that time have similar descriptions. A book from A.D. 202 by Hippolytus (who was a student of Irenaeus, a student of Polycarp) includes the full text of such a credo. According to a tradition that we can find in a book written in A.D. 404 (but which is probably based on much older sources), the apostles themselves supposedly settled on this formula when they split up to spread the Good News around the world. Whether the story of the apostles' authorship is true or not, the formula is undoubtedly very old. It's traditionally known as the Apostles' Creed. It's about as fundamental a statement of Christian beliefs as you are likely to find. And it's short, sweet, and to the point.

A Christian, according to this credo, is one who can say, in complete sincerity:

165 ≷

I believe in God, the Father, Almighty, Maker of Heaven and Earth. I believe in Jesus Christ, his only son, our Lord, who was conceived by the Holy Spirit, born of the Virgin Mary, suffered under Pontius Pilate, was crucified, died, and was buried; he descended to the dead, and on the third day he rose again; he ascended into heaven, he is seated at the right hand of the Father, and he will come again to judge the living and the dead. I believe in the Holy Spirit, the holy Catholic Church, the communion of saints, the forgiveness of sins, the resurrection of the body, and life everlasting.

It's a pretty concentrated lump. It would take some time to unpack and dissect it all, seeing what each of those phrases is talking about and why they're considered so essential to what it means to be Christian.

In what follows, I give my own reflections on the Christian God. I offer them not because I think I have a special or unique take on these ideas but just the opposite: I think my views are pretty typical for a Christian techie. At least, they're a sketch of how one techie, me, understands who he believes in.

Fundamental to my Christian understanding of God is the concept of the Trinity. Jesus spoke constantly of the Father, the Spirit, and himself in relation to them but always in reference to the One True God. If I am going to call myself a Christian, I have to take this description of God seriously, even as I struggle to understand what it means.

Thinkers and writers far better than I have struggled to make sense out of the concept of the Trinity. Every attempt to put it into simple words gets it wrong. For example, it's tempting to try to say something like "the different persons represent different aspects or modes or personalities of God." But church councils have specifically rejected that kind of language, saying, in effect, "No, that's not what we mean at all." It kind of reminds me of trying to explain subatomic particles to my students: if you think you understand it, you've got it wrong. The Trinity is a reality that does not easily lend itself to human words; indeed, even the word *person* is but the best that English can do with the more technical Greek term *hypostasis*.

Unlike physicists, theologians can't even retreat into mathematical equations to express what they mean. But at least, as with modern physics, I'm left with the comforting realization that while you may never understand it, if you live with it long enough, you can at least get used to it.

It is, on the face of it, so counterintuitive a concept that I can't help but find it credible. I believe that it is worth believing and really from God, principally because there's no reason why some mere human theologian would have thought to invent such a difficult idea. In some awkward way the word *Trinity* is trying to communicate an important and profound truth. It's just a truth that's really hard to get your head around.

≷ God the Father ≷

Of the three persons of God in the Trinity, the easiest and most direct for a techie to come to grips with is God as Creator. In the Creed, the name Father is linked to God as Creator not because God is supposed to be male but to emphasize the peculiar mixture of intimacy and distance that this Creator has with creation. God is not Mother Nature but more like, well, a father.

The image works well for me, in no small part because I have had a very good relationship with my own father, someone who has unquestionably always loved me and been there for me, to listen to me and give his advice, but who was always careful to step back when it was time for me to try my own wings. He was not someone who would always carry me but rather someone who would let me walk on my own while being there to catch me and help me up when I fell. So "God the Father" works for me. But for that very reason, however, God as Father can be a much more problematic image to someone who's had a rotten relationship with his or her own father.

So what does the Creed say about God the Father? The Christian believes in God the Father, Almighty, Creator of heaven and Earth. ("All that is seen and unseen," adds the Nicene Creed, written in the fourth century as an expansion of the Apostles' Creed.) And that's it. But of course, that's everything.

Creator of heaven and Earth. What does that mean?

It means a lot to us who are scientists. To believe in the God of Genesis, who creates the world in an orderly fashion and calls it "good," is the foundation of all our work.

We've talked before about the basic assumptions that every scientist, believer or not, makes before starting any scientific work. But notice, now, how those assumptions flow directly from our belief in this credo in a Creator God.

Beyond the most basic assumption—that the universe is real and not a figment of our imagination, though the quantum physics people will argue about the nature of that reality—any scientist must assume that the world does make sense, even if the sense can't be easily perceived. The universe is intelligible. A scientist has to believe that there is some kind of logic and order and regularity to it.

That seems obvious to us today because we've seen that science actually works. But it was not at all obvious a thousand years ago, when Western science was in its infancy. If the ancient monks and clerics who were our first scientists, like Albertus Magnus and Roger Bacon and Nicholas of Cusa, had believed that the universe was nothing but chaos, arbitrary and random, as the cultures of India and the East did, then like India and the East they might have developed wonderful philosophies and even phenomenal mathematics, but they'd never have seen any point in studying natural science. They would have thought that there was nothing there to be studied. On the other hand, a Creator God, the God of the holy books of Judaism, Christianity, and Islam, gave them the hope that there are reasons behind the way things work. No matter how hard it may be to fathom those reasons, they're there for somebody to ferret out eventually.

Another side of this assumption is that this rule-based universe can be understood by us mere mortals. It's not enough to know that the rules exist; we also have to have the arrogance to think that, at least in some small and incomplete way, we can grasp them. That's quite an assumption to make. If the universe is the activity of God (or the gods), then presumably only God (or a god) would be in a position to understand it. By saying that we can understand it, too, you'd think we imagined ourselves as having, in ourselves, the "image and likeness of God." Where did we ever get such a notion? But again, without that belief, there'd be no point in doing science.

But the wildest assumption of all is this: not only is the world understandable, and not only can we somehow be capable of grasping that understanding, but every scientist must accept, as a tenet of faith, with no reason to believe it ahead of time, one ultimate, crazy notion: that understanding the natural world is an endeavor worth spending your whole life doing, just for its own sake.

Not only does this belief in a Creator God give you confidence that the universe does have some underlying set of laws, but it also gives you a good excuse to get the funding from the authorities to look for those laws. It assures you (and your sponsors) that doing science to make sense of creation is a way of coming to know the Creator. It is a profoundly religious act.

Indeed, it's been argued that it's no coincidence that you find pure science, studying nature for its own sake (and not just to cast horoscopes or make better crops), only in cultures that accept the Genesis story of a Creator God: Judaism, Christianity, and Islam. You may find excellent ethics, philosophy, and mathematics coming out of ancient China, Japan, and India, but not pure science. For example, the systematic classifying of the flora and fauna of India was done by Jesuit missionaries, and although ancient Chinese scholars did record events in the heavens such as the "guest stars" that we now recognize as supernovas, the Imperial Beijing Observatory was the work first of Muslims and then of Jesuits.

So if doing science is ultimately a religious act, why does the story of a split between science and religion exist in our culture today? Because too many religious people have been scared away from science by the very stories of this split. Because most scientists keep their religion private, as is their right. Because the religious people most likely to be heard in the news are those whose strong bent in engineering hides their very limited education in science: the creationists. Because the scientists who do speak publicly about these topics have been precisely those whose very limited education in religion (people like Richard Dawkins or Stephen Jay Gould) have made them "science fundamentalists," every bit as narrow as the religious fundamentalists and probably not the best representatives of their fields—just the best known.

But it is important to remember that God the Creator is also God the Father. If to us God is nothing more than a scientific hypothesis invoked to explain planetary orbits or the rise of life on Earth or the source of the Big Bang, we are guilty of believing in the God of the Gaps. And we hold our religion hostage to new advances in science that may close those gaps. The science fundamentalists are right to reject such a God.

What sort of God would these images give us—God as nothing but an indifferent clockmaker, the Prime Mover, who starts things off but then abandons us? What do you call a Father like that? God is no deadbeat dad.

Nor is he the kind of Father who would let us think we were living our own lives but who secretly—without our knowledge—pulls strings to make life "easier" for us: uses his influence to get us into college, arranges for us to meet the love of our lives, in general never letting us grow and try and stumble and try again. Any parent knows, as any teacher knows, that the hardest part of the job is knowing when to keep your mouth shut. Which is not to say that sometimes, like our natural fathers, this one might not pull a few strings, arrange a few coincidences perhaps, to help us out to get past our own blind spots and onto the direction we're trying to get to. But usually, he does us the courtesy of waiting for us to ask for help before getting involved. He likes to be asked.

Besides, the deist or clockmaker image of God, who winds things up and then steps back, is not the God whom we experience every day in prayer and contemplation. And it is far removed from the God who sent his only son to save us from our sins.

God is not just the Father of Jesus. In Jesus we have become co-heirs to creation—I am quoting Saint Paul again—and as the letter to Hebrews says, we are to be raised and taught as such. He is, as our oldest prayer says, *our* Father.

God is a Father who gives life to the universe, yes, but one who watches as he allows it to grow and evolve. Yes, *evolve*; as Pope John Paul II himself stated, evolution is more than a theory; it's an observation of how God has set up his universe. The universe evolves, and life on Earth evolves, according to rules that we can begin to understand, rules that reveal the personality of the Rule Giver.

In creation, I see a Creator who loves to produce amazing complexity from the interplay of a few simple rules. I see a Creator who is both extravagant with his abundance yet works with great economy (even if I can't always see the logic of his economy), ignoring nothing. And I see a Creator who puts a high value on elegance and beauty. There have been, I'd guess, a hundred thousand images returned by the Hubble space telescope; I don't know of a single one that's ugly.

My religious faith does not control or directly influence the day-to-day details of my scientific work. I do not "lay on hands" to stop my computer drive from crashing or open the Bible to a random page to find the solution to a differential equation. Nor does my science direct me to an explanation of the mysteries of my faith, to define scientifically the true presence in the Eucharist or to explicate definitively on the nature of the Trinity. But my science helps me get used to the style of my God, to search out explanations that are beautiful and elegant.

And my faith reminds me that my study of creation must be based not on dreams of power or fame but on love.

It's a mystery that no theology can predict and no science can account for. We study the world for the love of it. And love makes the world go round.

≷ The New Testament God ≶

The second part of the Apostles' Creed is the longest and the most difficult. Whereas few people would probably have much trouble accepting at least the possibility of some vague, external God the Creator of heaven and Earth, it is this specific belief in Jesus as the second person of the Trinity that sets Christianity apart from any other religion.

Recognizing that this is the crucial and most difficult part of the faith, the Creed is quite specific about what is being asked for here. That there can be no doubt about it, we are asked to accept as our head the real Jesus, a particular human being who was known to have been born at a specified time, in a specified manner, of a specific mother; who died a real death in a specified historical time and place and manner; and who really rose from the dead at a specified, real time. And we must also affirm our belief that he was conceived in a miraculous way, that he has the status relative to the Father that in human terms can be described as equal to the only son and heir; and that, finally, this Jesus is given equal billing with God the Father. And we affirm that he is Lord; the boss; the one who knows us best, having been one of us, and whose ultimate role is to judge us.

Heady stuff.

There is no room in this statement of the Creed for soft-pedaling "spiritual" or "symbolic" interpretations. It's not that Jesus was such a good guy that he was as good as a son to God; it is that he was literally, biologically, sired in a miraculous way by the direct action of God. It's not that his resurrection occurred in a symbolic sense of his spirit "living on" in his followers; rather, in resurrection his was a real body, flesh and blood, one that you could touch and feel, a body so real that it ate a piece of fish with his friends.

Before I became a Jesuit, my experience of God—like that, I expect, of most techies—had mostly been with God the Creator. I didn't have a "personal relationship" with Jesus. I felt called by God, not called by Jesus. I felt close to God, not to Jesus. When I prayed, I prayed to God, not to Jesus. Jesus did not feel like a brother but more like a distant cousin whom I'd heard some nice things about and maybe might like to meet some day.

One of my instructors in the Jesuit novitiate pointed out that this was a pretty strange attitude for a person wanting to enter the Society of Jesus (which is, after all, the official name of the Jesuit order). It became one of those things I had to start working on to become a better Jesuit.

And so I went back and started rereading the Gospels, trying to get a flavor of who this Jesus was all about. In essence, I was being asked the same question that Jesus once asked Peter: "Who do you say that I am?"

One thing that struck me reading the Gospel stories was that Jesus seemed to share his Father's sense of humor. One cannot study creation long without appreciating the Creator's economical sparseness of style, his ability (mirrored in human terms by people like Bach) for creating harmonious complexities by the trick of counterpointing a few simple themes. And he does it with a sense of surprise and delight that conveys the personality of someone with a sense of humor.

But read Mark 2:1–12 or Matthew 9:1–8, the story of the paralytic. In the middle of Jesus' visit to someone's house, a bunch of people climb up on the roof, pull away the thatching, and lower down a paralyzed man on a stretcher for Jesus to cure. That, by itself, sounds like something worthy of Monty Python. Yet then, rather than curing him, Jesus says to him, "Your sins are forgiven." Bizarre; but he's got a point: What is more important, the state of someone's inner life or the state of his legs? And when we ask God for material help, what are we really looking for—just a free handout? And what good is getting that handout, what good is winning the lottery, if we lose all our friends—and our soul—in the process?

When challenged by the Pharisees regarding his power to forgive sins, he asks them, "Is it easier to say, 'Your sins are forgiven,' or to say, 'Take up your pallet and walk'?" Ouch. Few of us have the power to heal broken legs, but we all have the power to forgive our neighbor. Yet how often do we do so?

And now, having set them up, he delivers the punch line—wild, surprising, but completely logical in a way that, like a good joke, suddenly forces you to see a familiar scene from a completely new perspective. To show that he's not just blowing smoke, Jesus turns to the cripple and says, "Oh, and by the way, you can pick up your stretcher and walk out of here now." And the guy does it. Pandemonium.

In the nineteenth century, parallel to the attitude in science that believed Newtonian physics had everything explained and there was no more room for miracles, there was a great movement among the more liberal biblical scholars to try to "explain away" the miracles in the Gospels. They wanted to remove anything that was just a little bit unbelievable (or uncomfortable) about the Gospel version of Jesus and reach back to the "historical" Jesus. As one twentieth-century theologian put it, looking back on these efforts, the result was like trying to see Jesus at the bottom of a dark, deep well; and the face of Jesus that they saw down there, reflected back at them, looked suspiciously like the face of a nineteenth-century liberal theologian.

Perhaps it is my scientist's skepticism of anyone in *any* field who claims to be able to prove anything, but in the biblical criticism classes I took during my Jesuit training (most of which, to be sure, was excellent stuff), I also saw enough bad literary criticism to know just how bogus some of it can be. I've seen enough of how real people behave in enough different cultures—my Peace Corps years in Africa were eye-openers—that I can't rule out passages of the Gospels as "unhistorical" merely on the basis that they seem unreasonable or unlikely to my contemporary Midwestern American eyes or even just because they could be easily explained in another way (by pretending, for instance, that certain hard-to-explain passages in the Gospels must have been added by mistake). The fact is, human beings act in unlikely ways all the time. For that matter, so does God the Creator, whom I know so well.

Being a techie, I try to treat the Gospel stories like experimental evidence. In other words, on the one hand, I always have to keep in mind the prejudices and reliability of the experimenter; but on the other hand, I have to have extremely strong reasons before I can let myself throw any of the data points away, especially if my only reason to doubt them is because they seem "unlikely" to me—because they don't fit my preconceived notions about God and the universe. I know as a techie that you find your new insights precisely in the data that don't fit.

So based on that evidence, who do I say Jesus is?

He is God and Man, born of a virgin like so many ancient cultures predicted would happen. (Funny that those other stories no longer have the power to fascinate us.) He completed all the prophecies, but—good comedian that he is—he did it by playing against our preconceptions. For example, the prophets predicted a savior who would be the Son of God and the Son of David. I could easily have believed a biological descendent of David who was God's adopted son; so of course he is instead the biological son of God who is in David's family by adoption. His whole life makes you laugh, shake your head, and walk away with a new perspective on things like power and majesty.

Curiously, Jesus deliberately chose to be born of humble birth in a conquered race, seemingly illegitimate. He chose to live a life without wealth, without the respect and honor of the important people in the community, without a wife and family or even a girlfriend. (What does it say about our sex-obsessed culture that modern interpreters of his life keep wanting to invent some secret affairs for Jesus, usually with Mary Magdalene? The world is terrified of celibacy.)

And he chose to die like a criminal.

In every case, he chose the option that the world would have us believe was inferior. (He also chose to be born male; given the pattern of all the rest, that tells you something about the esteem in which he holds my gender!) And then again, the punch line: he rose in glory from the dead.

And there again, you can see another example of his sense of humor, a now familiar twist to the obvious. It's a cliché for a human leader who knows he's about to be executed to encourage his followers by saying, "As long as you remember me, I'll never die." But what does Jesus say in this situation? "As long as you remember me, *you'll* never die."

In the life of Jesus, the plot of every good story is foreshadowed. His mother Mary is the teenager who saves the world. The apostles are the archetypal bumbling but lovable sidekicks who at the end of the day live up to the hero's expectations. In Pontius Pilate we have the tragic antihero who thinks about doing the right thing but flinches at the last minute.

As a result, Jesus begins to look like a larger-than-life hero. If one decides to buy into Christianity (or even if one merely follows the inertia of one's upbringing) and accept these tenets of the Creed, it becomes very easy to see Jesus as God. But that is only half of the story.

The psychologist Karl Stern, a Jew who converted to Catholicism, has an essay in his book *Love and Success* titled "Some Religious Aspects of Anti-Semitism" that ends with the comment, "Many years ago Jacques Maritain remarked to this writer that, just as to Jews the divinity of Our Lord is a seemingly insurmountable obstacle, Christians have a similar difficulty with his humanity.... I believe that the inner experience of the humanity of Jesus for the 'cradle' Christian is a mystery on the level of grace just as the experience of his divinity is for the Jew."

The nineteenth-century biblical scholars who quested for the historical Jesus in the Gospels were actually asking the right question. The only problem was, they didn't recognize their question as a mystery to be contemplated, not a problem to be solved, and thus they frustrated themselves trying to find a limited, concrete answer in the text.

The fact is, human beings are always too complicated to be completely understood. We understand ourselves poorly, and we spend much time and money on everything from psychiatrists to astrology books in the vain hope of finding "self-knowledge." Understanding another person is hardly any easier. The trials of understanding a lover or a spouse, so frustrating and unachievable, are standard fare for the sitcom writer. So getting to know intimately a man who lived in a foreign culture two thousand years ago based on a few short manuscripts about him written years after his death is clearly a losing proposition.

And yet as a Jesuit, someone trying to follow Jesus, that's what I'm trying to do.

One might hope that getting to know Jesus is most quickly achieved by direct prayer. And yet the Jesus encountered in this way tends to be Jesus as God, and it is quite easy to overlook Jesus as man.

I can fall back on the rational approach and make some labored progress that way. For instance, notice that to consider Jesus as man raises the question of what it means to be human. Humans exist with both reason and emotion; we are capable of both wisdom and aesthetics; we possess both body and soul. It's challenging to apply this picture to Jesus. God as Love is fairly familiar and safely abstract; but God experiencing the emotion of love, the pain as well as the warmth, is startling. An otherworldly God I can compartmentalize with my reason; a right-here-and-now God with happiness and hurt is one whom I must deal with in a far more immediate way. An abstract God is one whom I can deal with on my own time and my own terms; a God who is also human, participating in my human limitations of space and time, makes real demands on my real emotions and makes those demands in real time.

I can return to the Gospels and ask the question, Who is Jesus? Was he someone who knew all along what his mission and message were? I suspect that he did; but if so, recognizing that he was human, I am thunderstruck by the incredible burden this knowledge must have placed on him.

Did he know ahead of time the outcome of his mission? Hard to say. Maybe he did; and yet that didn't make things any easier for him. After all, we can go to a Hollywood movie knowing that there'll be a happy ending, and we still worry over the hero's predicament. We can see a favorite play, reread a favorite book, hear a favorite opera, having memorized every detail of the plot, and still experience the thrills and chills of the plot's twists and turns. Indeed, for some books, knowing how it's all going to turn out adds to the poignancy of the situation portrayed. Perhaps that's something like what Jesus was going through.

And yet Jesus was human. Being human means living with uncertainty. And being human means having free will and living among a population of millions or billions of free-willed individuals. Anything less is less than human.

So which was it? How much did he know about what the future held for him? I don't know, I can't tell, and I don't even want to tell. Instead, I can only hold it as an object of contemplation.

How does my knowledge of the Gospels help me answer the question, Who is Jesus? They're frustratingly unhelpful, as it turns out. After reading the Gospel according to John, I know a lot about John but not nearly enough about Jesus. After reading Mark, I can see where Mark was coming from; but I'm still left unsure about Jesus. And the same is true with Matthew and Luke and Paul.

Another route is to parallel my old thoughts of how science leads me to know God, how personally I have experienced God through studying his creation; the natural world and its laws are the Creator's Gospel. And so if through the created universe I see God the Creator, then perhaps through the human universe I can see God the human, who is Jesus.

Somehow, in some way that keeps flickering in and out of clarity, in a way that I can only intuit and can't put into words, Jesus dances before me in the lives of the people around me. I especially get the totally subjective sense that I am somehow in his presence when I am with someone who is weak or helpless or scared; "the least of my brethren" as the Gospel says (Matthew

25:31–46). One odd observation that has been passed on to me from my Jesuit teachers is that the more unusual the people, the easier it is to notice him in them. So of course I could detect him in Africa and I could detect him in the inner city, in people whom I am not used to being around. But even though it is harder to see, he must also be in my fellow white male techie suburbanites, the people I encounter at the mall or on the freeway at rush hour.

He's also in the lives of the saints, in the Jesuits I live with (not all of them saints), and in my atheist friends. Sometimes the shape of Jesus is most noticeable by its absence, in people who have chosen evil—in the death squads, the terrorist bombers, the politicians who exploit our needs and our fears (big or small) to advance their own power.

But if you can find the outline of Jesus in the lives of all those other people, it must mean that you could likewise find Jesus in *my* life. What a bizarre idea! God does dwell in each of us; moreover, in each of us is the humanity that is the clue to understanding Jesus.

Of course, hearing that Jesus is the way that God took on a human nature didn't necessarily help me, as a techie, get closer to God. I have often felt pretty alienated from other human beings, and there's something rather irritating about having to think that Jesus lived and died not only for me but also for that bullet-headed baboon who gave me so much grief in high school.

And yet I have indeed had the experience of really glimpsing God in other people, even—sometimes especially—people who were far from saintly. Could it be that Jesus the human is a person like those people at those instances?

Maybe. I may have seen a glimpse of God in my friends. But I'm still seeing my friends. They each have unique personalities, none of them the personality of the real unique individual human who was that obscure rabbi two thousand years ago. Again, I'm seeing the God, not the human.

The mystery of the incarnation is not that God exists or that he created the universe or that he speaks to us in nature or through our fellow humans but simply that he himself truly became human. We have to get back to that.

He was human. He was once a baby. He had a mother.

And so this leads to a comment perhaps of interest to those non-Catholics who puzzle over this aspect of Catholicism: one route to understanding the human side of Jesus, popular among Catholics, has been to contemplate his mother, Mary—the person who knew him best as a human, who is unquestionably human herself, and who is in a position to bridge the gap of my understanding. In the Holy Family, I can start to understand the humanity of the child Jesus. In the setting of the family, I also begin to understand the humanness of myself and my friends, friends who are experiencing marriage at its best and worst, raising families or losing the ability to have a family, confronted with success or full of self-doubt. This is what it means to be human. In this I find Jesus.

≽ iGod ≼

The third part of the Creed, about the Holy Spirit, is on first sight quite an odd laundry list of beliefs. "The Holy Spirit, the holy Catholic Church, the communion of saints, the forgiveness of sins, the resurrection of the body, and life everlasting." What do they have in common? And what is this Spirit who is passed over so quickly?

For better or worse, the images of Father and Son are pictures we can immediately grasp. They carry emotional weight—and baggage. By contrast, the classic image of the Spirit, a dove, is much harder to grasp. I'm with the Japanese convert who, the story goes, was having difficulties understanding the Christian idea of the Trinity: "Honorable Father, I understand; Honorable Son, I understand; Honorable Bird, I don't understand."

And yet it's an image that is ultimately at the heart of what we believe and why we believe it. Go into Saint Peter's in Rome and see where the architecture draws your eye; eventually, at the end of its travels, high above the main altar on the far wall, the eye rests not on a cross but on the image of a dove.

(I am also reminded of my first year at the Vatican Observatory, working in an office that overlooked the pope's summer quarters. About my third day there, I was startled to notice a certain white bird hovering around one of the pope's windows. I had to laugh. It was just a pigeon looking for crumbs, of course. I think.)

My own understanding of what the Spirit is supposed to mean can be tied in to the three questions asked in Part One about why we look for God in the first place. God the Father made the universe, whose existence caused us to infer his existence as the answer to the question "Why is there something instead of nothing?" Jesus Christ gives us poor human beings an example of how a life finds meaning, a fixed point against which we can compare our own progress or regress. But that ultimate yearning that we get at three in the morning that comes like the odd snatch of a forgotten tune or a whiff of perfume on the wind, that's the Spirit.

But there's more to the Trinity and to the Spirit than those longings. It's perhaps best seen in the context of what the concept of the Trinity is trying to describe. In fact, I could easily imagine a religion based only on the Creator God, but to me, the Spirit makes sense only in the context of a Trinitarian theology.

So how do I understand the Trinity? I am really struck by the image that Dorothy L. Sayers, the mystery writer who also translated Dante and wrote plays and apologetics, presented in her book *The Mind of the Maker*. She was a kind of techie, a "theater techie" at least, and as a playwright she used an analogy for the Trinity from her experience in the theater. I present here a technological techie version of her analogy.

Consider the iPod, the first really popular small music player based on personal computer technology. To paraphrase Sayers, you can actually see in this little gizmo three different iPods, in a way that mirrors the three aspects of any creative endeavor—and in a way that ultimately reflects how the Trinity works.

You wouldn't have an iPod without the concept in the first place: a very portable, high-quality, large-storage music system designed to work with your home computer, which in turn manages music that has been downloaded from the Internet (or from your own CD collection). According to an article in *Wired* in 2004, the basic idea came from an engineer named Tony Fadell, though Apple chief Steve Jobs was ultimately responsible for driving the elegant interface and design. It's not just a small player that stores thousands of songs in a box the size of a credit card; it's a gizmo that does all that with flair, elegance, and an operating system that lets you get at the songs simply and easily. And it sounds great. That's the iPod we mean when we say "Tony Fadell and Steve Jobs invented the iPod."

But the design would have been pointless if it couldn't actually be built. The incarnation of that design is the actual iPod itself, the little box of metal and plastic and chips and wires that we carry around in our pockets. Not only is it beautiful, but it's also beautifully built. The headphones alone are worth the price. Nobody cut corners; there's a reason why the darn things are so expensive.

But writing this from the perspective of the twenty-first century's first decade, the real meaning that comes to anyone's mind when you say the name iPod is the way it has changed not just the way we listen to music but the way we possess it. In college, I had a big wooden crate full of vinyl albums and an ultrafastidious roommate who trained me never to play the same record twice without giving the grooves twenty-four hours to relax after that heavy (one-gram) stylus had scraped the music off them. (Training me wasn't very hard; I was pretty much ultrafastidious myself.) In the 1990s, I carried around cassette tapes by the shoebox, tapes that I was always losing—leaving them at friends' houses or in the front seat of the car where they'd melt into blobs of plastic under the Arizona sun. Now my music, all of my music, is kept in a tiny device that fits into my shirt pocket. (That's why you never see pocket protectors there anymore.) It's with me everywhere, giving my life its own personal soundtrack.

The iPod and its imitators have changed the way we purchase music, the way we share music, the way we learn about new music. It has also created a whole new medium for communication in the form of podcasts, which can use the bandwidth of the Internet to provide coverage of a wider range of topics and interests than any dialful of radio stations. Or television stations, with the advent of video podcasts. The revolution is well under way.

And here's where Sayers draws the parallel with the Trinity. The Father represents the creative God, the idea; the Son represents the incarnation of that idea in the physical universe; and the Spirit represents the way that the idea is alive in those of us who have been touched by it.

And that's why all the other things in the Creed are tagged on after "the Spirit." Just as you can see wind only in the things it moves, so you can see Spirit in the things it moves.

The Spirit moves in the church, as seen in the fact that we are surrounded by a community of people who are responding to the same gentle stirrings as we are so that we find ourselves all in the same place on a Sunday morning instead of sleeping in or reading the funnies over a cup of coffee. The Spirit is one thing we all have in common, in spite of all of our personal differences and shortcomings. We're all sinners, including our ministers and leaders, and yet somehow the church remains capable of being "holy"; we come from a wide variety of cultural backgrounds, and yet this catholic mixture is still capable of coexisting as one body in a single parish.

That catholicity extends, in fact, to the whole community of human beings in our history whose lives show that they've been moved by the Spirit. What they believed counts for us as well. As G. K. Chesterton so nicely put it a hundred years ago, "[Tradition] is the democracy of the dead.... All democrats object to men being disqualified by the accident of birth; tradition objects to their being disqualified by the accident of death." The last two millennia of Christians believed in the same God we believe in; the truths they fought for are truths we too need to preserve. Or to put it another way, if there is any formulation of that truth that we're ready to revise, we should equally be prepared to have it revised away yet again by our descendants. Because soon enough, we too will be among that communion of the past.

In addition, the movement of the Spirit inside us is the only thing that can give us the strength to forgive. To forgive that bullet-headed slob who tortured us in high school. To forgive the political leaders whose veniality, incompetence, and greed result in the sufferings of millions. To forgive our family. To forgive the guy who picked our pocket. To forgive ourselves.

And most astonishingly of all, the Spirit is the source of the reassurance we get in contemplating the example of Jesus Christ's rising from the dead. His resurrection is an act that carries with it the implicit promise that our lives too are neither finite nor pointless.

CHAPTER 13

The Supernatural in Nature

⇒ Cleansed and Quickened ⇐

Consider the famous line from John 3:16, "God so loved the world that he gave his only Son…" It says at the start, "God so loved the world…" Note that the Evangelist doesn't say God just loves people or goodness or souls or some abstract theological ideal. God loves the world. From the very beginning of the Bible, the first chapter of Genesis, we see God proclaiming that his creation was good.

Christianity is an incarnational religion. The physical universe matters to this religion. God so loved it that he became part of it. So what happens to it also matters. That, of course, is one reason why doing science—being a techie—is a very Christian activity. Writing *On the Incarnation* around the year A.D. 300, Saint Athanasius said that the universe "was cleansed and quickened by his indwelling." That's why if you believe in the incarnation, doing science—being a techie—is also a sacred act.

But that means that if we embrace Christianity, we have to deal with the possible contradictions of a free God messing about in a universe subject to the laws of physics. In becoming incarnate, God too accepts being subjected to those laws, the very laws that originated with God the Creator. Jesus gets cold and hungry, and to use his divine powers to turn stones into bread for his own convenience is a temptation from the devil.

We techies are intimately familiar with the physical universe, the universe that Christianity says God so loved. But we know it well enough to see beyond romantic visions of butterflies and postcard sunsets. It is also a violent place. Indeed, the very atoms in our bodies were fused together at unthinkable energies inside of stars or formed in the cosmic explosion of a supernova.

In a world controlled by the laws of physics, how can a techie believe in miracles? And if there is a good God, capable of performing miracles, why is there evil in the world? These questions are variants, or slivers, of the much more general question: How does a Christian techie think that God acts in the universe? And what happens to that God—and us—when the universe comes to an end?

≥ Natural Disasters ≤

As I write this chapter, a couple of natural disasters are fresh in my memory: a tsunami that killed more than two hundred thousand people around the Indian Ocean in late 2004 and Hurricane Katrina, which wiped out New Orleans in the summer of 2005. By the time this chapter is read, those events will be a more distant memory, but undoubtedly they will have been replaced by more recent natural disasters. You can count on nature to be powerful and deadly.

When you ask where was God in a hurricane, you're really asking, where is God in the activities of nature? It's the flip side of the intelligent design argument. If God were deliberately responsible for the path of evolution that led to the human eye, would not God be equally responsible for the path of a hurricane's eye?

I'll say this right here at the start. You cannot blame God for hurricanes. You can't blame him for my bad eyesight, either. And yet as a Christian, I believe that God is there in both of them.

Let me also dismiss another argument. Yes, in an important way, the widespread tragedies that result from disasters can often be attributed to human failures to prepare properly or respond adequately. I'll grant you that in a world without sinners, we would all be well warned, well protected, and well assisted afterward. Unfortunately, most of us don't qualify to live in a world without sinners.

But the real question is, why in God's name do there have to be hurricanes and earthquakes in the first place? Why do we have to suffer? Couldn't he have designed a gentler universe?

There's an odd divide in Western culture nowadays. We've become separated from nature. We have air-conditioned homes, air-conditioned cars, air-conditioned offices, air-conditioned lives. We spend most of our lives wrapped in cotton. If we feel pain, we want it to stop, *now.*

Well-lit streets at night means that most people never see the Milky Way—or at least not until the lights go out. After the Northridge earthquake in southern California in January 1994, the phones at the Griffith Planetarium started ringing off the hooks as people wanted to know why the earthquake made the sky look so scary. The earthquake struck at 4:30 A.M., while it was still dark outside. When people rushed through their blacked-out homes to the outdoors, a million people saw something in the skies over Los Angeles they'd never seen before: stars. And they were terrified.

In the last hundred years, for the first time in human history, our entire population in the West, rich and poor alike, has been able to stay up after dark as a matter of course. The night holds no more terrors for us; the wolf is far from our doors—until the lights go out.

I spent two years in the Peace Corps in Africa. I saw there how we used to live, back before flush toilets and neon lights. People lived close to nature, in a way that hardly anyone in America does anymore. And I learned in Africa that there's a word to describe people who live close to nature: starving. When we have a drought here in America, the cost of bread goes up a few cents. When they have a drought in Kenya, people go hungry.

A lot of us Peace Corps types went to Kenya with romantic ideas of leaving behind our shallow American existence, our nine-to-five jobs, and our evenings with nothing more to do than drink beer and watch TV. We wound up in a country just aching to have the luxury of being able to quit work at five and knock back a brew.

I've been an ecology freak since the 1960s, and I have been horrified at what unchecked development can do to a countryside. But I also see the irony of rock bands that preach "green" ecology with electrically amplified plastic guitars on their jet-setting world tour advertised over the Internet. Our lifestyle exacts a heavy toll on the environment; but so does the lifestyle of the desperate people in Kenya or Haiti, who strip the forests bare in their day-to-day struggle to stay alive. So I don't necessarily mean to disparage our cotton-swabbed existence. My point is just to point it out, because the shock we experience when a natural disaster hits us is precisely the wrench of being jerked out of our cotton womb and forced to confront nature. Nature can be hostile as well as beautiful; nature gives us food and gives us death.

The people in Africa, God help them, are used to living with pain and death. It is very close to the surface there. And I experienced God very close to the surface there, too. Atheism is a luxury of the well-to-do; it goes hand in hand with flush toilets.

But I like flush toilets, they are a great idea … until the storm comes and they no longer work.

The glory of technology is based on the glory of science; and the glory of science is that it works. Its laws are simple, you can calculate and predict outcomes with them, you can test your predictions against results, and you can use them to invent the gizmos that make our life simpler, easier, more reliable, more pain-free.

Newtonian physics assumes that the universe is predictable and orderly, and four hundred years of experimental science has given us confidence that the rules of cause and effect are very good at predicting how the universe works. Sure, there are places at relativistic speeds or at the subatomic quantum level where the physics gets more complicated, but for human-scaled events, we can use this cause-and-effect physics to build airplanes that fly and bridges that don't fall down. We can understand the mechanics of how life works and design drugs to finally cure diseases that have cursed humankind for all its history. We have progressed; we continue to progress; this progress is good; surely it will only get better; why, by the year 2000 we'll all live in flying domes and we will have conquered the common cold!

Right. Well, what happened to that 1950s future? If we can put a man on the moon, why can't we cure the common cold? Or predict earthquakes? Or control the path of a hurricane?

We thought that by making our calculations finer and finer, we'd get closer and closer to the truth. But a funny thing happened along the way. Around 1960, the meteorologist Edward Lorenz at MIT noticed that his computer models for the weather would predict remarkably different results if he varied his starting conditions even very, very slightly. It opened up a new branch of mathematics called chaos theory.

A favorite example in the textbooks for illustrating chaos theory is to imagine that you're shooting a BB gun at the bow of a battleship. As you move the gun from left to right, the BBs bounce off to the left, to the left, to the left, until suddenly you pass the center point and they bounce off to the right. That "extreme sensitivity to initial conditions" caused by the fact that the pointy end of the boat, where the two "linear" sides meet, is itself nonlinear: not smoothly varying but abrupt in its change of direction. Forces in nature can change abruptly, too. The concept of a "tipping point" is another example of this phenomenon.

We've learned that you tend to get essentially unpredictable changes, "chaos," when you have a system subjected to two different forces that interfere with each other in a way that is not linear. It turns out that sooner or later, most systems have more than one force acting on them, and quite often they descend into chaos. Weather is the most obvious example, with nonlinear fluid dynamics equations being tweaked by all sorts of different forces, from the heat of the sun to the friction of the ground that the wind blows over. This classic case gives rise to the old cliché about the butterfly who disturbs the atmosphere in such a way as to affect the weather a thousand miles away.

Of course, not every butterfly hits the sweet spot. But even planetary orbits, whose regularity let Newton demonstrate his simple laws of gravity and motion, can become chaotic; when Saturn and Jupiter both pull on an asteroid just right (or just wrong), it can be sent into an orbit that hurtles it on a collision course with Earth. The result: a natural disaster. Goodbye, dinosaurs! And then the dinosaurs' theologians ask, Where was God?

Now, mind you, just because we can't predict the future doesn't mean that at this level, it is not still subject to the same deterministic forces of Newton's laws. After all, we can make short-term predictions (depending on, well, lots of things) for tomorrow's weather or the path of a near-Earth asteroid. But even if we knew perfectly all the things we would need to know to make the calculation, in the long run we would eventually need to carry our calculations out to an infinite number of decimal places, which is to say, we wouldn't be able to calculate the system any faster than the system plays itself out. Eventually, our predictions always come too late.

But there's a joker in the natural world.

As an astronomer, when I get an image from a satellite looking down on a planet, I want a natural explanation for all the bits of information I see. Now imagine that I am an astronomer from a distant star, looking down on the night side of Earth, and I see the aurora borealis as charged particles from the sun are swept up by Earth's magnetic field and dashed against the upper atmosphere of Earth, ionizing oxygen atoms and lighting up the skies over the north pole and arctic Canada. But looking further in my image of nighttime Earth, I also see pools of light farther south: Chicago, Mexico City, Rio de Janeiro, and all the other places where people live and turn on their lights. The auroras I can explain as natural phenomena. The cities, however, are the action of intelligent creatures; the result of their decisions to live *here* and not *there,* decisions powered by history and economics and happenstance—and free will.

Now, free will is not the same thing as the butterfly effect. It is not due to the quantum uncertainty in the brain; you can't look for the tiny gaps and cracks in Newtonian physics and try to stuff God or man in there. For lots of reasons, both philosophical and scientific, that doesn't work.

But free will is something I am sure exists. You can't convince me otherwise, for to be convinced would mean that I would have to be free to change my mind, a contradiction. (But then, if I can't be convinced, does that mean that I am not really free? If nothing else, a paradox is a good sign that you've defined your question too narrowly.) Free will acts in the universe, but it is something somehow a little more than of this universe. It has a touch of the supernatural to it. It's one of the traits of the human soul.

By contrast, hurricanes are bound by the rigid laws of physics, by fluid dynamics, by laws that may be chaotic but are still deterministic.

And so here is the tension. There's the world of nature, the world I study as a scientist, nice and neat and well described by some beautiful equations, elegant in their simplicity. And there's the world of human beings, strange fleshy bundles of ego and free will, who can sometimes be described in a statistical sense but who as individuals never cease to surprise you. And yet human beings are a part of nature, with bodies that respond to the laws of biology and the laws of physics, capable of sinning and suffering and dying.

And those free-will-controlled bodies are inserted into the physical world of cause and effect, capable of acting at the sweet spot where the butterfly wing will have the biggest effect, and if we're clever enough, we could even be capable of calculating where that sweet spot might be. We're the joker in nature. The free will decisions of individual puny little human beings like you and me can affect the paths and the effects of hurricanes.

And if a human person can do it, so can God. So yes, God can act in a universe of cause and effect. If God can act, where is He?

One benefit that I have as a scientist who gets to know God through his creation is that I can learn to get used to the way God acts. God is God; he can, in theory, do anything he likes. But by seeing what it is he actually does and how he does it, I can begin to get an idea of what it is he likes to do and how he likes to do it. And I would have to say that the God who created this universe is someone who loves to act with elegance, economy, predictability, and consistency. God is the same from age to age, as the Psalmist tells us. He is a God, incidentally, who so fine-tunes things that the human eye comes about naturally and doesn't need his divine intervention at some particular point to jiggle things to make it happen. He's a God who doesn't have to interfere in the ordinary course of events but who will interfere if he is asked to.

And certainly, in the life of Jesus Christ, all bets are off: He rewrote the rules, by his incarnation and in the way he lived a life of miracles—from the least of his gestures (water into wine at a wedding feast) to his resurrection.

So yes, I have room for prayer and miracles. I'd be a pretty poor scientist if I rejected the evidence of so many experiences (including my own) that prayers are answered and that miracles do occur, just because they don't fit my preconceived theory for the predictability of the universe.

But I also try to observe not only the fact that God answers prayers but also how he answers them. He acts by acting on the human heart before acting on the laws of nature, by using divine coincidences and maybe urging a butterfly at just the right moment so that, for example, the Exodus of Moses and his people could just happen to have coincided with a rare but not impossible weather effect that gave them a dry path through the sea to safety.

Which is to say, yes, God could have acted during that latest natural disaster. Why didn't he?

Or did he?

I repeat the point I made earlier: you might argue that our human weaknesses, our sinfulness, made the results of the hurricane or the earthquake hurt more than they had to, but our sins did not cause the hurricane or earthquake. Each disaster arises because of the interaction of physical forces and the fluids of air and water and molten rock that are well described by Newtonian physics, ordained by a Creator who sets the rules of the universe and plays by them. But by those laws, God could have deflected the hurricane just a little, couldn't he? Or caused Earth to tremble someplace else? And who's to say that he hasn't done just that, a hundred times before, and we never noticed it? So why not one more time?

I've run out of glib answers. I can't answer that one.

In December 2004, I got an e-mail from a friend of mine that his grandmother had died. She was an outstanding person in so many ways, a talented concert pianist, a devout Catholic, an organizer of a league to help people with a certain debilitating disease (which she had suffered from herself when she was younger), a devoted mom and grandmom. I'd met her and fallen for her charm myself. I was sad to hear she'd passed. She was ninety-seven years old.

A few days later, I got another e-mail that a friend from my Peace Corps days, active in water resource projects to help the poor around the world, a beloved wife and mother to a seven-year-old boy, had died unexpectedly of complications from pneumonia. She was forty-three.

And every day that month, it seemed like another dozen people were killed by some car bomb in the Middle East.

And at the end of that same month, on December 26, 2004, a quarter of a million people died in a tsunami in Southeast Asia.

Where was God?

Numbers can be numbing. Every astronomer knows that; we readjust our figures, changing centimeters into light-years to give ourselves numbers that our brains can comprehend. The death and devastation following a natural disaster cannot be comprehended in the same way as the death of an individual friend. But ultimately, every death is an individual affair. And every time we can ask, where was God?

We can believe in a God who controls on a string every atom, every event, deliberately setting up life and tragedy. Such a God would indeed be a God immune to our sense of cruelty. Another possibility is a God who observes but does not intervene: the deist God of the eighteenth century, who set up the laws of the universe, wound up the spring, and let it loose to run independent of any further effort on his part. We can deny the existence of any God at all. Or we can deny the reality of those tragedies and continue living as if we ourselves were immortal.

None of these are gods that prayer and reflection tell me I can accept. But they are not mere straw men I've set up for a Jesuitical argument. They are versions of God that all of us believe in some of the time and some of us believe in all of the time. And so we rail at God when our business dealings flop, our favorite politicians lose elections, our love affairs go bad.

But my experience as a believer, as a scientist, and as a human being is that the situation is far more complicated—and confusing.

The laws of entropy are relentless. The universe, it appears, is fated to a gradual death as all energy dissipates into a uniform, featureless, ever-expanding ocean of cold. But in the meanwhile, on the surface of Earth, plants take sunlight and use a variety of unlikely chemical reactions to reverse entropy locally, making flowers and weeds. Savagely ripping that vegetation from the ground, bugs and bunnies populate the fields. Amazing in their own beauty, they are fed upon by the beautiful and majestic predators of Earth: the birds, the mountain lions, the humans.

Humans, who are free to act for good or evil and are capable of consciously creating beauty and ugliness. Humans whom, beautiful or ugly, we mourn when they die. Why do we mourn them? Because we find them worth mourning.

Pick up any newspaper, and hardly a week goes by when you don't read of some natural disaster. In that disaster, someone died. It was another grandmother. It was another mom of a seven-year-old. The fact that it may have happened again, over and over, a thousand times or a quarter of a million times, neither intensifies nor diminishes the meaning of each individual death.

Does God understand human suffering? Well, the Christian in me answers, it's not as if he himself had not also experienced betrayal and suffering and death.

Is death, then, but a natural part of life? Part of "God's Plan"? Are pain and mourning the price we pay for being alive? For a Christian, that can't be the answer. Instead, we are faced with the final contradiction: our God came to Earth and lived a life of pain and mourning and death precisely to proclaim an end to death itself.

God does play by the rules. He set up the thermodynamics that gives us mountains, earthquakes, tsunamis, and hurricanes; and yet those same laws of physics and chemistry allow for a human brain capable of calculating that thermodynamics and of understanding—albeit, terribly imperfectly—how to recognize and avoid the dangers of living on Earth. God respects cause and effect, and he is reliable enough for us to be able to understand his universe with confidence and some comfort.

But that same God also does intervene in individual lives. After the 2004 tsunami, the *New York Times* described how one young mother in a small Indonesian village fled for safety to the highlands, carrying her child, because she "heard a voice" telling her to flee. The mother next door, apparently, heard no such voice. We hear the survivors' stories; we never hear the victims'. We can't tell if God intervened in those cases, much less why or why not.

And each human soul, capable of acting freely, is capable of disturbing the universe and capable also, I believe, of responding to an urge from (or toward) the transcendent to make that disturbing act. Maybe we're meant to be his butterflies. It may not be the only way that God acts or can act in nature. But manifestly, this is one way that God does act in the universe: through us, as his free agents.

⇒ Heaven or Heat Death? ⇐

Beyond the death of an individual or our own death is the greater question of the ultimate fate of everything. What does traditional Christianity say about the end of the universe? Less than you might think. Or maybe more than you might think. It depends on what you think.

Throughout the ages, many people have spoken of or hoped for an eternal afterlife. Others, of a more practical bent, have looked for immortality of a kind in their achievements or at the very least in their offspring. In the global scheme, of course, even this sort of immortality is limited. We may still recall Caesar two thousand years after Brutus and Cassius did him in, but sooner or later, every monument, every book with his name on it, will be left on the surface of a cold, lifeless planet orbiting the dead ember of a star, just as the same laws of entropy have by now already turned Caesar's body into dust. If the universe is fated to what astronomers call a *heat death*, the final cessation of the heat flow responsible for all activity in the universe, then no kind of living eternity is possible in nature. It must only be possible outside of nature, hence in the supernatural.

This split into a natural world that ends and a supernatural one that continues forever is so obvious to a modern Christian that few believers are bothered by the contradictory pictures of

end time given in science and religion. But this kind of understanding, this simple split into natural and supernatural, is to a
large degree a product of the seventeenth-century scientific revolution, which appeared to demarcate a mechanistic Newtonian
universe split from the religious universe of God and eternal life.
It is not traditional Christianity.

Indeed, if our experience after death is supposed to be wholly
supernatural, then why does Jesus never speak of life after death
but always instead of "eternal life"? And why do the Gospels say
that he, in his risen form, came in a body so physical that it still
bore the scars of the crucifixion and could still enjoy the plea-
sures of a fish dinner?

Yet if this physical world itself does have eternal meaning,
how can you reconcile that with the scientific result that predicts
at best a gloomy (and utterly boring) view of its eternity?

Our Apostles' Creed says that Jesus will come to judge the living and the dead, and the Nicene Creed adds that his reign will
have no end. If Jesus will be around and reigning eternally, there
must be something more than just cold dust in the universe for
him to be reigning over. And this also means that not only Christ
but we too are expected to be around and alive eternally. Now
that you and I have come into existence, it appears that we are
going to stick around forever, in one form or another.

Christ's resurrection itself is not described in the New Testament. The Gospels only report the discovery, some days after
Jesus' execution, of the empty tomb that his dead body had been
put in and some appearances of the risen Christ to his friends
and disciples. But what did this resurrection actually mean?

Both the discovery of the empty tomb and the appearances
of the risen Christ—eating and drinking, able to be touched
(remember the story of doubting Thomas)—is clearly meant to
indicate that his resurrection is not something merely spiritual. It
concerns him in his bodily reality. There is a fundamental identity between the crucified Jesus and the risen Christ. This recog-
nition and identification happens through the senses: by seeing
the Risen One, hearing him speaking, touching him.

At the same time, we cannot understand this resurrection as
a kind of zombielike reanimation of Jesus' dead body. The New

Testament reports appearances of the risen Christ in which even his closest friends don't immediately recognize him; and he is able to appear inside locked rooms and come and go in ways an ordinary body could not do.

Likewise, in the Christian view, the death of a human individual does not mean that the person is completely dissolved. This is in deliberate contrast to ideas in some Eastern religions that would have the individual subsumed and lost in a mass of "consciousness" like a drop of water falling into an ocean. Instead, the church insists on identity and continuity between the deceased person and the resurrected one.

The key tool borrowed from Greek and medieval philosophy that seems to be needed to make this existence while waiting for a body work is the concept of a soul. But what do we really mean by "soul"?

The scholastic philosophers of the Middle Ages were able to use the rich language of form versus matter from Aristotelian philosophy to describe soul and body in a formal way. But the division of the human into components of body and soul may be merely a philosophical convention, useful to explain a theological truth in terms of a given human philosophy. It does not presuppose that this same truth could not be expressed in other ways by other philosophies.

Perhaps a more modern analogy, useful for those of us who are not schooled in ancient philosophy, is to think of the soul as analogous to the data in a computer. Like all analogies, this one will fail miserably when pushed too far; but at least perhaps it can help illustrate some of the issues involved in defining just what it is that survives after death.

Let's say you and I own identical computers. But I know mine is different from yours (beyond the fingerprints on the screen and the scratches on the case) because it has a completely different set of files from yours and perhaps even a completely different operating system.

It's not a matter of a physical difference. The computers could be identical models and be exactly the same in terms of size, shape, weight, and other details. The only physical difference is that certain metal grains representing ones and zeros are arrayed differently on my hard drive than the metal grains on your hard drive. But even the ones and zeros by themselves have no significance except in terms of the operating system that interprets them, and even the operating system can only translate those ones and zeros into bits of light on the screen, and those pixels have meaning only when we can identify them as letters, words, or pictures, which requires a human intellect to translate into ideas.

Consider how the subtlety of this point has led to all sorts of modern issues involving copyright law. When you buy a piece of software (or a music CD, a videotape, or a plain old-fashioned book for that matter), no one denies that you now own the piece of aluminum or polyester on which the information is written. But you do not own the ideas encoded on that medium. You own the paper that a book is printed on; you do not own the words themselves.

The point is to draw the distinction between the "wet ware" of the human animal—our bodies—and the ideas, memories, and emotions, and most essentially, the self-awareness, intellect, and free will, of the human person. Defining the soul as intellect and free will goes back at least to Saint Thomas Aquinas, and the usefulness of this definition is obvious. But in another sense, isn't this division artificial? Isn't it the case that the soul, like the program in a computer, has no *physical* existence without the physical existence of the body containing and operating on it?

Yet just as the idea behind a computer program could continue to exist long after every computer designed to run it has been made obsolete and sent to the junk yard, in the same way, couldn't a person's awareness and free will survive the destruction of the body? You might envision some science-fiction scenario with these components stored on some future computer; but who is to say that God even needs that kind of storage device?

(Let me emphasize again, this is an analogy to illustrate the issues. I am not saying that souls are the same thing as computer programs.)

Think again of our computer analogy: Is a computer program that's been copied to another disk the same program as the one on the original disk? Is someone transported by a Star Trek transporter beam, disassembled at one point and reassembled out of different atoms someplace else, the same person at the other end of the transporter? What happens if more than one copy gets made? With these speculations, you can begin to appreciate the importance of the physical body, not just the soul, in defining the individual.

Is the body at the end of time the same as the body the person had when death occurred? What do we mean by "same" in this context? We have no difficulty identifying an eighty-year-old man as being the same person as the baby he was eighty years ago, even if he has not a single atom left in his body from the body he had when he was born. But some software vendors insist that any computer that has had any of its major components replaced cannot legally run software licensed to the "original" computer.

In the time to be passed from the end of a person's life until the resurrection of the body (at the "end of time"), can the human soul be thought of—does it exist, like the idea of a poem that is not written down—without any kind of materialization whatsoever? Or in the absence of a physical expression, is the whole idea of time itself meaningless?

It's clear that trying to derive a physical, scientific implication for the end of the universe from religious principles is a hopeless task. But there is one important implication for the science in all this: the realization that physical science by itself isn't the whole story.

Yes, there is an interaction between the way we look at ourselves and our universe in a philosophical sense and the way we do it in science. Each can learn—by analogy—from how the other operates. But neither should assume that it's the entire story or that one is able to trump the insights of the other.

Saints walked in this universe before Newton or Einstein explained it. Understanding Calculus is not a prerequisite to gaining the kingdom of heaven. But a God who created the universe of Einstein can be seen to be much bigger and more subtle and more elegant than the nature gods of the Babylonians reflected in the opening pages of Genesis. Philosophy alone could never conceive of the richness of the universe that science has revealed.

And yet by the very fact that it cannot even begin to handle the existence of free will choices, science in its turn has proved to be incomplete. If the point of science, like all other human endeavors, is to provide a reflection of our universe, then science has left out a big chunk of the universe in its reflections. No scientific theory is capable of coming to the most important conclusion of Genesis, that God looked on this creation and said that it was good.

And that's only right. That is the whole genius of art: true art, be it painting or novel or drama or music, selects and arranges. A videotape is not the same thing as history. The genius of human understanding is to choose what to study and what to set aside. A science that tried to contain everything would no longer be science and would no longer be art. Even in the scientific world, we filter our data so that we can look at one phenomenon at a time.

Van Gogh's paintings are not photographs. I can't do spectral photometry of the stars imaged in a painting like *Starry Night*, nor did the artist ever intend it to be used that way. Instead, it is up to us to take his odd colors and splashy bits of paint and add in our own imagination to complete the picture. In that way, the picture—and a bit of the painter—enters into our soul.

In the same way, the scientific painting of the universe has deliberately set aside many of the most pleasing parts about being alive. That's not to criticize it, any more than we would demand that every van Gogh should come with a piece of French bread and a bottle of wine. Because by limiting itself, by removing certain facets of human existence from the picture, the scientific portrait of the universe allows us to bring to the surface other equally pleasing facets of existence that we might have otherwise missed: the order and reassuring predictability in nature and the logic that allows gloriously complicated things like stars and galaxies to arise from the simplest of scientific principles.

Our resolution of how the human person, incarnate in a universe that appears to be destined to an ultimate state of heat death, nonetheless obtains eternal life with a God who is himself eternal (and incarnate in this universe as well as being outside of space and time) admits to no simple scientific or theological explanation. The best we can do is speak in poetry and paradoxes of bodies that are at the same time the same but different from those we now possess.

It is paradoxical; but that is not to say it is unreal or even unfamiliar to us. We can understand that in some sense, the center of human identity, call it if you wish the soul, can maintain a hypothetical existence even in the absence of a particular physical manifestation in the same way that the idea of a song or a poem can live on even after every copy of it has been destroyed. Perhaps it is in the power of abstract ideas, the nature of words themselves, that we get our best analogy for understanding how we can exist even when our bodies turn to dust.

Maybe we've been given our clearest hint from him who was the first example of that eternal, physical existence. Jesus himself, before his death and resurrection, put it simply and directly: "Heaven and Earth will pass away," he said, "but my words will never pass away" (Matthew 24:35).

PART FIVE

The Confession of a Vatican Techie

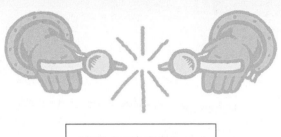

CHAPTER 14

Why Would a Techie Be a Catholic?

⧚ Why I Am a Catholic ⧛

As noted by many of the techies interviewed in Part Three, Christianity is divided into many different religions and sects. To some, it's a scandal that invalidates any religion ("They can't all be right, so they must all be wrong"); to others, the different flavors of Christianity are merely an assortment from which one is free to choose whatever pleases most, analogous to tastes in music or different computer operating systems.

I don't accept either of those characterizations.

So why am I, specifically, Catholic? How do I navigate all the pitfalls of being a Catholic? And at the end of the day, what do I get out of it that makes it all worthwhile?

Let me emphasize as strongly as possible what I am trying to do here. I don't intend this section to be a replacement for the Catholic Catechism. Nor do I want this to be a book of apologetics, trying to convince you that I'm right and you're wrong. (I am, and you aren't, but that's a different book.)

Nor am I trying to convince you that what I am about to say is the ultimate truth. (If I happen to think this stuff really is the truth, well, that's my problem.) Even less am I trying to say that anybody else but me, any church, or any subset of any sect thinks that what I am about to say is the truth. (If I am so foolish as to think that what I am about to say is a reasonable way of describing Catholicism, well, again, that's my problem.) What follows comes with no warranty. And not only may your mileage vary; it absolutely, with certainty, will vary from mine.

Because what I am trying to illustrate in this final part of the book is not how other people might understand religion or how they've told me they actually do understand it; here, all I am trying to do is to illustrate how I myself understand my own religion. And while I might entertain fantasies that everyone who reads these sterling words will become amazed by their sagacity and elect me emperor of the universe, in reality my only possible excuse for foisting them on you is to show you a detailed example of how a particular religious life works for the only techie I know who will sit still long enough to answer all my questions: me.

The point of this exercise is to illustrate how this particular techie makes sense of a religion that most assuredly was not invented with techies in mind. That means that I'm giving you my very personal take on things, *not* an official Catholic position. That means that the way I put things may look downright weird to a practicing theologian, never mind an ordinary nontechie Catholic. And that means that what I am about to say could be—almost certainly is, somewhere—completely wrong, where "wrong" means not really an accurate description of what the Catholic church is trying to teach, much less a valid description of how God and reality itself work.

I am not the pope. I am not even a priest. I have no degrees in philosophy or theology; though I have taken a smattering of graduate-level classes in both, it was by no means a unified or systematic study—indeed, mostly it was just enough to show me how little I know of either field. I have absolutely no authority, in other words, to teach anybody about what the Catholic church teaches, much less to pass judgment on anybody who does not agree with me. I'm a techie; I respect expertise, and I know when I *don't* have it myself.

And for that matter I also note here that virtually nothing I say is original. Few things in anyone's brain are. We're all magpies, collecting and gathering stray pieces of thought and making a nest out of them. It's cluttered and inconsistent, odd-looking and smelly, but comfortably homey as well. And it does the job we need done.

Indeed, the only thing that I guarantee is "right" about what follows is that I promise to try my hardest to give you a blunt, honest description of how my strange techie mind works—including laying bare all my prejudices and foolishness. I don't even pretend that there is another techie in the world besides me who thinks and believes the way that I do. But I'm the only techie in the world to whose innermost thoughts and fears I have unrestricted access.

And part of that honesty—the scariest part—is that what I will be revealing is not necessarily logical or even defensible. In fact, a lot of it is sheer prejudice. I recognize that. I do not defend it. If any non-Catholic is offended by my comments here, I can understand that, and I feel sorry for that, because I understand that these prejudices can be hurtful to people whom I love, whom I do not ever want to hurt. But I lay them out here in the open because I think they are not all that atypical of the kinds of prejudices that American Catholics of my background and generation are likely to hold, even if most of us are too polite to express them out loud. And I concede readily that the choice of religion that each of us makes is based on a wild mixture of reason and prejudice, fear and desire, motives at times base, at times silly, but still driven by a hunger for the transcendent.

Thus I start with the question of why I am specifically a Catholic. In one sense, it's simple: it is because I am half Irish and half Italian in ancestry; my parents were both Catholics, as were their parents going back more generations than I can know. It was the church they were brought up in, and so it was the church they brought me up in. I had nothing to do with it.

As it happens, I have always gotten along well with both of my parents. Neither of them was ever a fanatic or a monster or even someone who "didn't understand me"; rather, the most disconcerting thing about the home I grew up in was that, frankly, my parents and my siblings understood me all too well! Likewise, the nuns and lay teachers who taught me in parochial school (Our Lady Queen of Martyrs, in the northwest suburbs of Detroit) were wonderful people who did great things to encourage my talents and rein in my excesses. In other words, there was absolutely nothing unusual about my early exposure to the church except perhaps that judging from stories I have heard from other people's growing up, my childhood experiences were remarkable for not being remarkable.

I think that is important, because it means that I can approach the church I was brought up in without having to correct for any of the serious issues that too many other people have had to deal with. My experience of the church was about as good as you could expect to find, and it comes with a lot of warm and fuzzy memories. There was no emotional reason for me to leave; and so, not surprisingly, I didn't. Here I am.

⧽ Why I Am Not an Ex-Catholic ⧼

I have many friends who belong to other Christian churches and who seem perfectly happy in them. And I have run into my share of ex-Catholics, especially those who want to tell me in great detail all the horrible things that drove them from the church. Have I ever been tempted to try out the other flavors? And if not, why not?

In a funny way, my attitude is well reflected by a comment I heard once from one of those ex-Catholics, a woman I met informally at a wedding who heard that I was a Jesuit and so laid into me with all the horrors of her Catholic upbringing. If you've been around the church long enough, you've heard the hit parade: the sexist attitudes of its leaders, the intolerance of its teachers, the rigidity of its system of rules, the inelegance of its liturgies, and on and on and on. She wanted a religion that would ordain women, that would allow priests to marry, that would give a wide latitude for individual communities to invent their own style of worship.

I pointed out to her that there was indeed a church that did all the things she asked for. Why didn't she just become an Episcopalian? (And leave me alone!)

She looked at me funny. "I suppose I could," she said, "but it wouldn't be the real thing, now, would it?"

And I could only agree. Maybe it's the result of the propaganda that all those nuns fed me when I was a child, but I do have to admit that to me all the Protestant sects of Christianity smack of being "Christianity Lite." Christianity without the hard parts. Catholicism, only without that heavy-handed bureaucracy. (Of course we also complain when the bureaucracy fails to do its job of reining in the clerical crooks and fanatics and child abusers.) Catholicism, only without the hard-to-swallow stuff like God's real presence in the Eucharist. Catholicism, without the bit of how, despite our best efforts, we all continue to be sinners in constant need of forgiveness. Catholicism, without all the self-doubt.

A science-fiction aficionado friend described it to me this way. Take the archetypal space opera hero, Flash Gordon or Buck Rogers, who's pure of heart, always hitting harder and shooting straighter than the bad guys: he's a Calvinist, inexorably predestined to be good. Then look at Frodo the Hobbit, full of self-doubt, in need of forgiveness, and all too liable to fail at the crucial moment: clearly a Catholic. I favor Catholicism for the same reasons I recognize that *The Lord of the Rings* is a greater piece of literature than *Buck Rogers in the 25th Century*.

Like a lot of people who have made these complaints to me, my friend at that wedding had described a couple of nuns who taught her in her youth; one was good and understanding and encouraging, and the other was rigid and spiteful and mean. And as usually happens in these tales, the good one wasn't good enough, and the mean one managed to drive my friend away from the church. I wonder, why do we always let the mean ones win?

It's human nature and a human right to gripe about our leaders; and while on balance I think the popes of the last hundred years have been remarkably good men (albeit with their share of human weaknesses and faults), I also have to admit that the church has had its share of papal scoundrels, not to mention its share of scandalous bishops and priests. But why should that stop me from being a Catholic? There hasn't been a president of the United States whom I could be proud of since John F. Kennedy, and yet that doesn't stop me from being a good citizen, one who loves my country—proud enough to represent my country in the Peace Corps, proud enough to feel a deep sense of shame at some of the ways its leaders have behaved. Likewise, I have known scientists who backstab their colleagues, fiddle their grant funds, cheat on their spouses—but that doesn't mean I dismiss their scientific results.

Would I like to see things different in the Catholic church? In its fundamentals, not at all. I would rebel against any watering down of its essential theology, just as I cringe at the way I see a sort of creeping Protestantism infecting the American church, both in the efforts of some people to downplay its hard truths and in the efforts of others to instill a rigid fundamentalism in the way those truths are expressed.

A particular strength of Catholicism over denominations whose worship depends totally on music and preaching is that even the most tasteless liturgy with the most inane homily from a priest who's an outright scoundrel doesn't stop a Mass from being a valid and worthwhile source of grace. That also means that on controversial issues like married clergy or women in the hierarchy, I have an attitude that I am sure will be treated as heresy on both sides: I don't care. The things I get out of my church, the functional techie reasons I belong—its truths, its sacraments—don't depend on who gets to be bishop. That's just administration. I'm not interested in management. (I'm a vowed brother; I will never be ordained a priest, much less a bishop.)

And I note, in passing, that the Episcopalian solution hasn't spared that church a whole set of wrenching problems regarding these issues.

I've been speaking here of Protestantism, but of course there is another completely independent side to Christianity represented by the Eastern Orthodox churches. Their claim to historical continuity ("apostolic succession") looks to be every bit as good as the Catholics', and their theology is as rich—indeed, to modern eyes, it is indistinguishable from Catholicism. On the one hand, it looks like the only thing keeping us separate is our common human history. On the other hand, I am puzzled by the impression I get that in its thousand-year history, the Eastern churches have not produced either the achievements or the failures, the saints or the scoundrels, that have come out of the West. This may simply be ignorance on my part—or the lack of English translations. Probably I am missing something. But it does make me wonder if it is missing something, too.

⧽ Why I Remain a Catholic ⧼

Finally, I have to ask myself, Is being a practicing Catholic worth the cost? Does it lead me to places I would never have known about, tell me something I didn't already know? And in the final analysis, does it bring me in touch with that God who gives meaning to my life, a goal for my desires, and a rationale for the universe I meet in the lab every day?

In other words, is it true? Is it beautiful? And is it fun?

Well, what did you think I would answer? Would I have anything to do with it if it weren't all those things?

Now, don't get me wrong. I admire and at times I deeply love the things I have learned from non-Catholic writers, non-Catholic traditions, and my non-Catholic friends. I really do find God in those places. They are true and beautiful and fun. And heaven knows, there can be plenty of ugliness in the Catholic world. But at its best, well, it's the world I want to be in.

I made a comparison before between *Buck Rogers* and *Lord of the Rings*. Admittedly, that's an unfair fight; they're not even the same genre, and in any event, *Buck Rogers* will look junky by almost anybody's standard—even if it is still a lot of fun. (There are times when what you really want is a fast-food burger, not caviar.) Why not contrast the best with the best—say, C. S. Lewis with J. R. R. Tolkien? One is Anglican, one Catholic. And I love Lewis—I have stolen lots of his best stuff for this book. But compared to Tolkien, Lewis's universes are a bit stilted, filled a bit too much with the cardboard settings and characters of a toy theater.

You can play this game with the whole of twentieth-century British literature, where half the giants of the age were in fact Roman Catholics. Shaw versus Chesterton? George Bernard Shaw was by far the better playwright, but the philosophy behind his work is awfully creaky today. By contrast, G. K. Chesterton's writing style may be dated, but his thinking is remarkably fresh even in circumstances far different from when he wrote. You read Shaw for his style and wit; you read Chesterton for his wisdom. Poetry? T. S. Eliot the Anglican was brilliant; the Jesuit priest Gerard Manley Hopkins outshines him, and did it all fifty years before him, in obscurity. Satire? Kingsley Amis, the atheist, produced memorably biting humor; Evelyn Waugh, the Catholic, did so too—but he also produced *Brideshead Revisited.*

You can continue the game in many other fields, the best against the best. In this book I've cited Bach, a German Lutheran, as an exemplar of someone whose music like no other's mimics God's creative style, producing complex beauty out of the interplay of simple themes. I love it. But it can be just a bit, I don't know, mechanical or soulless compared to, say, Mozart or Beethoven, products of the Catholic German culture.

Do these illustrations help you see what I am trying to get at? Catholic intellectual achievement is probably a little less sure of itself, but for that very reason, it is also ultimately a little bit richer. I think it's because it has human fallibility, with all the accompanying richness and pathos, at its center. I think that's why even shaky Catholics or ex-Catholics (Graham Greene, Anthony Burgess, James Joyce) outdo their Protestant rivals, simply because they are far more aware of—and more in sympathy with—the friability of their own (and thus their characters') souls. By contrast, the Protestant tradition going back at least to Milton's *Paradise Lost* has the problem that the villains are always more interesting than the oh-so-perfect heroes.

The Catholic heroes experience sin and redemption, yes. But more than that, it's sin the way that the Mediterranean culture understands it. It's not enough to be sorry for your sins; you have to have a certain comfort with that sorrow, the ability to accept that neither you nor your neighbor will ever achieve perfection under your own steam. Acceptance then means sorrow without despair. This stands in contrast to the Protestant alternatives to such an attitude, which too often become either unjustified optimism or denial.

In fact, the only honest way you can look forward to a brighter future is to start by admitting that the present could use some improvement. The Protestant believes that he or she is "saved"; the Catholic has a faint hope for a time when that might be true but isn't so sure just yet.

So what is the real cost of being a Catholic? It isn't having to eat fish on Fridays or having to get to church once a week (I actually rather enjoy both of those things). It's having to admit, and live with, the fact that I am not perfect.

This is not just me saying so, out loud, because it's the socially correct thing to do, a way of fishing for contrary compliments from my neighbors. And it is not a complacency that lets me be comfortable with my corruption so that I don't really feel I need to change. I can't echo Claude Rains playing Captain Renault—no doubt, a French lapsed Catholic—one-upping Humphrey Bogart in *Casablanca* when he claims, "I'm just a poor, corrupt policeman"—by which he really means, "I'm a smoother, cleverer fellow than you with your superficial American morality." Admitting my failings means feeling sufficiently bad about them that I really do try to change and not being too surprised or too discouraged when I find that change is harder than it looks. (Even at the end of the film, we can't help but be still a little wary of Captain Renault's change of heart.)

If you do that right, then it really does hurt; it really does cost you. The benefit is that the more you can see your shortcomings, the more you are seeing the truth. It also puts a whole new wrinkle into the commandment to love one another as you love yourself. When you can hurt without despair at your own faults, you can likewise be less despairing of the faults of others. And as a nice side benefit, once you know how to recognize your own faults, sometimes you actually get to overcome some of them. It admits the possibility that anyone can be redeemed—even Captain Renault.

I notice an interesting thing about this discussion. To explain my bent for Catholicism, I've reached into my love of literature, music, movies—all the examples I have given, all the arguments, have been decidedly nontechie in nature. I think that's significant. Why is being a Catholic so important to me? Maybe it's because the church is the only thing out there that's big enough to balance out, or at least hold in check, my techie arrogance.

But recalling my techie roots, when I judge Catholicism by the functions that I demand from a church, it passes the test. It does have the deepest, richest, most challenging, and most embracing history of God's interaction with humanity, incorporating the history of Judaism and willing to embrace the wisdom of the world's other great thinkers. It has a systematic theology that gives me a handle on that history without ever ceasing to challenge me to look deeper and grow further in my faith. It has a full suite of

liturgies for every possible occasion in life. And its spiritual teachings give me a way of describing, understanding, and appreciating those odd moments I do experience, those moments that my
religion successfully gives me the space to experience: when the
transcendent God becomes immanent in my life. And at its best,
it does it all with verve and joy.

The ultimate reason why I stay a Catholic is because it works.

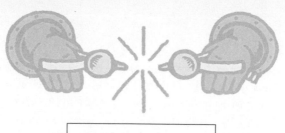

CHAPTER 15

How I Stay a Catholic

≳ Popular Misconceptions ≲

When I was a sophomore at the local Jesuit high school in Detroit, our theology teacher was a shy mouse of a fellow I'll call Mr. Smith. He was very smart, very well educated, and I'm sure quite a sweet man. In other words, he should never have been released unprotected into a roomful of fifteen-year-old boys. We were merciless.

Our favorite tactic for driving him nuts was to interrupt his lectures with irrelevant and, if possible, embarrassing questions. So one day, the class clown—not me!—interrupted a rather technical lecture on biblical form criticism, waving his hand and shouting, "Mr. Smith! Mr. Smith! I have a question!"

A familiar mixture of bewilderment and fear appeared on Mr. Smith's face.

"Is it true," asked the clown, "that if I get my girlfriend pregnant, I have to marry her?"

Mr. Smith's face turned a deep shade of red. "Th— th— th— that's," he stuttered, "um,... a, a *popular misconception.*"

And then, along with all the rest of us, he realized what he had just said.

Alas, Catholic teaching and theology are subject to many popular misconceptions. I hear them from my non-Catholic friends all the time.

There are things they think we believe that we don't. "YOU MUST BE A ROMAN CATHOLIC TO GO TO HEAVEN!" proclaimed a sign

I once saw an earnest young woman carrying down the streets of Hoboken, New Jersey. Well, no. Back in the 1950s, even before the reforms of Vatican II, there was a famous priest who insisted on that doctrine; he wound up getting himself excommunicated from the Catholic church for it, a fitting bit of irony.

But there are also a number of areas where actual traditional Catholic teaching is quite far from the usual assumptions in our culture, often flying in the face of "common sense." What about prayer candles and novenas and plenary indulgences? The flying house of Loreto, the liquefying blood of Saint Januarius, the shroud of Turin? The miraculous apparitions at Fatima or Lourdes?

Well, I wanted a religion that was bigger than me, and so I'm not disappointed when it turns out to have all sorts of expressions of spirituality that are clearly very important to lots of people but may not speak very strongly to me. That's OK; it's a different language, and I don't insist on being able to understand every language. I have my own ways of showing how I love God, and I don't expect everyone else to appreciate my ways, either.

It is curious, however, that so many of those odd spiritualities in Catholicism are based on real objects that people can see for themselves. That's more than you can say for any of the evidence for, say, UFOs. They're not, shall we say, golden tablets that have somehow gotten lost.

I mean, I may be skeptical that an ancient Palestinian house was miraculously flown to Loreto, Italy, by angels. But for more than five hundred years, there has been such a house in Loreto that I can actually go visit, regardless of how it got there. (And I suspect that how it got there is a story nearly as strange as the flying angels bit.) My faith would not be shaken over a perfectly natural explanation for the blood of Saint Januarius, a dark, solid substance kept in a vial in Naples that turns liquid and blood-red when brought out on special feast days. (One of those days, the saint's feast day, is my birthday.) It doesn't nullify the profound psychological effect that this ceremony has had on the citizens of Naples for nearly seven hundred years—and the fact that whatever the stuff is and however easy (or hard) it is to make for yourself, it's really there and really behaves the way it's said to behave. For nearly two hundred years, people have gone to Lourdes and been cured. Maybe it's psychological; maybe it's coincidence; but for the people involved, a cure's a cure, and that's what matters.

The skeptics who invest so much effort in trying to debunk these expressions of spirituality are missing the point of what they're all about. It's not that people have faith because of these holy things; rather, these things are holy because people have faith. These things serve as a focus for faith.

Besides, it's not an essential trait of Catholicism that you must believe in any of these curiosities. You can be skeptical and still call yourself a real Catholic. Indeed, the church hierarchy itself is usually the most skeptical of anyone about claims of bleeding statues and mystical visitations. It knows from experience how easy it is for us to fool ourselves.

But there's another class of Catholic beliefs that are not at all easy to dismiss—and hard for a skeptical techie to swallow— because they make important claims about the universe that might seemingly be susceptible to being "scientifically" demonstrated to be false.

For example, there's the doctrine of original sin. Original sin is a shorthand way of explaining the incontrovertible fact that people do bad things. Indeed, we do bad things even when it is clearly not in our own best interest to do them. Why? What makes us do such things? The question should not be controversial, but the church's answer is.

There are two issues involved. One is trying to figure out what the church actually means by "original sin"; the other is trying to figure out how it applies in a universe much bigger than Planet Earth. The answer to the first question would deserve an entire book to itself. The answer to the second is that nobody even pretends to know.

Let me sketch out the problem so that you can see what we are talking about. The traditional explanation of why there is human evil in the world (not merely physical evils like natural disasters, discussed in Chapter Thirteen) is based on a concept first expressed in the epistles of Saint Paul, who drew a parallel between the "fall" of the human race through one person, Adam, and its salvation through another, Jesus. The nature of this fall has been elaborated on by a number of theologians from Saint Augustine through Saint Aquinas through the Council of Trent. The favorite way to express it is that Adam, by sinning, rejected the special abilities ("grace") that he—and his descendants—had been given by God to resist evil, and as a result, the world is now open to both death and sin.

Now, there are a number of important things about how one is to understand evil that comes out of this formulation. The first is that evil and death are *not* the way things are supposed to be. We are not "rebelling against the will of the gods" when we fight against evil and death. Quite the contrary. But along with that comes the realization that we can't get ourselves back into the Garden. While the fight against evil and death is indeed the only time we can be confident that we're fighting God's fight (and of course the real question is not if God is on our side but if we are on God's), this is a fight that is bigger than any individual person. We can't do it on our own.

From this follows another lesson from the Adam story: the actions of one person affect everybody else. No man is an island. The adage that "it's OK to do what you like if you're not hurting anybody but yourself" is false. If you are ever less good than you could have been, you're ultimately hurting the rest of us. We were counting on you. We all need everyone else to be good, all the time, in order for us to be able to overcome evil ourselves. And that, of course, is another reason why we can't realistically expect to accomplish anything without the only person who can forgive us all and make us whole for all the times we're less than good.

Because most deeply and subtly within the doctrine of original sin is the understanding of what evil actually is. Evil can appear and act and be fought as if it were an entity in itself, but in actual fact, evil does not have an independent existence. Evil is merely the absence of good. It's not that something bad has been let loose on the world, like the monster in a teenage slasher movie; rather, it is that something good has been held back. And every time the good that should be there is denied, evil results.

Incidentally, the way that a *lack* can feel like a *presence* is a concept that anyone familiar with the physics of solid state semiconductors will recognize. Semiconductors operate by pushing electrons in and out of crystals. But some kinds of crystals are doped (impurities are deliberately introduced into the pure crystal structure) in order to make the crystal have a slight shortage of the proper number of electrons. What results are referred to as "holes." And it turns out that you can do all the mathematical calculations that predict how such doped crystals behave if you pretend that you have a perfect crystal and then introduce a mythical hole that has a negative mass and a positive charge (that is, opposite that of the missing electron). So instead of trying to solve for the motion of Avogadro's number of electrons moving in one direction, you can solve for the motion of one of these mythical holes moving in the opposite direction. The absence of an electron looks mathematically like the presence of a hole, just as the absence of good can look like the presence of an entity called evil.

Well, it makes sense to me.

The point here is that all of these ideas about evil—its being an unnatural state of nature, the absence of good, something generated whenever anyone is less than perfect—have some pretty profound implications for the way we live and behave.

Unfortunately, the traditional explanation of how evil got let loose on the world—Saint Paul's parallel between Adam and Jesus—depends on taking the Genesis story of Adam and Eve at face value.

I have no problem accepting that there was at some place and time some common ancestor to the human race; if nothing else, the mean value theorem tells me that if there was a time when there were no human beings and there is a time now when humans do exist, there must have been, somewhere, somehow, a first human. And indeed, various studies of human genes (and the observation that all human beings everywhere are capable of interbreeding) is completely consistent with the idea of a common ancestor.

But our science has also shown us that the history of the human race is much longer and more complicated than the simple story of Genesis—which is, after all, a kind of "children's book" version of the origins of our world, written a very long time ago for people with a very different understanding of how things worked. So what does it actually mean to talk about a "first human"? Did intellect and free will come suddenly to one individual? Or did the ability of the human animal to recognize good and evil, and one's relationship with God, slowly evolve along with brain size and opposable thumbs? Or are those even the right questions to be asking?

And then, when we say that death and sin entered "the world," are we speaking specifically of Planet Earth or of the whole universe?

How do I, as a scientifically literate twenty-first-century techie, deal with these strong challenges to the traditional formulation of the doctrine of original sin?

Easy. I throw up my hands and say, "I don't know."

But it doesn't bother me that I don't know. In fact, I am rather delighted to be able to admit that something we once thought we had pretty much under control turns out to be a whole lot trickier than we had realized. Because when this kind of paradox comes up in my own scientific life, which happens all the time, I have learned to recognize such a challenge as a great opportunity to learn something important and new.

Every time we come up against something new in a field we thought we understood, be it quantum physics or the structure of planetary rings, we find out that the universe is richer and more subtle than we had realized before. There's nothing in the Cassini spacecraft images of Saturn's rings that tells me that the law of gravity is no longer true. But the complexity in the rings that those images reveal tells me that this law of gravity does stuff to the particles in those rings that I still can't explain completely. I have no doubt that the laws of gravity are at work there, but the details of how each bit pulls gravitationally on each other bit is more complicated than even the biggest computer can handle, and I just can't see all the gears and levers yet. It's not that our old explanations are wrong and we have to throw them away; it's that all this time, they have been incomplete or incompletely understood. Once we finally realize that and have a hint of where the inadequacy lies, we can move on to understand them in some deeper, richer way.

Likewise, there can be no doubt that the source of human evil, the urge that people have to choose to do things they know are wrong, has been a part of our human experience since before the beginning of recorded history. Original sin is a fact. But explaining it in light of what we now know of human origins is going to be a lot trickier than the theologians would have guessed five hundred years ago.

And that's OK. More power to them.

Meanwhile—and here's the real techie attitude coming through—I have confidence that if I live my life and make my choices as if the traditional "sin of Adam" explanation solved everything, I won't go far wrong. Functionally speaking, the old explanation is sufficient for the job it is supposed to do, just as I can use "obsolete" Newtonian physics to solve most terrestrial engineering problems. I don't need to know the instant or the process when human beings first became capable of making free choices. It's enough for me, today, to know that I do have the power (and responsibility) to make free choices myself and that for whatever historical reasons, I can't depend on my own strength to make the right choice every time. In a practical sense, that's what the doctrine of original sin is all about. And that's true, regardless of how it came to be.

So if I can't do it myself, then how do I get the strength from day to day to make the right choices? According to traditional Catholic teaching, this sort of help comes through the sacraments, especially reconciliation (confession), the Eucharist, and the anointing of the sick. (The other four sacraments—baptism, confirmation, marriage, and ordination—are more or less one-offs, things you normally don't do more than once. But likewise, they are designed to give you what you need to get through certain turning points in your life.) But this raises another challenge to techies: How can a real change in the nature of my relationship with God, or indeed the presence of that God in some physical way, be effected by a guy in a funny outfit saying a bunch of words over me?

This is a particular problem for techies, because we are not always in tune with how words can shape reality. To us, things are either one way or the other, and "saying doesn't make it so." Certainly that's true in the physical universe.

But there are all sorts of ways that words change reality. Think of the words "I do" in a marriage ceremony or the words "I'm sorry" between friends. Think of "We are pleased to accept you to the incoming freshman class at MIT" or "Your proposal does not meet our needs at this time" or "You're fired." Indeed, to see the power of words in a scientific context, one need look no further than the endless heated debates on whether or not to call Pluto a planet.

Rites and ceremonies are an important and unique function of religion. Alas, too many techies don't understand them. This is a weakness, a lacuna, in the techie way of viewing the universe. Where does that weakness come from? I don't know, but my hunch is that it's related to a kind of insecurity, the fear that a lot of techies have of not being taken seriously.

Consider, as a silly but perhaps illustrative example, a comparison between how a Catholic understands the Eucharist with how a little kid understands a birthday cake. There are lots of cakes out there; but for any cake to be a real birthday cake, any kid can tell you, it has to have candles; it has to be served only on one's birthday, not before or after; and it has to be presented by Mom (or, if Mom isn't available, Mom's truly authenticated and delegated representative). Everything else is just a nice cake.

You can probably see the parallels I am trying to make with the Eucharist, a special meal that is really what it claims to be only if it is presented at the proper time and in the right place and manner by a properly authorized priest.

But a lot of techies are not all that secure in their own self-worth, and their arrogance comes not of innocence but from this deep fear that someone, someday, will "find them out." (Nearly all students at MIT seem to be convinced that they got in by mistake because they can't possibly be as smart as all the other students they see around them.) Given that common insecurity, a techie may sniff out the parallel and see both Eucharist and birthday cake, scornfully, as a kind of childish make-believe. It's the same logic that says, since there is no Santa Claus, there must not be a God either. And their lives are poorer as a result.

And for some reason, some of us are terrified of being considered childish—even as we glory in our childlike sense of wonder. I think it comes from too many of us not having been taken seriously when we were children—children who were, more likely than not, already smarter than the adults who had power over us but would not take us seriously. We're all still looking for the pat on the head from the grown-ups, even as we cynically scorn such approval.

Ironically, a child has no problem sorting out the make-believe from the real. It's the cynic who can't tell the difference.

≹ Infallibility, Rules, and the Cloud of Witnesses ≸

But what about issues that are closer to my emotional center? What if, say, the church insisted that all Catholic universities must teach as fact the idea that Earth is fixed in the cosmos and the sun goes around it? That once did happen, after all. And there's no guarantee that it couldn't happen again. That's the danger of a big, bureaucratic, hierarchical church.

Of course, to its credit, the church has also been opposed to ideas that were well worth opposing, like astrology or various types of parlor room spiritualism. And it was one of the few voices to speak out against "eugenics" long before that once highly fashionable pseudoscience reached its logical conclusion in the Nazi death camps. Indeed, it is often at its best when it is most unpopular, telling us to look again at the easy answers we so desperately want to believe in.

If they are neither always wrong nor always right, how do two thousand years' worth of edicts from the Vatican make sense to me? How do I live with all the "rules" that seem, to a techie, to form the structure of this church? And most of all, how do I deal with the rules that come from a mere human being who, by the accident of being elected pope, is somehow defined to have the ability to be "infallible"?

First, it helps to understand what those rules are really all about. Even more important, it is essential to see that not all rules have the same function. Some of them do indeed define the essentials of the religion. Others are conventions, useful to make sure that we are all singing from the same page of the hymnal.

And others are rules of thumb: hard-won lessons learned through painful experience about how to avoid behaviors that can look really inviting but turn out, more often than not, to be very bad ideas.

To see what I mean, consider the various rules of basketball. There are some rules that are essential: if you don't have a round ball and hoops to throw it through, you aren't playing basketball. Indeed, the rules about dribbling versus carrying the ball, about how many players are on each team, about the general shape of the court and how high above the floor the hoops must be are all essentials that define the game. If you claim you scored a record number of points but the hoops were lower that day, it doesn't count.

Then there are rules like where you put the three-point line (or even if you should have one) or whether or not there's a shot clock. These sorts of rules may change from league to league or from season to season, yet you can recognize that everyone's still playing basketball. They are arbitrary, to some degree, but everyone must agree to one version or another before we can all play the game.

But there's a third kind of rule, the things that good coaches pound into their players at every practice. Rules about who should be chosen to play the center position and what talents are better suited to a point guard; about looking up-court while you dribble and the importance of passing the ball before you shoot; about the proper way to set a pick-and-roll. None of these rules are in the rule book. No one will call foul if they are not followed. But you ignore them at your own risk; and if you do, more often than not you'll lose the game.

The rules of religion follow the same format. Some things—the essentials of the Apostles' Creed—define what a religion is. Some things—rules for ordination, rubrics for rituals—are essentially arbitrary but necessary to make sure everybody's clear on who does what, what counts, and what doesn't. But a third set of rules is there to help the followers of the religion come closer to their goal of being in a good relationship with God. There's nothing inherent about meat on Friday that makes or breaks a believer; but if you don't learn to control your appetite in small ways, you're far more likely to break under the more strenuous tests that life can send you.

Type 1 rules, rules that define the church, are essential. There is no messing with them. Type 2 rules, rules that outline the day-to-day operating of the church, are things that everyone has a right to complain about, but unless you enjoy causing traffic jams by driving on the opposite side of the road from everyone else, you really have to follow them. Type 3 rules—well, there may be times when you have to use your common sense, but you should be aware that when you open that box, you're voiding the warranty.

The Catholic church's edicts on type 1 rules are few and far between. For one thing, it's a basic principle of the Catholic church that its essentials do not change. We're not suddenly going to discover a fourth member of the Blessed Trinity. The only such edicts one can expect are clarifications, not new additions. And there are only two places that such authoritative statements on these sorts of definitional rules are found: in the decrees of ecumenical councils, which are gatherings of all the bishops worldwide; and papal statements that are defined to be infallible (more about that in a minute). In the two-thousand-year history of the church, there have been only twenty-one ecumenical councils. And since the doctrine of infallibility was defined by the first Vatican Council, there has been only one ex-cathedra infallible statement.

Type 2 rules can be issued more often, but they are limited to topics such as revisions of rites and canon law. If the Vatican says all candidates for the priesthood must study *these* courses for *that* many years or at the Mass we'll stand *here* but kneel *there*, then that's the way it is. One can argue whether they're good ideas or not, but there's really no true-or-false sides to argue.

It's with the third kind of rules that the confusion arises the most.

The Vatican is a big place, with a lot of people, and it's been around for a long time. Over its history, there have been countless directives and statements issued by all sorts of people at the Vatican, people with a wide range of authority (and wisdom) or lack thereof.

As a techie, I picture each of these statements as something like a data point, weighted according to the authority of the person giving the statement. A press release issued from "the Vatican" without a specific citation of who is saying it and under what authority carries the least weight. Carefully thought-out statements from specifically named cardinals appointed to do a specific job carry a lot more weight. Official encyclicals (essentially, circular letters from a pope to the church, usually worked on for many months by a team of experts) carry significant weight indeed.

And as with data points, you have to look at the whole cloud of edicts, not only from today but from the entire history of the church. As with data points, you have to be aware of possible "systematic" biases due both to the human limitations of the persons making the statements and to the historical times in which they were made. All of theology, like all of life, is a balancing act, and when there's a threat from one direction, the natural response is to exaggerate the opposite trend. (And in this regard, it's useful to remember the old adage that "every heresy is based on an important truth." Just because somebody has overstated a point and needed to be reined in doesn't negate the bit of truth that was being overstated.)

In any event, no one Vatican statement by itself can be used to justify a particular line of action that you wanted—or feared. Only the sum total of teachings over a long period of time can really indicate where the truth is to be found.

Yet what about papal infallibility? When does that kick in?

Frankly, if you want a complete and learned discussion of what infallibility does and does not mean, go to some authoritative source like the *Catholic Encyclopedia* or the Catechism. I have neither the space nor the authority nor the wisdom to top those sources.

But to show that I am not hiding anything, let me quote the appropriate words from the decree of the Vatican I ecumenical council (held in 1870) that specifically defined the pope's infallibility. It stated:

> The Roman Pontiff, when he speaks *ex cathedra*—that is, when in the exercise of his office as pastor and teacher of all Christians he defines, by virtue of his supreme Apostolic authority, a doctrine of

faith or morals to be held by the whole Church—is, by reason of the Divine assistance promised to him in blessed Peter, possessed of that infallibility with which the Divine Redeemer wished His Church to be endowed in defining doctrines of faith and morals; and consequently that such definitions of the Roman Pontiff are irreformable of their own nature (*ex sese*) and not by reason of the Church's consent.

Faith and morals. Faith, here, implies the definitions of what it means to be Catholic: rules of type 1. Morals may be better translated as *mores,* the customs and conventions of a community, "the way we do things"; in other words, rules of type 2. Nothing in the definition of infallibility refers to rules of type 3.

There's a lot more stuff in this definition that we need not get into, but the point I want to emphasize here is that the definition in fact actually limits the infallibility of the pope. Unlike some of the other bosses I've worked for in my life, this one admits that he's only infallible under certain extremely limited conditions. Not everything he says is infallible; quite the contrary. To quote the *Catholic Encyclopedia,* "the presumption is that unless the Pope formally addresses the whole Church in the recognized official way, he does not intend his doctrinal teaching to be held by all the faithful as *ex cathedra* and infallible." And such formal statements have occurred only at the rate of one per century and always to reaffirm and specify an item of faith that was already a long-held tradition.

There's one final item about how I as a techie understand church teachings. Ultimately, when it comes to any church teaching, be it an essential definition or a coach's dictum, I am guided by an assumption that is very much a part of the Jesuit tradition and yet also very techie. I acknowledge that the people who came up with these sometimes unlikely teachings—which can be as strange as relativity or quantum theory at times—were not stupid people. If the ideas don't make sense to me, then that says more about me than about the ideas. I cannot dismiss these ideas out of hand; certainly, at the very least, I ought to at least do my best to understand what they are trying to say before I judge them. And that can only be done by trusting from the start that there is some content to these ideas, something true and important in what they are trying to say. To dismiss them out of hand is as intellectually dishonest as dismissing any particular data point merely because it doesn't fit my pet theory.

≳ Sinners and Fools ≲

It was a Sunday morning Mass in Saint Cecelia's Church, an almost empty edifice in Back Bay, Boston. I was twenty-seven years old, a postdoctoral research fellow at MIT. My life as a Jesuit brother was still ten years in the future, a future I could never have imagined.

Sitting in this church was a homecoming of sorts. I had just moved into a gentrified apartment not far from where, seventy-five years earlier, my grandfather had gone to school. And now I was attending the same parish that my grandparents had gone to during the years of World War II. There was even a plaque in the back of the church listing the men of the parish who were "serving in action," and my father's name was on that plaque; when his parents lived here, he was flying bombers out of Britain and was later held in a prisoner of war camp in Germany.

And now, at the start of the 1980s high-tech revolution, I was living in this same neighborhood and attending this same church. The neighborhood had changed a lot since the war years. As the Irish and Italian immigrants had risen in economic status, they'd abandoned the city for the suburbs. Row houses had turned into slum houses. Then the baby boom and the high-tech boom had launched a new generation of young urban professionals like myself who had rediscovered the charms of living in the heart of a vibrant, trendsetting city like Boston. We were transforming those slums into very posh neighborhoods.

But when I looked around the parish that Sunday morning, I realized that I was the only Yuppie in the pews. Well-educated, well-off single folk in their twenties and thirties went to nightclubs and cafés, bookstores and record shops. Not churches. On Sunday mornings, they slept in.

Instead, the few people I saw across the aisles from me were just the opposite of my contemporaries. They were old. They were poor. Their clothes had a Salvation Army look to them. Some of them were street people. Some of them were minorities. Some were grossly overweight. Others were handicapped or disfigured. One of them was drooling.

All of them were definitely uncool. None of them, I realized, were people I knew—or wanted to know.

Or even wanted to be seen with.

I was sufficiently insecure, unsure of my own coolness, that I was getting very nervous at finding myself in company like this. Wasn't I on the appropriate path to social success? A university job, an apartment with hardwood floors and exposed brick, season tickets to the Boston Symphony and the Boston Shakespeare Company. I wore the right clothes, had the right stereo, went to the best ice-cream shops. But my status was not yet secure. I still didn't have a tenure-track job or a good salary at a high-tech start-up. I didn't even have a girlfriend. I hadn't yet *arrived*.

So what was I doing here in a church? Wasn't my presence there more than just a little bit dangerous to my social status? Should I really be hanging out on a Sunday morning with this ragtag congregation of life's losers? Surely, I was just a victim of a mindless routine, dating from the compulsion—guilt—that my grade school nuns had instilled in me. And wasn't it about time that I broke free from those childish habits?

I took a deep breath.

I had come to church to be with God. And these people around me, these "life's losers"—here, with them, was precisely where I would find him.

In fact, compared to my soft life, the challenges that every one of these people must have to face every day, challenges that would terrify me to contemplate, meant that I was flattering myself to think of myself as their equal.

That may have been the moment that started it all, the moment that made me uncomfortable enough with where I was headed that I turned down a job at an up-and-coming software firm, left my research position at MIT, and joined the Peace Corps. (By the way, that up-and-coming software firm went belly-up while I was serving in Africa.) After the Peace Corps, I spent four wonderful years teaching at a great little liberal arts school, Lafayette College, while I finally figured out that the girlfriend I had been pursuing so intently really wasn't right for me—something she'd been trying to get me to see for some time. Then I joined the Jesuits, thinking I could keep teaching in small liberal arts colleges. Instead, the order sent me to the Vatican Observatory.

Now, instead of a luxury apartment in Boston, my home is an ill-furnished ten-by-sixteen-foot room, cold in the winter and too hot in the summer. But it's a room in a palace.

Living in Rome these past ten-plus years, I have seen my share of venal, ambitious, foolish, pompous churchmen. I see one every morning in the mirror. This is where I belong. Not in a church of saints but in a church of sinners.

Admitting our sinfulness in all its depth is the first step in the Jesuit spirituality known as the Spiritual Exercises, but it is just the opposite of a breast-beating guilt trip. In fact, it is a joyous occasion, for only when we understand the depths of our failings can we appreciate how deep and real is God's forgiving love. And the more you'll admit he's had to forgive you for, the more you can realize that he loves you. The same is true for a church as for an individual.

In my studies as a Jesuit (which never end; I seem to forget more than I learn), I have taken special delight in reading church history and the biographies of saints. A common theme in the lives of many saints is the fierce opposition they endured from within the very church they loved and served. For example, even Robert Bellarmine, the great Jesuit theologian and defender of the church during the years of Reformation and Counter-Reformation, had to fight to keep his greatest works off the church's own Index of Forbidden Literature. When the church later made him a cardinal, he noted wryly that of all the Jesuit saints and blesseds up to his time, none of them had been in the church hierarchy. He finally broke the streak; but it took three hundred years after his death before he was canonized, thanks to his enemies within the church.

(That's another reason, in case there was any doubt, that I know I'm not a saint; I don't have those enemies, I haven't suffered like that. Mind you, I'm not complaining.)

And it is clear that all the fools in Rome today have nothing on the incredible parade of knaves who have populated the history of my church. Disagree all you want with recent popes, but there's no question that at least they've tried to be holy men, sincerely attempting to do what they thought was God's will. That's more than you can say about a lot of popes in history, whom I wouldn't entrust my car keys to, much less the keys to the kingdom of heaven. And yet somehow the church and its doctrines have survived. I am only half-joking—less than half—when I say that this is the ultimate proof of God's existence, a miracle only God himself could have pulled off.

I'll be honest: the first few times I had a chance to meet Pope John Paul II, I was disappointed. I saw a mere man whose English wasn't all that great (of course, neither was my Italian), just reading to the public from a page that someone had handed him. But by the end of his life, even when his illnesses made him almost impossible to understand, I saw this incredibly frail old man radiate a power and a holiness that had nothing to do with the mere words he spoke. It wasn't just me; everyone I know who saw him at the time felt it. It was fun to watch how our visitors at the Vatican Observatory, friends and family, reacted to meeting him: the more skeptical they were about it all beforehand, the more awed they were when they finally shook his hand.

God is in our weaknesses. God is in our frailties. God is in this pompous, sinful, arrogant, scandal-ridden, and tired old church of mine. He is constantly reproving her, constantly forgiving her. He whispers in the still, soft voice that has echoed down the centuries through her voids and vacancies. How he must love her!

I love this church with all her faults (which are, after all, only my own faults writ over and over again, a billion times in its billion members). I love her in the way that as adults we can appreciate the human frailties and triumphs of our parents and love them more deeply than we ever could when we were children.

It is through the church that I have come to know God. I love her because I love Him.

Acknowledgments

Many people have helped me put this book together. I must first thank all my Jesuit brothers, in so many places, who taught me so much and listened to my long-winded attempts to describe the shape of this story. That includes a debt of gratitude to many specific Jesuit institutions: Parts One and Two originated as talks given at Loyola University in Chicago and the University of Detroit Mercy; Part Three is based on my notes while working at Santa Clara University; and the two final parts were completed at Fordham University, which gave me the Loyola Chair for visiting Jesuit scholars during the 2006–2007 academic year. And through it all, I was supported in many ways, including spiritually and financially, by my home institution, the *Specola Vaticana* (Vatican Observatory).

I've also had the privilege of having a regular column in the British weekly Catholic magazine *The Tablet*, which has also published longer articles of mine, as has the American Jesuit magazine *America*. In those columns and articles I first explored some of the topics expanded on here.

My Jesuit provincial, Father Tim Brown, S.J., passed my first draft on to a theologian who graciously hunted down the worst of my theological howlers—five pages' worth. I am eternally grateful for his efforts in the service of truth and for keeping me from embarrassing myself even more than I have already here.

This book would never have been completed, however, nor would it have found a home with Jossey-Bass, if it had not been for the faith in it (and the extremely practical advice) of my agent, Gillian MacKenzie. And of course my editors at Jossey-Bass, Julianna Gustafson, Sheryl Fullerton, and Catherine Craddock, are the ones who made it a book.

Most of all, however, I have to thank all the glorious techies in my life—with a special hat tip to Dan Davis, Dennis McCarthy, Bill Higgins, Barry Gehm, Jaclyn Allen, Steve Gruenwald, Cliff Stoll, Grace Wolf-Chase, and Moshe Yudkowski—who have supported me, challenged me, fought with me, and taught me so much about how to see religion (especially, my own religion) from a techie frame of mind. *They* are God's mechanics.

Five years have passed since my first conversation about religion with the techie friends from MIT whom I describe in the Introduction. Today they're a part of their local Episcopal parish, where the husband is a church warden. Their eldest son, a young techie who's into building robots, used to sing in the church choir. But the boy's a teenager today, and a skeptic—for now.

The Author

Brother Guy Consolmagno, S.J., was born in Detroit, Michigan. He earned undergraduate and master's degrees from the Massachusetts Institute of Technology and a doctorate in planetary science from the University of Arizona, was a researcher at Harvard and MIT, served in the United States Peace Corps in Kenya, and taught university physics at Lafayette College before entering the Jesuit order in 1989.

Consolmagno was appointed to the Vatican Observatory in 1993. His research explores connections between meteorites, asteroids, and the evolution of small solar system bodies, observing Kuiper Belt comets with the Vatican's 1.8-meter telescope in Arizona, and curating the Vatican meteorite collection. He is the author of more than one hundred scientific papers and articles and a number of books including *Turn Left at Orion* (with Dan Davis), *Worlds Apart: A Textbook in Planetary Sciences* (with Martha Schaefer), and *Brother Astronomer.*

Consolmagno has served on the governing board of the Meteoritical Society and as chair of the Division for Planetary Sciences of the American Astronomical Society. He is a past president of Commission 16 (Planets and Satellites) and secretary of Division III (Planetary Systems Sciences) of the International Astronomical Union. He has held chairs as a visiting Jesuit scholar at Saint Joseph's University and at Fordham University.

Index

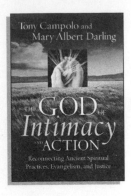

The God of Intimacy and Action

Reconnecting Ancient Spiritual Practices, Evangelism, and Justice

Tony Campolo & Mary Albert Darling

Hardover
ISBN: 978-0-7879-8741-1

"There was a time when those who most passionately pursued intimacy with God in their souls were the same folk who most impatiently worked for justice in the streets. They were called prophets. Sometimes saints. Tony and Mary ask: 'Why not you and me?'"
—John Ortberg, pastor, Menlo Park Presbyterian Church

In *The God of Intimacy and Action*, beloved author and activist Tony Campolo teams up with spiritual director Mary Albert Darling to show how contemplative spiritual practices can lead to greater intimacy with God and fuel passion for reaching out to others through spreading the Good News and fostering justice for the poor and oppressed. The authors reveal why this combination is not only crucial but historical and is vividly demonstrated in the lives of saints such as St. Francis of Assisi, Ignatius of Loyola, and Catherine of Siena.

Campolo and Darling explain mystical spirituality and its practices and integrate them with evangelism and justice to illuminate what they call "holistic Christianity." They suggest specific ways to nurture and energize one's spirituality and show how to go beyond living a Christian life that merely emphasizes right beliefs and right behaviors. They encourage followers to develop a sense of personal unity with Christ that will compel them to help share Jesus' message and mission in its totality. The ultimate goal is a unity with God that involves a connectedness with those around us—especially the lost, poor, and oppressed.

Tony Campolo is professor emeritus of sociology at Eastern University. Previously he served for ten years on the faculty of the University of Pennsylvania. Dr. Campolo is a media commentator on religious, social, and political matters, and hosts From Across the Pond, a weekly program on the Premier Radio Network in England.

Mary Albert Darling, associate professor of communication at Spring Arbor University, is a Protestant who has been trained in spiritual direction in the Jesuit tradition. She also teaches in her university's Spiritual Formation and Leadership graduate program.

The Battle Over the Meaning of Everything

Evolution, Intelligent Design, and a School Board in Dover, PA

Gordy Slack

Hardover

ISBN: 978-0-7879-8786-2

"For six weeks in 2005, a courtroom in Pennsylvania became a forum for intense debates about the most fundamental matters: science, faith, and what we should teach our children about them. Gordy Slack takes us inside that courtroom, where his personal and intellectual engagement with the subject serves him exceedingly well. He has written a lively, lucid account of a fascinating trial."
— **Margaret Talbot, staff writer, "Darwin in the Dock," the** *New Yorker*

The Battle Over the Meaning of Everything is a compelling eyewitness account of the recent courtroom drama in Dover, Pennsylvania, that put evolution and intelligent design on trial. Journalist Gordy Slack offers a riveting, personal, and often amusing first-hand account that details six weeks of some of the most widely ranging, fascinating, and just plain surreal testimony in U.S. legal history—a battle between hard science and religious conservatives wishing to promote a new version of creationism in schools.

During the *Kitzmiller* vs. *Dover* trial, members of the local school board defended their effort to require teachers to present intelligent design alongside evolution as an explanation for the origins and diversity of life on earth. The trial revealed two essentially different and conflicting views of the world and the lengths to which true believers on each side will go to promote their own. The controversial ruling by George W. Bush–appointed Judge John Jones III was full of surprises and had a profound influence on America's educational landscape.

This engaging story of high drama and unforgettable characters is a sophisticated examination of the deep cultural, religious, and political faultlines that divide America. But it is also a personal account of how those same divisions cleaved Slack's own family in two.

Gordy Slack is a science writer whose articles have appeared in *Mother Jones, Wired, The Scientist,* and *Salon.com.* He is a former senior editor of *California Wild,* the science and natural history magazine published by the California Academy of Sciences, and a frequent contributor to San Francisco's KQED radio. His writing often focuses on evolutionary biology and the relationship between science and religion.

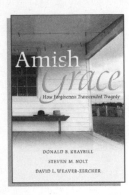

Amish Grace

How Forgiveness Transcended Tragedy

Donald B. Kraybill, Steven M. Nolt, and
David L. Weaver-Zercher

Hardover
ISBN: 978-0-7879-9761-8

"A story of forgiveness informed by deep faith, rooted in a rich history, and practiced in real life. In an American society that often resorts to revenge, it is a powerful example of the better way taught by Jesus."
—**Jim Wallis, author of *God's Politics* and president of Sojourners/Call to Renewal**

On October 2, 2006, a thirty-two-year-old gunman entered a one-room Amish school in Nickel Mines, Pennsylvania. Ordering the boys and other adults to leave, the killer opened fire and shot the ten remaining girls execution-style, killing five and leaving the others critically wounded. He then shot himself as police stormed the building.

Before the sun had set on that awful October day, members of the Amish community brought words of forgiveness to the family of the one who had slain their children. Those in the outside world were incredulous that forgiveness could be offered so quickly for such a heinous crime. The story of Amish grace eclipsed the story of violence and arrested the world's attention.

Amish Grace explores the many questions this story raises about the religious beliefs and habits that led the Amish to forgive so quickly. It examines forgiveness embedded in a separatist society and questions if Amish practices parallel or diverge from other religious and secular notions of forgiveness. It also asks why and how forgiveness became international news. "All the religions teach it," mused an observer, "but no one does it like the Amish." Regardless of the cultural seedbed that nourished this story, the surprising act of Amish forgiveness begs a deeper exploration. How could the Amish forgive so swiftly? What did this act mean to them? And how might their story provide lessons for the rest of us?

Donald B. Kraybill, Ph.D. (Elizabethtown, PA) is senior fellow at the Young Center for Anabaptist and Pietist Studies at Elizabethtown College and author of *The Riddle of Amish Culture*. His commentary on the Nickel Mines killing was featured in dozens of broadcast and print media sources including *the New York Times, the Washington Post, the Guardian* (London), *the Australian, Newsweek,* NBC, ABC, CBS, CNN, NPR, BBC Radio.

Steven M. Nolt, Ph.D. (Goshen, IN) is associate professor of history at Goshen College. His books on the Amish include *A History of the Amish* and *Plain Diversity: Amish Cultures and Identities*. Nolt also fielded dozens of inquiries from media around the world.

David L. Weaver-Zercher, Ph.D. (Grantham, PA) is associate professor of American religious history at Messiah College. He is the author or editor of numerous books on the Amish, including *The Amish in the American Imagination* and *Plain Talk: The Amish and the Media*. In the aftermath of the Nickel Mine shooting, he was contacted by numerous media outlets.